One-Year Dynasty

Also by Matthew Silverman

New York Mets: The Complete Illustrated History
Swinging '73: Baseball's Wildest Season
Baseball Miscellany: Everything You Always Wanted to Know about Baseball
Best Mets: Fifty Years of Highs and Lows from New York's Most Agonizingly Amazin' Team
Mets Essential: Everything You Need to Know to Be a Real Fan
100 Things Mets Fans Should Know Before They Die
Shea Goodbye: The Untold Inside Story of the Historic 2008 Season, with Keith Hernandez
Mets by the Numbers: A Complete Team History of the Amazin' Mets by Uniform Number, with Jon Springer

One-Year Dynasty

Inside the Rise and Fall of the 1986 Mets,
Baseball's Impossible One-and-Done Champions

Matthew Silverman

Guilford, Connecticut

For Jim Jasensky, one of many Mets fans for whom the 1986 season was the pinnacle of life as a fan. Should I ever see them win it all again, I will think of you when the gloves go airborne, Jimmy Jim.

An imprint of Rowman & Littlefield

Distributed by NATIONAL BOOK NETWORK

British Library Cataloguing in Publication Information Available

Library of Congress Cataloging-in-Publication Data

ISBN 978-1-4930-0909-1
ISBN 978-1-4930-2420-9 (e-book)

∞™ The paper used in this publication meets the minimum requirements of American National Standard for Information Sciences—Permanence of Paper for Printed Library Materials, ANSI/NISO Z39.48-1992.

Contents

Part I. Dominance

1

The Waiting

April 1962 to October 1985

ONLY GARY CARTER STOOD BETWEEN THE METS AND OBLIVION. Two outs, last inning, last hope. At the end of a long season, the veteran catcher's battered knees were a constant source of pain, but he ignored the hurt, stared intently at the pitcher, and held his bat high, like always. Staring back at Carter was a hard-throwing right-handed reliever who was having the best season of what would be a short career. Now the pitch: Carter swings, and it's . . . a routine fly ball to the outfield. Caught. Game over. Season over.

The 1985 season came to an end the night of October 3 in St. Louis on right fielder Andy Van Slyke's catch of Carter's high fly. The Mets had come to Busch Stadium three games behind the Cardinals with six games left on the schedule. New York needed a sweep to forge a tie atop the National League East. First place or nothing. No other option was available.

The divisions were not yet realigned to place St. Louis out of the way in the National League Central. There was no Wild Card in 1985, no National League Central, no postseason for the New York Mets.

Gary Cohen watched the devastating climax unfold from the stands at Busch Stadium. Two decades later he would watch

Gary Carter NATIONAL BASEBALL HALL OF FAME LIBRARY, COOPERSTOWN, NY

another devastating Mets defeat to the Cardinals from the Mets radio booth, but in 1985 he was a Columbia grad turned minor league announcer whose season was over and who wanted to see the team he'd watched (at age 11) win a world championship keep its dream alive for a second title. So Cohen and a friend hopped a People Express flight—"The first airline where attitude is as important as altitude"—to see what unfolded in St. Louis. Cohen had been worried about wearing Mets garb "in enemy territory," but he found plenty of Midwestern hospitality and dismissiveness inside the red-clad confines of Busch Stadium. "People were incredibly friendly and didn't see the Mets as a threat at all," he recalled. "By the night of the third game there was a little more edginess to it."

Peter Golenbock felt the edge from his vantage point among the media. Writing a book that year with Mets manager Davey Johnson, he was banished from the Busch Stadium press box for clapping after Darryl Strawberry's monster home run off the digital scoreboard clock in the 11th inning for the only run in the first game of the series. Cohen and Golenbock were among the few in St. Louis who were happy to see Dwight Gooden win for the 24th time in game two. Heading into the decisive third game, Golenbock, the lawyer turned *New York Times* best-selling writer, was looking for a great ending for his Davey Johnson diary of the '85 season and the chance for the book to succeed like his recent collaborations with Yankees Sparky Lyle, Ron Guidry, Graig Nettles, and Billy Martin. The Mets had become the hot property in the Big Apple, and the clapping came naturally—even as the glares from the Midwestern scribes told him they were protective of the old axiom of "no cheering in the press box" and perhaps a little defensive of the hometown nine. Anyway, Golenbock conceded, "It wasn't the first press box I was kicked out of."

Though the Mets had won the first two games and were going for the sweep, the math still favored the Cardinals on that first Thursday night in October: four games left on the 1985 schedule,

97 wins for the Mets, 98 for the Cardinals. If the Mets won, the standings would be even. If the Cards won, it would be all but over.

NBC's heavily promoted "Must-See TV" Thursday night lineup of *The Cosby Show* followed by *Family Ties*, *Cheers*, and *Night Court* (all among the top dozen shows in the Nielsen ratings) was just so much fluff for hard-core baseball fans in New York and St. Louis. Those in other markets could read about the game in tomorrow's paper, or perhaps point a transistor radio in the direction of St. Louis and listen for the booming voice of Jack Buck. There was no national TV outlet broadcasting midweek baseball games, no matter how crucial or captivating the game might have been.

The first inning was far more compelling than the Huxtables' troubles with their son and many daughters in reimagined Brooklyn Heights. *The Cosby Show* was quickly forgotten as four of the first five Mets singled against Cardinals starter Danny Cox. Then up stepped George Foster. The most costly—and least productive—extravagance to date by Mets general manager Frank Cashen, Foster was making the third-highest salary in baseball ($1.94 million). He'd homered the previous night, but this time he grounded to third base, resulting in a force-out at home. Cox then retired Howard Johnson to escape the inning trailing just 1–0. The Mets needed to provide rookie Rick Aguilera more support than that.

Between them, Dwight Gooden and Ron Darling had 70 starts, 40 wins, 10 losses, and 20 complete games in 1985, but that pair had already started the first two games of the series. Another stellar second-year starter, Sid Fernandez, was pitching the following night back in New York. El Sid, a heavyset southpaw who'd begun the year on the disabled list, had pitched on short rest just twice all year and the Mets lost both times. Ed Lynch, the veteran of the staff at age 29, hadn't been right since a scuffle with Mariano Duncan of the Dodgers a few weeks earlier and hadn't won in almost two months. Manager Davey Johnson was loath to start sidewinding righty Terry Leach against a team with so many left-handed bats. So Johnson had no real choice but to go with Aguilera, who'd gone 10–6 with a 3.09 ERA since making his major league debut in June. With four starting pitchers under age 24, Johnson obviously had plenty of confidence in his young staff, but this was the biggest game the franchise had played in a dozen years. To top it off, the rookie was facing a lineup capable of slapping the ball all over the Busch Stadium artificial turf. And that's just what they did. Ozzie Smith, Vince Coleman, and Willie McGee—three of the five switch-hitters in the St. Louis starting lineup—drove in all four runs.

The Mets collected 13 hits in the game but never caught up after St. Louis took the lead in the fourth inning. Keith Hernandez, who endured abusive howls from St. Louis fans and was lambasted by the same local media that had hung on his every word as a team leader when he was a Cardinal, knocked in two of the three Mets runs. Hernandez had a 5-for-5 night, yet he was stranded on base each time, including in the ninth inning when he represented the tying run. He stopped running somewhere between second and third when Van Slyke grabbed Carter's fly ball.

"A winner! A winner!" Cardinals announcer Jack Buck's voice echoed on radios throughout the stadium and across the country on the powerful KMOX signal from Virginia to Nevada. The KMOX reach—plus the Cardinals winning more world championships than any National League team—bathed large swaths of the Midwest in Cardinal red. That their ball club could beat New York's while calling them "pond scum"—a term first hung on the Mets by Midwesterner turned *Late Night* icon David Letterman—made it all the better. It didn't matter that New York outnumbered St. Louis 7 million to 400,000; what mattered was St. Louis 4, New York 3.

"I was crushed," said Gary Cohen, looking at a long, sad flight home on People Express, an airline that would soon be out of here. Peter Golenbock's book with Mets manager Davey Johnson, *Bats*, would end the way so many New York National League seasons had before it, with the line, "Wait til next year."

It officially became next year for the Mets on October 5, 1985. They needed to sweep three games from third-place Montreal at Shea Stadium; they needed the Cardinals to lose twice at home against the Cubs, the 1984 NL East champs who had long ago packed it in on 1985. When the Mets stumbled against the Expos on Saturday, St. Louis could paint the town red—if it wasn't that color already.

The Cardinals finished 1985 with 101 victories. The Mets won 98 games, the most wins in team history, save for the 1969 world champion Miracle Mets. There would be no miracle in 1985 in New York. And while Kansas City would find one in the '85 World Series against the Cardinals, that didn't do much for New York.

A quarter century earlier expectations were far lower. The original Mets didn't have to be good. They just had to be there.

Five years with no National League team had felt like death in a baseball town. For 68 seasons New York had identified itself with two NL franchises. Before the New York Highlanders—the original name of the Yankees—drew their first breath in 1903, the Giants and Dodgers had their own identities and deep-seated loyalties. Then the Dodgers got the deal of the century to relocate to California after the 1957 season. The Dodgers, in turn, lured the Giants out of New York, like Eve handing off the apple to the closest person because sin isn't as much fun alone. The Dodgers wound up in paradise in Chavez Ravine, winning more World Series in their first five years in Los Angeles than they had in seven decades in Brooklyn. The Giants got the bruised end of the apple with windswept Candlestick Park, almost moving out of San Francisco twice before building one of baseball's best ballparks, in China Basin. The Giants would finally win their first West Coast World Series 53 years into their San Francisco stay. Then they quickly won another two, or more titles than the team that replaced them in New York.

The Mets were born of a bluff. When the National League showed no interest in helping New York get a new NL team in the late 1950s, Bill Shea, name partner in the prominent New York law firm of Shea & Gould, was empowered by Mayor Robert Wagner to find the city a team by whatever means necessary. Shea came up with the idea of a new league: the Continental League. In a time before the American Football League, American Basketball Association, and World Hockey Association played their way into mergers with the established leagues, Shea got into the game without ever buying so much as a bat or a ball for the Continental League. Shea found enough filthy-rich, civic-minded folks pledging to back franchises in cities across the country to intimidate Major League Baseball. In Branch Rickey, who'd integrated the majors, started the farm system concept, and rebuilt three separate franchises from the ground up, the paper league had a lion as president. Though he was pushing 80, Rickey could still make baseball—and the press—pay attention to this upstart league. In August 1960 the major leagues caved: the Mets and Houston Colt .45s were approved as the first new National League teams in seven decades.

New Yorkers could now concentrate on what they had, instead of what they had lost. Yet the biggest crowds the Mets drew in their early years were invariably for games against the Dodgers and Giants. In the Mets' two-year stay at the Polo Grounds, 30 of the 34 largest crowds featured either the Giants or the Dodgers. And the Mets weren't any more likely to beat them than anybody else in the National League. The Mets went just 4–32 against the Dodgers those first two years, making the Giants look like pushovers at 10–26.

Everyone beat the Mets, as generations of Mets haters would taunt by manipulating the title of the team's theme song, "Meet the Mets." With Casey Stengel running the club, the early Mets played it for laughs. You'd better play it that way when your record in year one is 40–120 and you finish 60½ games out—the worst team of the century.

Shea Stadium opened a year behind schedule in 1964 yet perfectly timed to coincide with the World's Fair at Flushing Meadows. The fair felt like another smokescreen to hide the hideous play of New York's National League club. Lulled into a catatonic state by the relentless playing of "It's a Small World," clutching a still-warm, freshly pressed plastic dinosaur from Sinclair Oil, and chomping on a Belgian waffle, fairgoers could hang a left at the Unisphere and find themselves wandering to Shea, the strangest exhibit of all. The Mets were a display of futility and desperation. Yet by handing their guests 100 wins in their first two seasons at Shea—while winning just 62 at home in 1964–65—the Mets proved to be exemplary hosts.

Stengel broke his hip celebrating his 75th birthday with all his old pals in town for Old-Timers' Day in August 1965. The injury forced him to retire, and Wes Westrum was elevated to manager. The 1966 season marked the first time the Mets did not lose 100 games or finish in 10th place—95 and ninth wasn't miraculous, but it was progress. The not-as-terrible Mets actually drew even more fans than they had during the run of the World's Fair. The 1966 Mets saw 1.9 million come through Shea's gates, fewer than Dodger Stadium but more than the state-of-the-art Astrodome recorded in its second year. Most importantly, Shea drew 800,000 more patrons than venerable Yankee Stadium. With the Yankees having fallen off their lofty perch and into last place in '66, there were fewer reasons for borderline fans to stick with the staid old Yankees. If you were going to root for a bottom-feeder baseball team in New York, the Mets were at least fun.

When the modest gains of 1966 were followed by a retreat to the basement in 1967, Westrum quit before he could be fired. The team's obsession with its New York predecessors had left the Mets with a lot of old baggage with name appeal but no aptitude.

That grab for old Dodgers and Giants, however, served the Mets extremely well when it came to their next manager: Gil Hodges. A Brooklyn icon who still lived in the borough during the off-season—he opened Gil Hodges Lanes on Ralph Avenue in 1961—Hodges had returned to New York in the expansion draft and had even hit the Mets' first home run in 1962 before injuries ended his playing career. The Mets traded him to the Washington Senators to manage an expansion team barely better than themselves. But Hodges did well enough that the Senators weren't eager to hand him back to New York. That infuriated M. Donald Grant.

Every story has to have a villain, and in the first two decades of Mets baseball, that villain was the team's own chairman of the board. Grant served Joan Payson, matron of both the Whitney family and the New York Mets, a woman whose vast interests and obligations took her all over the world. Someone was needed to handle the team's finances, and that fell to Grant, her stockbroker. A native Canadian and the son of hockey Hall of Famer Mike Grant, Don Grant used his token stock holding in the baseball Giants as both an introduction and an invitation to Payson to indulge in her whim to become part owner. She came to own 10 percent of the Giants and was the lone dissenter in the vote to abandon Manhattan for San Francisco. She was a natural choice to help front the Mets in their Continental League phase, becoming sole owner by the time the team started in the National League.

Grant possessed few of the endearing qualities of Stengel, Payson, or any of the lovable losers who made it pleasurable to root for the early Mets. Though the son of a famous athlete—and recruited himself by the Montreal Canadiens (he turned them down)—Don Grant, stockbroker not stickhandler, considered athletes below his station. He treated players like redeemable property, which, before free agency, they more or less were. Managers were a different matter.

Grant thought that when Hodges was sent to Washington in 1963 (in exchange for oddball outfielder Jimmy Piersall), Gil could be summoned back to New York when needed. That was not the case, of course, but Grant would not take no for an answer from the Senators. Johnny Murphy, a former Yankees star reliever and a member of the Mets front office from day one, was sent to negotiate with old Yankees teammate George Selkirk, Washington's general manager. It took time to work out a deal—pitcher Bill Denehy and $100,000—but Hodges was a Met again by Thanksgiving. When Mets general manager Bing Devine left to return home to the world champion St. Louis Cardinals the following month, Murphy, having proven he could broker deals to Grant's satisfaction, was elevated to Mets GM.

The Mets had bushels of young players and a manager willing to work them in and out of the lineup through platoons at multiple positions. Hodges and Rube Walker, a friend since their days in Brooklyn and one of three coaches brought from the Senators, put together the innovative (for the day) five-man rotation to nurture the team's burgeoning stable of talented pitching. The 1968 Mets weren't much to look at, but they had one of baseball's top pitching staffs. And they only got better in 1969: Tom Seaver, Jerry Koosman, Nolan Ryan, Tug McGraw, Gary Gentry, and Jim McAndrew, all of them under 26, helped the Mets win 37 of their last 48 games to take the first NL East title. The players revered and respected Hodges, who was not only an eight-time All-Star first baseman but had earned a Bronze Star as a Marine sergeant during the bloody Battle of Okinawa during World War II. His demeanor did not suit everybody. Two of the worst trades in franchise history—Amos Otis in December 1969 and Nolan Ryan in December of 1972—were approved by Hodges. Both players blossomed elsewhere after being frustrated in New York.

Hodges's demeanor rubbed off in the locker room. When the Mets reached .500 for the first time in club history on May 21, 1969, the writers who had covered the team from day one were ecstatic and looked for reactions to match theirs. Tom Seaver wondered what they were talking about. "What's .500?" was Seaver's response after throwing a shutout in Atlanta. "Let us reach first place. That'll mean something. We're looking far beyond .500." The same press corps that suppressed laughter when Gil Hodges said before the season that the Mets could win 85 games was taken aback at the brash young team that didn't seem to know its place as baseball's laughingstock.

First place was months away, but the Mets made statements throughout 1969 that showed they were serious: a team record 11-game winning streak before school was out; brash young Seaver retiring the first 25 Cubs on July 9 and settling for a one-hitter in what is still probably the best-pitched game in franchise history; a return engagement in Chicago with the Mets taking two of three; and winning on pitching with just enough hitting to get by, including five straight wins during their August turnaround in which the Mets offense averaged just 2.5 runs per game. And then came September's miracle mania—hunks of fortune wrapped around feats of skill: a black cat appearing in front of the superstitious Cubs dugout as the Mets prepared to take over first; twin 1–0 shutouts in a doubleheader sweep with the pitcher driving in the lone run in each game; and Cardinal Steve Carlton striking out a record 19 Mets, only to lose on two home runs by strikeout-prone Ron Swoboda. The Mets went from 10 games out in the middle of August to 8 games up at the end of September.

The first National League Championship Series saw the Mets staff implode. The Mets pitched to a 5.00 ERA, but the Braves allowed almost two more earned runs per game—plus two additional unearned runs per game. New York swept Atlanta, but the World Series was still considered a mismatch. The Baltimore Orioles won 109 games, owned the lowest ERA in baseball, and scored 147 more runs than the Mets. New York recorded 100 wins while scoring just 632 times—fewer runs than the Seattle Pilots, the last-place expansion club Jim Bouton pilloried in his landmark book *Ball Four*.

The World Series began as most predicted. Tom Seaver, 25–7 during the year—plus a victory in the NLCS opener—allowed a home run to the first Oriole he faced and lost to Mike Cuellar. The Orioles plated four runs in the victory—and scored just five more runs the entire Series.

Jerry Koosman took a no-hitter into the seventh inning of Game 2 and Ron Taylor got the last out of a 2–1 win. The Mets won Game 3 by the one-sided score of 5–0 as Nolan Ryan saved it for Gary Gentry, but the game was really saved by center fielder Tommie Agee's two spectacular catches. The next gravity-defying grab was by Ron Swoboda in Game 4, when Tom Seaver went 10 innings and the Mets won on a throw that ricocheted off baserunner J. C. Martin's wrist. The next day the Mets were behind 3–0 in the sixth but stormed back, thanks to a bit of shoe polish that acted like instant replay 45 years before it became the rule in baseball. The umpire initially ruled the pitch a ball, but Hodges strolled out of the dugout with a baseball with shoe polish on it. Koosman later claimed that it was his shoe polish rather than Cleon Jones's—Kooz quickly rubbed the ball on *his* shoe at the behest of Hodges. With a man on first due to circumstantial evidence, Series MVP Donn Clendenon followed with a two-run home run. By then, the Orioles had to believe there were forces beyond man or nature at work.

Light-hitting Al Weis, who'd never before hit a home run at Shea Stadium, clubbed one to tie the game. Swoboda, who rarely played against right-handed pitching, hit a game-winning double off righty Eddie Watt in the eighth inning. Worn-out Koosman threw a pitch with nothing on it that Davey Johnson skied to Cleon Jones and the Mets were world champions. Simple as that.

Since the divisional era began in baseball in 1969, only four teams have repeated as world champions. The Mets are not one of them. A letdown was inevitable the following season. And the season after that. And the season after that.

April 2, 1972, was Easter Sunday, four days before a new season was scheduled to begin, but all plans were on hold. The first baseball strike in history had been called two days earlier by players to force increases in teams' contributions to pension and medical benefits funds. Still in limbo in Florida, the Mets coaching staff attended Easter Sunday Mass, where the deeply religious Gil Hodges ran into the equally devout Expos outfielder Rusty Staub.

"I'm on the other side of church, and when Mass is over I go over to chat with them," Staub recalled. "And I remember driving off saying, 'Wow! Easter Sunday brings out the best in everybody.' They just talked with me and were so nice. They knew I was a Met. I didn't!" Though a trade had been worked out the previous day with Montreal, nothing was announced because of the strike. Staub would not find out about the deal for four more days. There were more pressing matters.

After Mass, Hodges and coaches Ed Yost, Rube Walker, and Joe Pignatano played golf. As they left the course around 5 p.m., Hodges fell over dead in the parking lot, two days shy of his 48th birthday.

"The family, especially Gil's wife, Joan Hodges, told me how much he wanted me on his ball club and fought to get me," said Staub, who heard the news on the radio the night he'd seen Hodges at Mass. "It's probably the most disappointing thing in my career that I didn't get a chance to play for him."

Staub wound up playing for Yogi Berra, the one Mets coach not on the golf course that fateful Easter afternoon. Berra had been in Miami with friends before being hastily summoned to meet M. Donald Grant that night. He was offered the managing job, even as the Mets chastised the media for asking if the team had considered a successor. That did not stop press speculation about internal candidates like pitching coach Rube Walker or director of personnel Whitey Herzog. The Mets announced their new manager and new right fielder at a press conference tactlessly held the same afternoon as Hodges's funeral.

With the death of Hodges, no one in the organization could override M. Donald Grant. The stunned Mets seemed ripe for disaster when the 1972 season opened—nine days late due to the strike. Instead, the Mets got off to the best start in their 10-year history. Jon Matlack, who took Nolan Ryan's spot in the rotation, was sensational. Fellow rookie John Milner provided power and protection for Staub in the order. And the feel-good story of the year arrived on Mother's Day in the form of Willie Mays, the long-lost son of New York, a Giant bauble that Joan Payson had wanted back in the city since before the Mets played their inaugural season in 1962. Now he was back: age 41, shaky in the outfield, slow on the fastball, yet still able to knock one over the wall for the deciding run in his first game. It was nice to have Willie back, but the next year and a half was far from grand for New York's NL club.

From May 21, 1972, when the Mets had a 25–7 record and a six-game lead, until August 14, 1973, when they had a firm grasp on last place, they went just 110–131 (a .456 percentage). Though still in the basement on the last day of August 1973, and down 3–0 in the first inning to St. Louis, the Mets came back to win in extra innings. Then they came back on the National League.

Trailing in the NL East by 5½ games on September 5, the Mets took over first place two weeks later. A ball seemingly destined for the bullpen struck the top of the wall and turned into a 7–6–2 out that symbolized a comeback as staggering as 1969, if not as memorable—or as complete. Ten of the '73 Mets were veterans of '69, including Tug McGraw, whose mantra of "Ya Gotta Believe" was backed up by his truly inspired work in the bullpen. After blowing 7 of his first 18 save chances, he was almost perfect over his final 19 appearances, winning 4, saving 12, allowing batters to hit just .157, while posting an ERA of 0.88 over his final 41 innings. Most importantly, the Mets went 17–2 in his games. With Tom Seaver pitching his way to his second Cy Young Award, Jon Matlack recovering from a fractured skull to go 7–2 down the stretch, George Stone winning 12 of his final 13 decisions, and Jerry Koosman setting a club record for consecutive shutout innings (31⅔) that stood for four decades, the Mets clinched the unlikeliest of division titles in a makeup game the day after the '73 season was supposed to have ended. Never mind that their 82–79 record was the worst for any postseason club to that point in history.

The champagne was opened again nine days later, when the Mets shocked the Reds in the National League Championship Series. The Mets lost the battle (with Pete Rose during his memorable melee with Bud Harrelson in Game 3), but they won the war. And then ran like hell as the fans tore apart every inch of Shea Stadium.

The Mets held their own against the Oakland A's, who would win three straight World Series. The Mets took a three-games-to-two lead, but Yogi Berra's decision to pitch Seaver—whose right shoulder was not 100 percent—on short rest in Game 6 against Catfish Hunter is still a much-lamented move. Matlack, who had allowed only one earned run in his last 40 innings, finally cracked in his third start of the World Series. Though the A's were world champs, the Mets' express trip from last to first in one month made good on the newly coined Yogi-ism, "It ain't over til it's over." But now it was over.

The Mets made no moves that winter. When they found themselves in fifth place in August of 1974, winning 10 of 11 put them all of one game closer in the standings. They did not score for 20 consecutive innings—and that was in just one game: a 25-inning loss to the Cardinals that was the longest National League game ever played to a conclusion. Desperately short of offense, new general manager Joe McDonald momentarily loosened Don Grant's tight clutch of the purse strings, paying San Francisco $150,000 for all-or-nothing slugger Dave Kingman. Kong set the club record for home runs (36) and just missed the team mark for strikeouts (153), while walking as many times unintentionally (29) as John

Milner, who had 288 fewer plate appearances. Tom Seaver won his third Cy Young in six years, but the Pirates rolled to their fifth NL East title since 1970.

The 1976 season marked the end of a two-year forced living arrangement in Flushing with the Yankees.* The '76 season also marked the end of the Mets as top dog in New York. The Yankees reopened Yankee Stadium and grabbed an early lead in the AL East that they never relinquished. Kingman had 30 home runs at the All-Star break, earning him enough fan votes to start the All-Star Game, but an ill-advised dive by the defensively challenged Kong squashed any dreams of his breaking Hack Wilson's NL record of 56 home runs, or even dreams of becoming the first Met to claim a home run crown. Though Kingman recovered from his thumb injury to finish a close second to Mike Schmidt (38–37), the Mets never competed against Schmidt's Phillies, who followed the bicentennial script and claimed their first postseason berth in 26 years. Jerry Koosman won 21 games for the Mets, but the poorly conceived trade of Rusty Staub for Mickey Lolich—like the trade of Tug McGraw to Philadelphia a year earlier—meant the Mets were as incapable of taking leads as they were of holding them. The Mets addressed no needs that off-season—the first year of free agency—and set the stage for the saddest period in Mets history.

The death of matriarch Joan Payson in 1975 (one week after the passing of patriarch Casey Stengel) gave M. Donald Grant yet more unchecked power. Payson's daughter, Lorinda de Roulet, assumed her mother's role, but her father, Charles Payson, who had inherited the team from his wife, was not interested in doling out the capital required to compete in the new spendthrift age of baseball. The Mets stars looked at the exploding salaries tossed out

* The Giants and Jets likewise shared Shea Stadium for football in 1975.

by other teams and wondered when they would get theirs. They'd get theirs, all right. The date was June 15, 1977.

Seaver and Grant, who had cobbled out a contract extension before the game's salary structure changed, fought almost daily in the press. The *New York Daily News* was their forum. Beat man Jack Lang worked the Seaver angle, and columnist Dick Young was firmly in management's boat with Grant. The boiling point came the day of the trade deadline when Young insulted Seaver, his family, and his friend Nolan Ryan by writing that Nancy Seaver was jealous of Ruth Ryan because of the difference in their husbands' contracts. Seaver, who had gone around Grant and negotiated a new extension with de Roulet, called the whole thing off and demanded a trade after reading Young's column. GM Joe McDonald sent the three-time Cy Young winner to two-time defending world champion Cincinnati for four players—three of whom could never crack the Big Red Machine's lineup. That same dispiriting evening, Kingman, who'd announced he would become a free agent after the season, was shipped to San Diego for Bobby Valentine, whose playing days were on borrowed time. The Mets were off the tracks. Obscurity beckoned.

The Mets shipped almost everyone of value out of town, getting back pennies on the dollar for some of the best players the team had developed. They were the lucky ones. Those left behind saw their careers pass by unnoticed save for a stubborn few who still watched on Channel 9, listened on WMCA, or, rarer still, came to Shea Stadium.

"I think the owners made the decision to redo the team and that of course culminated in the Seaver trade. After that it took several years to get things going again," says catcher John Stearns, a four-time All-Star catcher with the Mets during the dismal years. "It was different then, mostly because [of] the money. Once the money started, things changed."

Attendance dropped 400,000 below the previous season. In 1978 the Mets were lucky to reach one million—a number they hit in each of the first 15 years of Shea. The 1979 gate was a franchise record low for a full season: 788,905. In the 1960s, when memories of the abandonment by the Dodgers and Giants remained fresh, the Mets were better than nothing; by the late 1970s the Mets were nothing.

The nadir of the nadir came during the final home stand of 1979, when the Mets lost four doubleheaders in five days before 22,671—that's not an average, but rather the *total* take for the four twin bills. The Mets won their last six games on the road to keep the odometer from turning over on 100 losses. Manager Joe Torre's 63–99 club possessed the worst record in the National League. By the time the Mets played again, they had a new owner.

As bad as the 1979 Mets were, they still sold high, shattering the record for highest price for a baseball team. The $21.1 million was paid by Doubleday Publishing, led by Nelson Doubleday and his eager team president, a 43-year-old real estate developer named Fred Wilpon.

The Mets hired former Orioles general manager Frank Cashen to run the club, or more aptly, to totally rebuild it. The slogan "The Magic Is Back" was splayed on the outside of Shea Stadium, which had been stripped of its signature blue and orange exterior panels as the new owners' first order of business. What was really needed was to scrape the dreck off the field.

Whatever magic Shea beheld on April 10, 1980, was seen by just 12,219, a pitiful number but still the largest Opening Day crowd in three years. The crowds didn't get much bigger through the first two months as the Mets played their familiar brand of listless, punchless baseball. Shortly after Memorial Day, however, the Mets picked up the pace. A Steve Henderson home run to complete a comeback from a 6–0 deficit was a high point for a lost generation of Mets fans. The team's brief summer fling with contention jolted back to reality with a 29–55 second half as the Mets lost 95 games for the fourth year running. The "magic" wasn't back; it was only a marketing campaign.

Playoff contention in 1981 wasn't magic—it was a mirage created by wiping out a third of the season with a devastating strike. When the powers that be decided to start a new season in mid-August, the Mets made a run at the second-half crown. A 24–28 mark put the Mets within a game of first place in a division no one seemed to want with two weeks to go, but a five-game losing streak ended the illusion. The day after the Montreal Expos clinched the NL East second-half title at Shea, the scoreboard bluntly proclaimed during the season finale that Torre and his staff had been terminated. Despite their second-half surge, the first half had been so bad that the club's 41–62 overall record translated into 98 losses under nonstrike circumstances. The 701,910 attendance prorated for a full season was about one million. Not good enough.

Nor was Torre's replacement, George Bamberger. The longtime pitching coach for the Orioles when Frank Cashen ran the team, Bamberger also managed the Milwaukee Brewers, engineering a turnaround of that franchise in the late 1970s. The thing was, the Brewers had emerging talent, including future Hall of Fame infielders Robin Yount and Paul Molitor. The Mets had little minor league talent close to fruition, and Cashen's first attempt at buying a big name failed miserably. Former MVP George Foster was on the downside of his career. Dave Kingman, reacquired in 1981, became the first Met to lead the league in home runs with 37, but he tied the club record for strikeouts (156) and batted just .204. As a team the Mets tied for last in the NL with a .247 average and struck out more times than anyone in baseball. Bamberger had the most promising athlete on the team, Mookie Wilson, bunt until he got two strikes. Then Mookie was shipped to Alabama to spend the winter learning to slap the ball and run in one motion, like fast-pitch softball. "It was all pure junk," he wrote in his autobiography.

The pitching, which Bamberger was supposed to fix, got worse. The 1982 Mets allowed the most hits, walks, and runs in the National League—by a large margin—and completely fell apart in the second half. A 15-game losing streak came within two Ls of matching the club record set by Casey Stengel's laughable 1962 crew. Bambi's team wasn't funny, it was pathetic. Six games over .500 on Memorial Day, the '82 Mets still lost 97 times. Joe Torre winning the NL West title with Atlanta, a team that had been as down in the mouth as the Mets in recent years, didn't make 1982 any easier to swallow.

Still, Cashen had to beg his old pal not to leave. Bamberger had quit on Milwaukee in 1980 because of a bad heart; in New York his health was OK but his heart wasn't in it. He resigned in the midst of a brutal West Coast trip in June of 1983. And that was after the Mets had brought up their most highly touted prospect: Darryl Strawberry. "The Black Ted Williams" won Rookie of the Year for a last-place team, Jesse Orosco turned into one of the league's top relievers, and Ron Darling showed plenty of ability during his September call-up, but the moment that shook fans awake was the June 15 trade deadline heist of Keith Hernandez from St. Louis for troubled reliever Neil Allen and questionable prospect Rick Ownbey. A perennial Gold Glove first baseman, the 1979 NL MVP, a former batting champion, and a hero in the previous year's World Series, Hernandez was the kind of player the Mets traded away—not traded for.

Shannon Shark, born in 1969, recalled his first Mets memory as the trading of Tom Seaver. He attended many games in the 1980s—thanks to a customer at the bar his father tended who tipped in Mets tickets. Though most Mets tickets cost under $5 and seemed as worthless as currency from a third-world nation, the tips and the trips to Shea in the early 1980s paid off down the line. Today Shark is chief of *Mets Police*, a fan advocacy blog that championed the return of Banner Day and hosts the annual Queens Baseball Convention. His generation of Mets fan will always hold a special place for 1984. "You didn't expect it; it came out of nowhere," he said. "Wow, we don't suck. And this is interesting, and these pitchers look good. So this is what good baseball looks like. That's fun."

Dwight Gooden's appearance marked a sea change in how the Mets were viewed in the city and, once Doc went around the league, on a national level. The fifth overall pick in the 1982 amateur draft, Gooden was better than the dreams of even the most optimistic Mets fan—and optimism was down after seven straight seasons with an average winning percentage of .404. Along with manager Davey Johnson, the Mets transferred their top layer of talent to New York from their Triple-A home in Virginia. *Baseball America* had recognized the Mets as owning the top farm system in baseball, and the best of the best was the 1983 Lynchburg Mets. The Class A club had almost a .700 winning percentage in '83, boasting 15 players who eventually reached the major leagues. Gooden won 19 of 27 starts for Lynchburg and fanned 300—at age 18. A year later he treated National League hitters like they were still in A-ball. Gooden struck out 276 to lead the NL in 1984 and set the rookie strikeout record.

Gooden and the resurgent Mets dusted off cobwebs in sections of Shea that hadn't been disturbed in a decade. The stadium rocked on nights Doc pitched, and as the team kept winning, the place was pretty lively on other nights as well. The 1.8 million attendance was an increase of 725,000 fans, outdrawing the Yankees for the first time since the two teams shared Shea in 1975. The 65 days spent in first place were more than the '69 and '73 Mets pennant winners combined, and the 90 wins in '84 were the most by the franchise since '69. But this time it was the Cubs' year. Midseason acquisition Rick Sutcliffe, 16–1 as a Cub, was the difference. Gooden, the NL Rookie of the Year, was runner-up to Sutcliffe for the Cy Young Award while Hernandez finished second in the MVP balloting to Chicago's Ryne Sandberg.

Then came 1985. The trades for Gary Carter and Howard Johnson were augmented by a new crop of rookies ready to contribute (Lenny Dykstra, Roger McDowell, and Rick Aguilera). Yet the ending in St. Louis was a punch to the gut. Hernandez, keeping a diary of the 1985 season that would be the book with

Mike Bryan, *If at First*, summed up the resolve of the team, and the reality of the math: "It's not a matter of trying harder. We just have to win more games."

Through 1984 and 1985, the Mets had turned around a dormant franchise and won more games than any team in the major leagues, but in an era before Wild Card baseball, you either won your division or you went home. And the 1985 Mets were home for the winter.

2

Life of Collusion

October to December 1985

Ninety-eight wins means that a team has arrived. Championship Series tickets are printed, the ornamental bunting is brought out of storage, and throats across the state prepare to go raw cheering, yelling, and occasionally nipping from a flask on chilly October nights. But the 1985 Mets and their fans experienced none of this. They were the first National League team since divisional play began in 1969 to win 98 games and not reach the playoffs. The Mets' inaugural season, 1962, was the last time an NL team won 98 or more times and did not play in October.*

Ten off-seasons into the first class of free agents, signing a player on the open market had proved an excellent way of filling roster holes. For some teams, at least. For every Reggie Jackson, who'd signed two big free agent deals and led both the Yankees and Angels to the postseason, there was a Wayne Garland, whose 10-year, $2 million contract signed in 1977 was still on Cleveland's books in 1986—five years after being waived in a Tribe career encompassing just 88 starts, 28 wins, and 48 losses. Trying to gauge future performance (and health) was the biggest gamble

* Thanks, no doubt, to the 120-loss Mets as pennant fodder, two NL teams were left out in the cold despite 98-plus victories in 1962.

of free agency, and there was always the risk that the open market could turn into a high-stakes poker game with other teams. There's no group more used to getting what they want than a bunch of old men (and Marge Schott) with enough money to own a major league team. So with general managers wagering with ownership's money, the pile in the middle of the table could grow quite large. Those were the hazards of the game, which would be fine—if only free agents panned out on the field the same way they did in a rich man's imagination.

Mets general manager Frank Cashen did not like free agency. For those who complain about 21st-century Mets GM Sandy Alderson's free agent track record, Alderson has nothing on Cashen. In his dozen seasons running the Mets, Cashen signed one "big-name" free agent, which came in his final year, 1991—and it was a mistake: Vince Coleman. Yet between 1980 and 1990 Cashen engineered the most productive period in franchise history. He mostly used free agents to fill small holes on the roster or, in the rebuilding years in the early 1980s, signed past-their-prime players to mask the fact that the team had hardly anyone who could play.

In his first six seasons with the team, Cashen signed a grand total of five major league free agents who played out their options with other teams. All were near the end of their careers, and three of those signings—Rusty Staub, Mike Cubbage, and Dave Roberts—came in a one-month span in Cashen's first full year as Mets GM. Staub, a fan favorite during his first tour with the 1970s Mets as the team's main run producer, signed with the Mets in December 1980 and emerged as one of the most productive pinch hitters in baseball. Cubbage did little as a Mets player, but he stayed on as a minor league manager, serving at every level of the farm system before returning to New York as a major league coach; he even managed the Mets for the last week of the 1991 season. Roberts, a 36-year-old southpaw, was released in May 1981 with a 9.39 ERA.

Cashen's other two free agents came in 1984 and were odd choices. He signed Jerry Martin on St. Patrick's Day, 1984, shortly after the 35-year-old spare outfielder finished serving a jail sentence for conspiracy to purchase cocaine. January of '84 signee Dick Tidrow, the former Yankees reliever late of the White Sox, seemed like an impulse buy. Cashen signed him one week after the White Sox claimed Tom Seaver in a compensation claim. Cashen, who'd built back fan equity lost during the George Foster debacle by bringing home "The Franchise" in 1983, erred mightily by not putting Seaver on the list of protected players. A rule—subsequently removed—allowed teams losing a free agent to select another major leaguer as compensation from a pool of unprotected players. There were bitter feelings between the Mets and White Sox, and though Chicago clearly didn't want Tidrow back, it was odd that Cashen chose this time to sign his first free agent in three years—especially one he wound up releasing a month into the season.

Whatever the reasoning behind his past dalliances with free agency, Cashen would not be involved in any such splurges for 1986. As it turned out, every team suddenly looked at free agency with the disdain of a Frank Cashen. It was no accident.

On the day of Game 3 of the 1985 World Series, major league owners convened in a private auditorium at the Anheuser-Busch Brewery in St. Louis. August "Gussie" Busch was the longtime owner of the Cardinals and, as president of the country's number one brewery, he truly could be called "The King of Beers." Yet the owners weren't there to listen to Busch, or even to drink beer—they were Scotch men, by and large.

"The Lords of the Realm," as John Helyar called the owners in his book of the same name, were addressed that day by outgoing Players Relations Committee chair Lee MacPhail. MacPhail, a second-generation major league executive and future Hall of Famer, had served as two teams' general manager and then American League president. His finest moment was helping finally settle the 1981 baseball strike, but he was best known for having ruled against the Yankees in the 1983 "Pine Tar Game," overruling AL umpires who had disallowed George Brett's game-winning homer because the bat handle had more pine tar than the rulebook permitted. MacPhail's report as outgoing PRC chair was his last act before retiring from the game, and he had the rapt attention of the owners convened at Anheuser-Busch. His report, in the wake of the two-day strike of that summer—a blessedly brief but still humiliating defeat for ownership—presented the facts and figures of how the last decade of ascending player rights and salaries had made the Lords, well, less Lordly. At the end of the 1985 season, major league teams were responsible for $50 million to nonplaying players, those who were either injured or so ineffective they had been released. The report surveyed 104 hitters and 57 pitchers, all with long-term contracts. All had experienced declining performances as compared to before the start of the contracts. These players, by and large, also spent more time on the disabled list than players with one-year contracts.

MacPhail's report concluded:

> *We must stop daydreaming that one free agent signing will bring a pennant. Somehow we must get our operations back to the point where a normal year for the average team at least results in a break-even situation, so that clubs are not led to make rash moves in the vain hope that they might bring a pennant and a resulting change in their financial position. This requires resistance to fan and media pressure and it is not easy. On the other hand, the future health and stability of our Game depend on your response to these problems.*

The pressure was on the owners like a 3–2 pitch with the bases loaded against the game's toughest closer. And that closer was Commissioner Peter Ueberroth.

Ueberroth, who was given to scolding without warning, went around the room asking who among them would be signing free agents in the coming weeks. Most said they would not, but Ueberroth had harsh words for the group as a whole anyway: "It's your own stupidity. . . . Let us try to operate in a businesslike way before we, as a sport, are bankrupt." The commissioner held neither the owners nor the game in any particular regard. His legacy was of more importance to him than the game's legacy; Ueberroth wanted to be remembered as the commissioner who got rid of drugs and put baseball back on solid fiscal footing. Owners were in such bad shape, they had little choice but to listen and follow.

Everyone listened to Peter Ueberroth in the 1980s. He had been *Time*'s Man of the Year in 1984 for resurrecting the Olympics and engineering a $200 million profit for an event that had come to be a burden for the hosts. A decade earlier, the city of Denver had agreed to give back the "honor" of hosting the 1976 Winter Games.* The 1976 Summer Games in Montreal gave birth to the lasting symbol of ceaseless cost overruns: Olympic Stadium, which became the Expos' home after the Games but remained saddled with debt as well as the moniker "The Big Owe." The 1980 Winter Games in Lake Placid had resulted in pride in American winter sports—thanks mostly to speed skater Eric Heiden's unprecedented five gold medals and the U.S. hockey team's fabled "Miracle on Ice," but even as the prestige helped soften the financial losses incurred in the determined little upstate New York village, any momentum was immediately pushed aside by a U.S. boycott of the 1980 Summer Games in Moscow as a protest to the U.S.S.R.'s invasion of Afghanistan. Ueberroth, who had made his fortune in the travel agency business, didn't just change the image of the Olympics at the 1984 Summer Games in Los Angeles; he changed the profit margins. It didn't hurt that the Soviet Union's retaliatory boycott had made medals easy pickings for the Americans in '84. Ueberroth also jacked up the cost for supporting the

* Winter Games veteran Innsbruck, Austria, jumped in and took over as host in 1976.

Games so that a $10,000 sponsorship fee in Lake Placid in 1980 cost $4 million four years later. Did baseball ever need a makeover specialist like him.

When the Lords eagerly tapped Ueberroth to replace Bowie Kuhn as commissioner, the owners were essentially saying they no longer needed a gatekeeper to keep the national pastime sacrosanct; they needed someone to boost the gate. As any outsider could see from a mile away, what the owners required most was someone to protect them from themselves: to once and for all stop fighting over players past their prime, to stop bidding up services against each other—or worst of all, against no competitor at all.

Baseball was rife with recent examples of teams pushing their payrolls into the stratosphere. The Royals handed out three "lifetime contracts" in an 11-month span to homegrown products George Brett, Dan Quisenberry, and Willie Wilson. The lifetime contracts were generally for less money per year than comparable stars were receiving. As Brett put it, to the revulsion of those reading his comments in the paper while waiting for, say, a city bus to take them to a $3.35 per hour minimum wage job, "The annual salary is nothing." He caught himself, yet too late: "It's not nothing. But there's a lot of people making more." Those people would soon include the first men to surge beyond the $2 million annual salary barrier: Ozzie Smith signed a four-year, $8.7 million deal in St. Louis, followed by Eddie Murray for $13 million over five years in Baltimore. All of the aforementioned players were 30 or older in 1985, and all of them signed before they could go on the open market. If they'd waited, those who were free agents in the fall of '85 would most likely have ended up where they came from—and for a lot less money.

As Ueberroth chastised the owners in St. Louis on October 22, 1985, he turned to the lawyers present: Lou Hoynes, baseball's all-purpose counsel; Jim Garner, American League counsel; and Barry Rona, PRC chair replacing MacPhail. The commissioner told the lawyers, "Stop this discussion at any time if at any point it smacks of collusion." The lawyers did not stop Ueberroth; it seemed like nobody could.

The commissioner reportedly ended the meeting with this admonition: "You all agree we have a problem. Go solve it." Those words would come up at a later grievance hearing regarding collusion. But that was a long way away. Baseball was in for a glorious summer—and fall.

When Ueberroth had taken over as commissioner a year earlier, his face still tanned from the glow of the Los Angeles Games, he was quick to put the owners in their place. He had been hired because the golden goose was on life support. Ueberroth's philosophy can be best summarized in what writer John Helyar described as a Ueberrothian "parable" given early in his tenure as commissioner. "Let's say I sat each of you down in front of a red button or a black button. Push the red button and you'd win the World Series but lose $10 million. Push the black button and you would make $4 million and finish somewhere in the middle." He paused and looked at the reduced Lords in his midst. "The problem is, most of you would push the red one."

Given the Mets' $17 million per year cable deal with Chuck Dolan's SportsChannel—the envy of most clubs and $10.3 million more annually than the Yankees—Frank Cashen could make the red button as profitable as the black button. And infinitely more satisfying.

Cashen was not a spendthrift, an attitude evidenced by his free agent abstinence. A baseball man of the old school, he'd come to the game after serving as a lawyer, a newspaperman, and a brewery manager. The owner of National Brewing, Jerold Hoffberger, also owned the Baltimore Orioles, and he'd put Cashen in charge of baseball operations in 1964, after Lee MacPhail left to join the Yankees. The Orioles won the 1966 World Series, the first of four pennants and six postseason appearances in his decade with the club (Cashen had taken the title of general manager in 1971). He was mentioned as a candidate for American League president, which, ironically went to MacPhail, and even was brought up as a potential commissioner during a failed attempt to oust Bowie Kuhn in 1975. Cashen went back into the brewery business at Hoffberger's request, but he wound up in the commissioner's office—as administrator for baseball operations. Kuhn, along with several teams, recommended him as the best man available to run the just-purchased Mets in the winter of 1980.

Cashen built the Mets from the ground up. He'd worked the draft, taking advantage of the Mets' high draft placement based on their lousy record in the early 1980s. He prudently made trades and learned from mistakes (relief ace Jeff Reardon for Ellis Valentine was arguably the worst trade of his first six seasons). And he scooped up players who had talent yet were ignored in the 75 rounds of the amateur draft, including Doug Sisk, Ed Hearn, and one of the organization's better finds: Kevin Mitchell.

As the Mets evaluated themselves after the painful end to the '85 season, they had to take a look at every aspect of the team and see where they could get better.

The 1985 Mets lineup seemed formidable, but their .257 batting average, .323 on-base percentage, 134 home runs, and 695 runs were just about average among the 26 teams in the major leagues. Though the Mets were better than most National League teams in these offensive categories, their strength was clearly pitching. The staff fanned more batters than any major league team while allowing fewer hits—and baserunners—than all but one club. The young guns put the emphasis on young: at 24.7 years old on average, Mets pitchers were nearly a year and a half younger than any staff in baseball. But that was actually a chink in the armor that Cashen sought to shore up.

In the final week of the 1985 season in St. Louis, the Mets lacked the poised veteran who could go into a hostile environment and get the team the win needed to tie the NL East race.

Rick Aguilera had been a key member of the '85 rotation—and would be again in '86—but the Mets needed a veteran. Preferably a left-hander.

Lefty John Tudor was a marvel, traded twice in as many years before blossoming at age 31 with the Cardinals. He was a difference maker against the Mets in 1985, just as the acquisition of Rick Sutcliffe by the Cubs in 1984 had helped push Chicago past the Mets down the stretch that season. Tudor lost seven of his first eight decisions as a Cardinal in '85 and then went 20–1 with 10 shutouts and a 1.37 ERA from June to the end of the year—even better than Sutcliffe's 16–1 mark in his final three and a half months in '84. Tudor would have won the Cy Young Award in any other year except for 1985. Dwight Gooden's poise and pure power—not to mention his jaw-dropping stats—awed writers, players, and fans alike. As had been the case with Sutcliffe the previous year, Gooden took all 24 first-place votes for the Cy Young by the Baseball Writers Association of America. For his 21 wins, Tudor got 21 second-place votes . . . and a National League pennant.

Tudor hadn't seemed like anything special as a Pirate in 1984. Three pitchers for last-place Pittsburgh had a better ERA and equaled or bettered his 12 wins. While New York was abuzz with the big-ticket acquisitions of Rickey Henderson by the Yankees and Gary Carter by the Mets, the deal that proved more significant for the season ahead was the relatively low-key deal between the Cardinals and Pirates that sent Tudor and catcher Brian Harper to St. Louis for 35-year-old outfielder George Hendrick, whom the Pirates would trade to the Angels that August in a cost-cutting move. Whitey Herzog liked Tudor's makeup as well as his apprenticeship in Boston, where he'd been a starter for parts of five seasons before he was dealt to Pittsburgh after the '83 season. Herzog's reasoning behind the deal was simple: "Left-handers who pitch at Fenway Park, with that short left-field, have to be smart or they get killed . . . I figured John Tudor would be a hell of a pitcher in a big ballpark like ours." Busch Stadium was cavernous in its pre–Mark McGwire configuration, and the logic was sound. If Fenway-bred southpaw Tudor could thrive in a big ballpark with a change of scenery, maybe the Mets could strike gold with a lefty from Boston.

November 13, 1985, was an especially busy day for the Mets front office. It was the day that teams had to get the roster down to 40, not an easy task for an organization brimming with blue chip minor leaguers as well as a win-now mantra. "In the last 48 hours," director of player personnel Joe McIlvaine said at the time, "one third of our roster changed. We made 12 deletions and 11 additions, and now we're back to 40."

In order to add eight prize minor leaguers to the protected roster, including future Mets Dave Magadan, David West, and Barry Lyons, the Mets started cutting. They released veterans Tom Paciorek, acquired in July of '85 as bench insurance; Kelvin Chapman, the right-hand side of the second-base platoon; and Brent Gaff, who spent the year on the disabled list with a rotator cuff problem and never pitched again professionally. Others were sent outright to Triple-A Tidewater: sidewinder Terry Leach and southpaw Randy Niemann, plus minor leaguer John Young and versatile veteran and future Manager of the Year Clint Hurdle. Hurdle had the kind of playing career that made people consider the legitimacy of a *Sports Illustrated* cover jinx. His smiling 20-year-old mug and wind-coifed hair graced newsstands in March of 1978, all of nine major league games under his belt in Kansas City, with the label "This Year's Phenom." When the phenom part didn't pan out, Hurdle became the hardest-working guy on every team he played for and even learned to catch, at the suggestion of his minor league manager, Davey Johnson.

Johnson told Hurdle, "Clint, first thing I'm going to do is get you to play third; that's going to help you get back to the big leagues."

Bob Ojeda NATIONAL BASEBALL HALL OF FAME LIBRARY, COOPERSTOWN, NY

"And he worked his butt off," Johnson explained. "Then at the end of the year, I said, 'Now I'm going to put you behind the plate and that's going to get you back to the big leagues.' Because he's big and strong and has a good arm. And he was a fast learner. And so St. Louis picked him up, took him back to the big leagues as a backup catcher, like a utility guy." With 24-man rosters on the horizon, a player like Hurdle was valuable enough for Herzog to scoop him up for the Cardinals in 1986 in the Rule 5 draft.

The other four players the Mets needed to cut down were shipped to Boston. At the time, it was projected that the main player coming back, Bob Ojeda, would be the fifth starter, or perhaps bullpen insurance in case Jesse Orosco had another poor season. The most intriguing part of the deal initially was the volume of players involved. The Mets got three other pitchers besides Ojeda: Tom McCarthy and John Mitchell, who had brief major league careers, plus Chris Bayer, who went 16–4 in the minors for the Mets in 1986 but never rose past Double-A. The Mets sent four players back: an outfielder who would debut in Boston that summer, LaSchelle Tarver, plus three other young players who already had major league experience. They were outfielder John Christensen, reliever Wes Gardner, and a first-round pick from 1983 the Mets had drafted before Aguilera and West, and who'd been the number one starter at the University of Texas, ahead of Roger Clemens. A pitcher named Calvin Schiraldi.

As usual, Frank Cashen preferred to solve personnel decisions via trade. The free agency slowdown did not affect the makeup of the Mets. Like everyone else, they'd lose cash when an arbitrator ruled later in the decade that owners had colluded to restrict player movement, breaking the rule against teams acting in concert in player dealings. The 1986 Mets benefited from competing clubs not signing free agents. But the Mets benefited far more from another Ueberroth decision that could have left the team without its best player in '86.

3

Exquisitely Bored

January and February 1986

Dwight Eugene Gooden was already known to the world simply as Doc, a just turned 21-year-old superstar supporting his parents, the front man for one of baseball's best teams, and a demigod in the cultural center of New York. But in the first weeks of 1986, like some Bret Easton Ellis character in *Less Than Zero* (soon to be a Brat Pack flick) with the name Clay or Trent or Rip, Doc actually was just a restless kid flitting place to place in his native Tampa, a six-pack in his lap in a Mercedes. Ellis, born the same year as Gooden, didn't need to put it on paper; the age and situation pointed to dangerous indifference. Dwight Gooden was bored.

Gooden was actually looking for marijuana, but he arrived at his cousin Bo's house and found none. Doc had tried pot a year earlier only to determine that it did little for him besides cause drowsiness. He planned to try weed again in the hopes of relaxing. Other athletes found it helped them wind down after a game, a road trip, or a season. Then maybe some magic grass could turn his parents' home back into the refuge it had been the previous off-season, when his unexpected success as New York's favorite teen had made time with his family the balm he needed after the excess

Dwight Gooden on the field at Shea Stadium before Game 6 of the 1986 World Series DAN CARUBIA

attention. Going from Rookie of the Year to pitcher of a generation in one year, plus hanging out socially with his hard-drinking teammates, had changed Gooden's perspective by the time the 1985 season ended. After winning 24 games and pitching's Triple Crown, he truly was a superstar, his likeness eight stories high on the side of a New York City building. He was no longer content to sit in the house with his parents and extended family, behaving like the same unspoiled son his father had drilled daily, transforming a tall, skinny colt into a Triple Crown thoroughbred. In two years Gooden had surpassed any father's aspirations, and his next contract would make him a millionaire. That so many strangers had placed so much faith and hope in Gooden made him even more restless.

Cousin Bo went out to find Doc some pot. He was prudent enough not to take his Cy Young–winning kin (make that his unanimous Cy Young–winning kin) along on a ride to buy drugs. Someone might recognize "Dwight the Great" from the cover of *Sports Illustrated*. But Doc was not alone at his cousin's house. Two scantily clad women—Cousin Bo also knew prostitutes—were in a back bedroom kissing each other, drinking vodka, snorting lines off a small mirror, and issuing a siren's call to Dr. K. He was still just a young man whose head could be turned by the prospect of something easy and fun. The girls lured him into the back bedroom. He emerged a different person.

By the time his cousin came back, Gooden was no longer interested in giving weed a chance. "Coke gave me a feeling I'd always wanted but didn't know how to find," he wrote many years and many rehab stints later. "It convinced me immediately that nothing else mattered at all. No pressure. No worries. No need to stop. I had never heard that cocaine had calming properties. But that night it made me feel calm. The drug hit quickly, and I had no confusion. This is how I wanted to feel."

At the same time Gooden was saying yes in the flesh, he was saying no in a coloring book. His likeness along with several other ballplayers, including Dave Winfield and Don Mattingly of the Yankees, was part of a 1986 activity book titled *The Pros Say It's OK to Say No to Drugs*. Having Gooden on the cover proved to be, of course, the ultimate irony, but so was the fact that the coloring book was produced by the MLB Players Association, which was working diligently to make sure players would not be subjected to random drug tests. Gooden was not the only one having trouble "just saying no," to borrow the line—so to speak—that First Lady Nancy Reagan had turned into a national rallying cry. It is a lot easier to say no on paper than when handed a mirror and a rolled-up dollar bill. "Cocaine didn't fill my days like a job or a hobby would have," Gooden confessed in his memoir, *Doc*, in 2013. "But cocaine was never entirely out of my mind again."

Even before Dwight Gooden tried his first line of cocaine, baseball had endured way too much of the stuff already. The go-to drug for the '80s chic, it was popular enough that Americans spent $80 billion a year on the drug at the height of the decade. And at first, it felt like money well spent. Cocaine has the ability to let the user be the life of the party all night long and into the next day. For ballplayers, with too much money and too much time away from home, the drug became a powerful lure. And far too many ballplayers went from enjoying cocaine parties with their pals, teammates, and hangers-on to instead being a party of one. The highly addictive drug can soon make heavy users value it over friends, family, and livelihood. Many in society lost jobs because of cocaine, but big league baseball is not some $16,800 a year job (the average salary in 1985). Being a ballplayer is the ultimate job. The 1985 average salary of $370,000 was the result of a 12 percent increase per year for a decade. Players have winters off and the eyes of attractive young women on their every move, and if a man is prudent with his money, fortunate in his health, and prodigious in his talent, he can provide enough money not just for his lifetime, but for the lifetime of his progeny.

Jeopardizing that security, or thumbing your nose at the genetic lottery that put you in that position, is something the average fan can't understand. They might understand why *they'd* do drugs, but they just can't understand why *you'd* do drugs if you were a ballplayer.

Those who grew up before the more lenient 1960s, or people of any age who thought drugs an anathema, were far from sympathetic in terms of narcotics use. That included most of the men in charge of the teams and the major leagues in the 1980s. And reasons given for using drugs often sounded flimsy in the light of day.

"Part of it was peer pressure," future Hall of Fame hitter and major league manager Paul Molitor explained in 1985. "I was single and in Milwaukee and I hung around with some wrong people."

Dick Davis was one of those wrong people. A major league outfielder and designated hitter, he was a member of the Kintetsu Buffaloes in the Japanese Pacific League by 1985. Davis told federal agents that while with the Brewers in 1979 and 1980, he and Molitor had "drug problems because of an identity crisis."

"I felt it was just an experiment I tried, and I got hooked," said Tim Raines, who started using cocaine with older teammates after his stellar rookie season with the 1981 Montreal Expos. His subsequent "sophomore slump" was more than just hitting into bad luck. "You find yourself liking it. You try it again and again. All of a sudden, it gets to the point where you have to have it." Raines admitted snorting coke in the dugout bathroom, carrying it in his batting gloves to conceal it on the field, and sliding headfirst into second to keep the gram bottles in his back pocket from breaking.

And, like Dwight Gooden, some players got deeper into the drug because they were bored. Lonnie Smith was a world champion who hit .339 in 100 games with the 1980 Phillies. He finished third in the Rookie of the Year voting to, ironically, Steve Howe, who would be suspended from baseball seven times for cocaine abuse. Smith soon had his own problems with the drug. After six years in the minor leagues, Smith was now an established player and no longer had to spend winters proving himself by playing in South America, where he had first tried cocaine. He had more time and more money than he knew what to do with. Cocaine filled the holes in his schedule. "I really went over the bend with it because I had nothing to do," he said. "I did it almost every day during the winter."

Though cocaine was far from a performance-enhancing drug, many players claimed to have experienced a good game after using the drug for the first time and kept on using it, thinking it positively affected their performance. "However, they eventually discovered that the drug hampered them and diluted their talent," two New York journalists wrote just as cocaine was about to steal the spotlight from baseball's tight division races.

It all came to light during a four-part investigative piece in the *New York Times* in mid-August 1985. The settlement of the two-day strike earlier that month left no smokescreen to obscure the game's drug problem from the populace. Or the media. Writers Murray Chass and Michael Goodwin bared the issue of cocaine in baseball for all to see. The investigative series—picked up by the wire services and run in newspapers throughout the country—also acted as a preview for a federal trial in Pittsburgh to begin the Thursday after Labor Day weekend.

The situation was such a circus that the Pirate Parrot—or at least the man in the mascot suit—played a major role. Kevin Koch (pronounced, um, Coke) made $30,000 a year as the mascot, debuting the year the Pirates won the World Series, 1979. Koch soon had a sideline arranging for cocaine for several Pirates and their out-of-town ballplaying friends. Federal agents came to his door in November 1984, and that same day he wore a wire while buying cocaine from his close high school friend Dale Shiffman. Koch received immunity from prosecution, but his days were over as the Pirate Parrot. Koch was lambasted nationally in the press as "Stool Parrot," but he flew off with no jail time. Shiffman was found guilty on 20 of 111 counts and served two years in a federal penitentiary.

Seven men who trafficked cocaine for baseball players were on trial, known as "the Pittsburgh Seven." A year earlier four Kansas City Royals had become the first active major leaguers to serve prison sentences for cocaine. The KC players' luck was especially bad because possession was pursued as a felony in the Tenth Circuit Court in Kansas while in neighboring Missouri, where the players actually played, similar offenders were usually charged with a misdemeanor. In 1985 in Pittsburgh only those who dealt drugs faced prison sentences. The players called to the stand were not on trial—except in the court of public opinion.

Dave Parker was an All-Star, a batting champion, a Most Valuable Player, and, at 6-foot-5 and 230 pounds, an intimidating guy, but he was grilled on the stand by attorney Adam Renfroe. He questioned Parker on the outfielder's Rolex watch and diamond ring—both valued at more than $20,000—and then dramatically asked Parker to account for himself. "How do you carry that burden, knowing that because of you the Pirates went from the world championship to being the worst in the National League?"

Parker fought off the question like a breaking ball on his fists: "I don't carry that burden because I don't take responsibility for what adults do."

Keith Hernandez was summoned from California to Pittsburgh with the Mets trying to win their first NL East title in a dozen years. Just as he mesmerized locker-room reporters with his gift for language, astute observations, and quick responses, his statements in court produced two of the most-used quotes from the proceedings. First, he shocked everyone by saying that "40 percent of all major league players used cocaine in 1980." He immediately regretted using that figure, saying in the diary he was keeping on the '85 season, "How could I know what the percentage was?" (His former manager, Whitey Herzog, had used the same 40 percent figure in the *New York Times* series to describe the number of drug users on the 1980 Cardinals.)

Hernandez also regretted calling cocaine "a demon inside me." He admitted using the drug over a three-year period, stopping on his own volition the year before he was traded from the Cardinals to the Mets in 1983. He lamented dramatizing his use, which he later identified as "never massive."

With a month to go before the end of the 1985 season, the courtroom histrionics in Pittsburgh proved far more riveting than a mid-September baseball game. Though the ballplayers had been granted immunity and were not on trial, their roles in the scandal would last longer than the jail terms handed out to the seven men sentenced for supplying the drugs for the players. As spring training 1986 loomed, baseball planned its retribution for the players involved.

The Kansas City cocaine case was the closest thing there was to a precedent for Major League Baseball in terms of punishment. After serving time in prison, the four Royals were handed suspensions during the 1984 season. Vida Blue, a former MVP, Cy Young winner, and three-time world champion and the first man to start the All-Star Game in both leagues, was suspended for the entire '84 season. But that was with Bowie Kuhn as commissioner.

The suspension of Blue was one of the final significant acts of Kuhn's 15½-year tenure, but the commissioner took his role as baseball's guardian seriously enough to visit the fan turned dealer in prison and administer a sworn statement. Mark Liebl let Royals players, plus the visiting players they brought, snort cocaine for free as long as they used it at his Dodge City home; doggie baggies were sold at the below-market rate of $80 per gram. Blue's involvement and his conviction for actual possession resulted in the yearlong suspension. The other players—Willie Wilson, Willie Mays Aikens, and Jerry Martin—had their yearlong suspensions shortened by an arbitrator. After serving his suspension, Martin spent the final four months of his career with the '84 Mets, batting .154.

If Keith Hernandez were to miss, say, one-fifth of the 1986 season—Martin had been suspended 33 games in 1984—it could have a devastating effect on a ball club that relied so heavily on its first baseman's bat, glove, and leadership. This was supposed to be the Mets' year. Finally.

Having recently returned from the Super Bowl in New Orleans, where the Chicago Bears put an exclamation point on a dominant season by crushing the New England Patriots, Hernandez granted one of the few interviews he gave that off-season. The Pittsburgh trial, his divorce, and falling just short against the team that had traded him, made 1985 a trying year for Hernandez, even as he hit .309 and finished eighth in the MVP balloting. He traveled the country after the season, receiving positive responses almost everywhere he went. That wasn't surprising when he was on a cruise with Mets fans in the Caribbean—he had been cheered long and loud in his first at bat at Shea following the Pittsburgh trials. Spending the holidays with his children in St. Louis was far more of a test because of the way he'd been booed roundly during the climactic series at Busch Stadium in October.

"People have actually been very supportive, even in St. Louis," he told Joseph Durso of the *New York Times* in early February of 1986. "But I have no idea what the commissioner will do."

No one knew what Ueberroth would do. And on any given day it was hard to be sure *where* he was. He had met individually with 23 of the 24 players mentioned during the Pittsburgh testimony.* Olympic-savior Ueberroth prided himself on being the man who would rescue sport from the scourge of drugs. Though

---

* Ex-Met John Milner, retired from the game and a key figure in the wayward nightlife in the Pirates clubhouse, refused to meet with the commissioner.

he longed to be the anti-drug commissioner, he was more like the commissioner who didn't enjoy baseball very much. When not lecturing owners at the quarterly meetings, he was not usually near his New York office or at the ballparks. He served on several corporate boards, negotiated mergers, and played a lot of golf. Spending February in frigid Manhattan instead of at home in Newport Beach, California? That was a crazier notion than owners spending money on free agents during his reign.

Finally, on February 28, 1986, Ueberroth emerged in midtown Manhattan to hand down baseball's sentence. He approached the podium just three days after National Basketball Association commissioner David Stern slapped a lifetime ban on Michael Ray Richardson of the New Jersey Nets for failing his third drug test in three seasons. That did nothing to lighten the mood heading into Ueberroth's press conference.

The first part of the baseball commissioner's ruling sounded exceedingly harsh. Joaquin Andujar, Dale Berra, Enos Cabell, Jeffrey Leonard, Dave Parker, Lonnie Smith, and Hernandez would be suspended for one year without pay. Six of the seven had testified under immunity at the Pittsburgh trial the previous September; the seventh, Andujar, a 20-game winner and All-Star the previous two years for St. Louis, had been subpoenaed but not called to testify in the drug trials. He was traded to Oakland over the winter.

But before teams or fans or players or Players Association lawyers could hang their heads, seethe, or file a grievance over the ruling, Ueberroth offered a lifeline: The players would not miss any games if they agreed to random drug testing for the rest of their careers, contributed 100 hours of community service each of the next two years, and handed 10 percent of their 1986 salaries to drug abuse programs. Another 14 players were given lesser penalties, but if any of these players failed a drug test they would be suspended immediately. The commissioner also cleared two key members of the Pirates' 1979 world championship "family":

four-time batting champion Bill Madlock and Pirates legend Willie Stargell. Dale Berra and John Milner had accused the pair of providing them amphetamines, the drug used to perk up major leaguers long before and long after the Pittsburgh trials.*

Drugs would never leave baseball. Even as the cocaine problem diminished—at least in the headlines—generations of players who grew up with weight training, vitamins, and supplements would push baseball in a direction that proved even more dangerous to the game's reputation. Later travails with steroids and other performance-enhancing drugs, which were seen almost exclusively as a football problem in the mid-1980s, would dwarf baseball's drug abuse situation in the Reagan era. But the cocaine issue was big news in the '80s—so much so that United Press International named drugs the number one sports story of 1985. It was not something anyone in the baseball hierarchy was happy about—especially Peter Ueberroth.

So before the commissioner dismissed the room on February 28, 1986, Ueberroth digressed into scolding mode: "I am obviously not pleased in having to make these decisions . . . But this is an emergency time for baseball. The seriousness of the transgressions demands the actions I have taken."

Hernandez said at the time that he was pleased he would be able to play, but he was stunned by his $135,000 fine, the largest penalty handed out by Ueberroth. He initially considered filing a grievance but soon dropped the idea. The players all paid their fines, abided by the conditions, and played in '86. Hernandez was the only player involved ever voted by fans to start an All-Star Game post-Pittsburgh.

Ueberroth continued to talk about making baseball drug free, but two such measures he tried to install in 1985 and 1986 were shot down by the Players Association, which contended that universal drug testing infringed upon players' rights. The

* John Milner also threw 1970s Mets teammate and Hall of Fame legend Willie Mays under the "greenie" bus, but Peter Ueberroth did not ask to meet with Mays.

commissioner's stand could not compete with the realities of law, collective bargaining, and the country's most powerful union—especially when the commissioner and owners were at the same time involved in collusion against free agents.

Though players who agreed to Ueberroth's terms in lieu of suspensions were required to be tested, the Players Association rescinded previous contract clauses requiring other players to take drug tests. The Mets, for one, were not in favor of tests for all. Frank Cashen, a lawyer as well as a general manager, stated during the winter of '86 that "irresponsible drug testing has no place in our league." He did note, however, that a letter was sent to players stating that if they wanted a drug test stipulation in their contract, "possibly to impress a future employer or for whatever reason, we will include it." That option for contract language would come back to haunt the club and its star pitcher, but as far as '86 went, it was time to play baseball. Or, as the sign being prepared for Shea Stadium's exterior said, "Baseball like it oughta be."

4

The Perfectly Strange Couple

March 1986

In March of 1986, two mismatched distant relations moved into the same cramped space; their awkwardness and misadventures were endearing enough to become a television mainstay for the rest of the decade. *Perfect Strangers* starred Mark Linn-Baker, a Yale-trained actor who had worked alongside Woody Allen and Peter O'Toole, but he was just the straight man. The new show was built around Bronson Pinchot, who'd appeared as a high school friend of Tom Cruise in the 1983 hit movie *Risky Business*, about a punk turned pimp turned Princeton freshman. Pinchot's biggest role to date, though, had been as scene-stealer Serge, an art gallery assistant with a weird accent and fondness for making espresso in the 1984 Eddie Murphy movie *Beverly Hills Cop*, which sold more tickets than any R-rated film since *The Exorcist* in 1973. Before you could say, "Don't be stupid," the New York–born Pinchot was doing another foreign accent and saying "Don't be ridiculous" as Balki, a cousin from an obscure Mediterranean island who comes to Chicago and moves in with Linn-Baker's character, Larry.

Perfect Strangers was ABC's latest incarnation of *The Odd Couple* premise, a show the network had canceled a decade earlier only to see it explode in popularity in syndication. That show

Whitey Herzog and Davey Johnson

NATIONAL BASEBALL HALL OF FAME LIBRARY, COOPERSTOWN, NY

featured two men—one a slob sportswriter, Oscar, the other a neat-freak commercial photographer (portraits a specialty) named Felix—who moved in together after their wives kicked them out. The incompatible roommate comedy came from prolific playwright Neil Simon, followed by a Walter Matthau–Jack Lemmon movie. *The Odd Couple* on ABC was the first of many shows produced by hitmaker Garry Marshall. Dale McRaven, who worked with Marshall on *Mork & Mindy*, an offshoot of Marshall's biggest hit, *Happy Days*, was a creator of *Perfect Strangers*. *Perfect Strangers* lasted almost two years longer on the network than *The Odd Couple*, but it did not have the writing, acting, or syndication staying power of the iconic show with Jack Klugman and Tony Randall, which hinged on the immortal question, "Can two divorced men share an apartment without driving each other crazy?"

Mismatched roommates was a recurring theme in baseball in March of 1986: the odd coupling of Mets and Cardinals. These division rivals played almost halfway across the country from one another each summer but shared the same ballpark in Florida every spring. By 1986 the teams had been spring roommates at Al Lang Stadium in St. Petersburg for a quarter century. Before the Mets, the Cardinals shared St. Pete with the Yankees, who opted for Fort Lauderdale after 1961. The Mets took the Yankees' spot in St. Petersburg, and the mood considerably lightened. With the Cardinals essentially playing spring straight man, Mets manager Casey Stengel entertained an army of eager scribes at the ready. Stengel, who had trained 10 pennant-winning teams in this same spring locale with the Yankees, played it strictly for laughs with his abysmal expansion club. Stengel pronouncements turned into comic bits worthy of Neil Simon: "Get yourself in shape now, you can drink during the season," and "There will be two buses to the park from the hotel. The two o'clock bus is for those who need a little extra work and then there will be an empty bus leaving at five o'clock."

The shared atmosphere wasn't always convivial, like when St. Louis's fierce ace Bob Gibson welcomed Tommie Agee to the National League by drilling him in the helmet in the first inning of the first spring training game in 1968—it took Agee until 1969 to get his bearings in New York. After the Mets won the World Series in '69, however, the Mets and Cards became NL East foes training in close proximity at a time when few teams shared spring facilities. The budding rivalry lulled as the Mets hit the skids in the late 1970s, arriving for spring training with their sights set on fifth place, not first. On a back field in St. Petersburg in a B squad game in March of 1984, the Cardinals regulars who'd shirked the travel associated with an A game got their first glimpse of a kid fresh out of A-ball: Dwight Gooden. It was like a resurrection of Bob Gibson, only younger, wilder, and dressed in blue. Enmity between the clubs bubbled to the surface once more as the Mets arose from the dead, raising the odd question: Can two division rivals share a spring training facility without driving each other crazy?

The answer came quickly in March of 1986. It was no.

Like the Mets, the Cardinals trained minor leaguers at one site in Tampa–St. Pete, had their major leaguers in another facility, and played in a third location. An assortment of major and minor league Cardinals bussed over to Al Lang Stadium one morning to play the Mets. Sharing a ballpark meant putting the two clubs on one another's spring schedules for convenience's sake, even if they were NL East rivals who played each other 18 times when the games counted. The Cardinals crammed into the small locker room with too many bodies trying to make the 24-man roster of the defending National League champions. A sign similar to a movie marquee on the Al Lang scoreboard reminded anyone who might have forgotten who won the previous year's pennant. The next seven months would be about establishing who was going to win the 1986 division title, unless you possessed a singular prescient T-shirt the Cardinals found hanging in their locker room.

The T-shirt greeted the Cardinals with the words: "New York Mets—1986 NL East Champions."*

The Mets couldn't stop talking about how good they were. Neither could anyone else. Prognosticators were all in with the Mets, from the supposedly pure at heart at Moral Majority founder Jerry Falwell's Liberty University in Lynchburg, Virginia—"The New York Mets should finally begin their reign as NL East champs" proclaimed the *Liberty Champion*—to the bookies in Sin City, where the Mets were installed as 4–1 favorites to win the pennant and 7–1 to take the World Series. The Las Vegas Club extended those same odds to a handful of select teams, including the Yankees, the Dodgers, the Reds, and, oh, the defending NL champion Cardinals. Only one of the corral of 12 *Sporting News* writers covering the National League picked the Cardinals to repeat in the NL East in '86—and "The Baseball Bible" was based in St. Louis! Cue Rodney Dangerfield: "I don't get no respect at all." Or ask Whitey Herzog. "The team to beat is still the Mets," the Cardinals manager growled that spring. "They think they won the last two years anyway."

The Cardinals were annoyed that the Mets got so much coverage, especially in *USA Today*, a paper started in September of 1982 by the Gannett Company and the closest thing there was to an accessible national news rag—or "McPaper," as detractors called it for its shorter stories, use of color, and fondness for charts. "They never understood what the deadlines meant with the time difference between New York and St. Louis and games starting an hour later," Steve Jacobson, who covered the first 40 years of the Mets at *Newsday* and coauthored *All Bets Are Off*, said of the Cardinals. "They didn't understand that was why the Mets were always on the front page of *USA Today* instead of the Cardinals."

* The Associated Press reported the existence of this mysterious T-shirt in 1986, but three decades later, confirmation from players on both teams and members of the media was hard to find. Ya gotta believe what you want.

The Mets and Cardinals shared more than just the Las Vegas odds, McPaper coverage, the National League East, and the spring ballpark in St. Petersburg. The 1986 Mets had Keith Hernandez, of course, the glue of their infield, just like he'd been for the world championship Cardinals in 1982. The Mets also featured Rafael Santana, who saw all of 9⅓ innings at shortstop as backup to Ozzie Smith in 1983. Frank Cashen claimed Santana the same day the Cardinals released him in January of '84. For their part, the Cards had three former Mets in camp in St. Pete in '86: Jose Oquendo (the starting Mets shortstop for most of 1983 and '84), Clint Hurdle (the former progeny turned utility player who was a Met in '85), and Rick Ownbey (all that St. Louis had to show for the Hernandez trade; Ownbey would win one game as a Cardinal). Even the Cardinals front office had Mets ties: GM Dal Maxvill, a former Mets coach, replaced Joe McDonald, who had run the Mets during their dismantling phase in the 1970s.*

There was another person with ties to both the Mets and Cardinals. Whitey Herzog had gotten his start in the front office side of the game with the Mets in 1966. Twenty years later it was his duty as manager of the Cardinals to beat the Mets' brains in. If that left a mess he could always clean it up with that Mets T-shirt left in his locker room.

Dorrell Norman Elvert Herzog actually got his start as a professional ballplayer on the other side of New York. He was a left-handed, light-haired outfielder in the Yankees farm system who had been christened Whitey at age 17 at his first minor league stop in McAlester, Oklahoma. Herzog was so well liked by Yankees manager Casey Stengel that the Ol' Perfessor made sure to get the kid out of New York. Stengel's Yankees won seven pennants over the course of the eight years Herzog spent bouncing

* Joe McDonald had the ill fortune to be the general manager on the wrong end of two of the most lopsided trades in Mets history. He was on the job in New York when Tom Seaver was dealt to Cincinnati for four middling prospects in 1977, and he was the Cards GM who arranged the trade of Keith Hernandez to Shea Stadium six years later.

around the American League's second division: Washington, Baltimore, Detroit, and Kansas City. If he'd spent those years with the Yankees, he might have won a World Series ring or four, yet he would have had nothing but time to shine up his jewelry while sitting on the bench watching Mickey Mantle and Roger Maris; or he could have been stuck, like so many others, in the Yankees' overcrowded minor league system. After a .151 average in 1963 brought an end to his big league playing days, he scouted for the team closest to home, working for the Kansas City A's and owner Charlie Finley.

"Finley was on a rampage, spending a lot of money and trying to sign as many nicknames as he could, you know Vida Blue, Catfish Hunter, Skippy Lockwood, and all those guys," Herzog said, still spinning baseball stories in his eighties as easily as he could pick a young ballplayer with a future. "But the big thing was I was able to sign 12 players for Charlie for about $125,000–$130,000 [total], and a year or two later, seven of them were on big league rosters."

Bing Devine took notice. Dismissed as Cardinals general manager by owner Gussie Busch despite one of the greatest heists by a GM in major league history—Lou Brock from the Cubs for Ernie Broglio—and putting the pieces in place for St. Louis's 1964 world championship, Devine was starting over with a Mets team that really needed to start over. He was general manager in waiting for the Mets as future Hall of Famer George Weiss plodded his way toward retirement. When Devine hired Herzog as third-base coach for the Mets in 1966, the Mets were so bad that the team's first season *not* losing 100 games or finishing last was cause for rejoicing. "The Mets gave us ninth-place rings," Herzog recalled, laughing.

After a year in New York as third-base coach, Herzog planned to return to Kansas City, where it was cheaper to live and closer to home. Devine intervened. "I'm not letting you get away," Devine told Herzog. "I'd like to make you my assistant."

"I did the double checking for the '67 draft," Herzog said, "which was a hell of a draft as far as high school players were concerned." He saw plenty of those prospects firsthand as manager of the Instructional League Mets in St. Petersburg. That club's roster featured 25 soon-to-be major leaguers, including Nolan Ryan, Jerry Koosman, Jon Matlack, Steve Renko, Jim McAndrew, Danny Frisella, Ken Singleton, Ken Boswell, Rod Gaspar, Duffy Dyer, and Ted Martinez. Herzog's first taste as a manager produced a .600 winning percentage in Florida. Even as Devine returned to St. Louis, Herzog rose through the ranks in New York. Though he claims, "I was kind of a nobody" initially with the Mets, manager Gil Hodges hopped out of his chair to greet Herzog when he spotted him at a celebration after winning the '69 World Series.

"Young man," Hodges told Herzog, who was all of seven years younger, "I want to congratulate you because every time I've called you and asked you who you had to replace this guy, you always sent me the right guy." Herzog was so stunned you could have heard the ninth-place ring slide off his finger and hit the floor. "That was really a big compliment coming from a guy that was a great ballplayer and had just won the World Series as a manager."

Hodges was more than just the manager; the power of the whole organization coursed through him. As *New York Times* beat writer Leonard Koppett put it, "It was painfully clear that Hodges and top management were as one, that there was no higher court of opinion to appeal to above the manager." Herzog's influence likewise grew as he became farm director, even if his opinion wasn't always followed. He advised the Mets against trading Amos Otis in December 1969, and Nolan Ryan two years later—deals that soon went down in infamy as two of the worst trades in Mets history. Herzog also felt the Mets were giving up too much by trading three of their best hitting prospects—Ken Singleton, Tim Foli, and Mike Jorgensen—to obtain Rusty Staub in April of 1972. But that trade was far from the team's biggest concern.

Gil Hodges's shocking death before the announcement of the Staub trade left a power vacuum in the organization that was seized by M. Donald Grant. The team's chairman drew the purse strings tighter and no longer had to worry about being vetoed by the most powerful man in the organization. With Hodges dropping dead in a golf course parking lot during baseball's first strike, it fell to Grant to name a new manager. And Grant did not like Herzog. The straight-talking Herzog, age 40, had made it clear what he thought of Grant's baseball acumen. That assessment would be proven over time.

"Herzog was too strong-minded and too opinionated for Grant's taste and he frequently told the Mets' chairman of the board in organizational meetings that he should let his baseball men make baseball decisions," wrote Jack Lang, a beat writer who chronicled every facet of the team in its first quarter century. "This rankled Grant, who fancied himself a much better evaluator of talent than his more experienced personnel."

"I was down in the Instructional League and they didn't ask me to come to the funeral," recalled Herzog. "That kind of hurt me a little bit. But by the same token, there were people in the press saying that maybe I'd be next in line to be manager. They hired Yogi, which was fine, because Yogi was a great friend of mine."

The Mets' stunning 1973 pennant under—and some might say, in spite of—Yogi Berra, plus a couple more years of contention, had more to do with the organization Herzog helped build than it did with the three managers the Mets went through between 1972 and 1976. Had the Mets opted for Herzog, who had a natural-born ability to manage and knew the team's minor league system intimately, Shea Stadium may not have become the hopeless abyss it turned into in the late 1970s. The organizational decay that followed Herzog's departure was a tribute to Grant's aptitude as a talent evaluator not just of ballplayers but of whom to put in charge. Grant's legacy is not just forcing the Tom Seaver trade—making "The Franchise" expendable to prove some point that the fans never understood—but also letting a Hall of Fame manager go.

Herzog, who had previously turned down chances to manage the A's and the Indians, stayed as Mets player development director through 1972, "even though I was frustrated and bored with the job." He left the Mets that fall to become manager of the Texas Rangers. "That might have been the worst decision I ever made in my life," he said. Another future Hall of Fame manager, Tommy Lasorda, was actually lucky Herzog beat him out for the job with the abysmal Rangers. Herzog was fired before the season was out, but when his Texas GM landed in Kansas City, he got a call about that club's managing vacancy in 1975. "I got a second chance to manage because Joe Burke . . . respected me enough that I'd done a good job in Texas, where I didn't deserve to be fired, and he hired me in Kansas City," Herzog said. "And I stepped into a wonderful situation in Kansas City with a good, young team."

As the Mets regressed, Herzog won three straight AL West titles with the Royals, breaking the hold on the division by Charlie Finley's powerhouse Oakland A's—the team whose system he'd helped stock in his first job as a scout. But just as Herzog did not get along with M. Donald Grant, he and Royals owner Ewing Kauffman did not see eye to eye. Kauffman fired Herzog in 1979 despite his .574 career winning percentage with Kansas City, still the highest in franchise history.

He had a far better relationship with Gussie Busch—despite Herzog's role as pitchman for Budweiser's chief competitor, Miller Lite! Unlike Grant and Kauffman, Busch appreciated Herzog's candor. It also didn't hurt that Herzog could hold his beer and talk a blue streak. He was hired in 1980 to clean up a St. Louis locker room that had drug and attitude issues. Herzog replaced Ken Boyer, who had been his roommate during his third-base coaching stint with the 1966 Mets. A couple of months later, Herzog replaced another former Mets colleague, John Claiborne, as Cardinals GM. Herzog handed the managing duties to Red

Schoendienst, who had already managed the Cardinals to two pennants and 1,000 wins. That winter Herzog showed what he could do when calling the shots.

He agreed to return as manager and maintain his GM duties for no extra money, so long as he did not get a lot of interference from the brewery or its army of lawyers. He looked at his big ballpark in St. Louis—the largest in the division but equipped with turf that made balls bounce higher and roll to the wall quicker—and decided to remake the team in the image of his park. Herzog did not beg ownership to make the park smaller; that happened a decade later under a later regime, much to Mark McGwire's benefit. Herzog worked with the home field he had and went about remaking his team.

The first thing he did was sign his catcher from Kansas City, Darrell Porter, just months after he'd become one of the first players to acknowledge a drug and alcohol problem and undergo treatment. Herzog already had one of the game's best-hitting catchers in Ted Simmons, but he had a plan to floor everyone at the Dallas Winter Meetings by waiting until then to announce the Porter signing. The Dallas poker game was on.

The next day he traded seven players, including two other catchers—Terry Kennedy and Steve Swisher—to the Padres for relief ace Rollie Fingers, lefty swingman Bob Shirley, and two more catchers: Gene Tenace and Bob Geren. Already stocked with more catchers than anyone could need, Herzog spent the next day cornering the market on Hall of Fame relievers. He sent hotshot rookie Leon Durham, prospect Ty Waller, and veteran third baseman Ken Reitz to the Cubs for Bruce Sutter—like Fingers, a future Cooperstown inductee. With the hot stove still burning with talk of Herzog's dealing, he sent Fingers, Simmons, and starting pitcher Pete Vukovich to the Brewers for lefty Dave LaPoint along with righty Lary Sorensen, hot outfield prospect David Green, and veteran right fielder Sixto Lezcano. A year later he would swap Lezcano and unhappy All-Star shortstop Garry

Templeton to the Padres for starting pitcher Steve Mura and a two-time Gold Glove shortstop about to turn 28: Ozzie Smith.

In short, Herzog wasn't afraid to make deals. Herzog took over the worst team in baseball and a year later had the National League's best record. It was his tough luck that the convoluted split season caused by the strike robbed him of a postseason berth because his team finished two games behind two different teams in the two halves. "We got cheated," he said later. No matter, by October of 1982 the Cardinals were world champions. And for added difficulty, he beat the Milwaukee club that was the one team to get the better of his wheeling and dealing, and even that was in the short term. The Brewers were without injured Rollie Fingers against St. Louis in the '82 World Series. Sutter, on the other hand, won one game and saved two, including the seventh game for the Cardinals.

But one of the tenets of Herzog's trade philosophy was you'd rather trade for prospects than give them up. In other words, "You never know how good a prospect will become. Instead, you try to move a player who has reached his peak, so you don't wind up giving away more than you know." By June of 1983, coming off the world championship, clinging to first place, and trying to appease an owner who realized his precious club still had drug issues, Herzog shook up the Cardinals. With Lonnie Smith leaving the team for drug rehab just before the June 15 trade deadline, the Cards called up top prospect Andy Van Slyke and traded for more young players. One prospect too many, as it turned out.

Neil Allen was happy to be part of such a lopsided trade—or at least that's the way it came out. "I've been traded for somebody who's somebody," he said the day of the trade. "They'll remember this trade years from now and they'll say, 'Who was Keith Hernandez traded for?' I'm honored." Fans in St. Louis had other ways to describe the feeling. They booed the announcement of the trade that night at Busch Stadium.

Fans in New York were . . . not immediately available for comment. The Mets had been in the dumps for so long that many people had stopped paying attention. *You mean the MVP, batting champ, perennial All-Star, Gold Glove winner, and the guy who got the big hit in Game 7 of last year's World Series is now a Met? And they got him for Neil Allen and a 13th-round pick who was in the bullpen because he wasn't good enough to make the rotation of the lousy Mets?*

"Were they drunk when they made that deal?" Mets catcher John Stearns asked of the Cardinals in an interview the night of the trade. Not drunk, but the Cardinals were worried about the locker room. Kevin Horrigan, a political reporter turned sports columnist for the *St. Louis Post-Dispatch*, who also wrote *White Rat* with Herzog, added insight to the Hernandez trade from the St. Louis perspective.

"We all knew the rumors that Keith had a drug problem, a coke problem," Horrigan said. "We couldn't print it back in those days. In St. Louis you never write ill of the Cardinals if you can afford to. Clearly the Mets picked his pocket on that one. Keith was such a good guy and he got it all turned around. Once the old man, August Busch, down at the brewery found out about the drug problems, he wasn't having any of it. So Whitey's hands were sort of tied there."

Hernandez couldn't believe the trade, either. He'd seen the Mets every spring training in St. Petersburg, getting ready to go north to go nowhere. He thought of Shea Stadium as "Baseball Siberia," an outpost of outcasts where he'd been dispatched for falling out of favor with Cardinals management.

Three decades and several grandchildren later, the principals had mellowed and had nice things to say about each other, though Hernandez admitted he steered clear of Herzog while a Mets player. "We kind of avoided each other," he said in a 2015 interview. "You don't see the other team when you're playing. They don't visit your locker room, you know."

In 1986 the feelings were still raw. Herzog was writing a book that year, and he was plenty fed up with both the Mets and their first baseman: "Getting rid of Hernandez was addition by subtraction," Herzog wrote in *White Rat*. "I really feel that if we had kept him, his attitude and his bullshit would have ruined our club. I know he never would have been as good as he has been with the Mets. Ballplayers are like Missouri mules—sometimes you have to hit them on the head to get their attention."

Hernandez hit the ball on the head, especially against the Cardinals. The year of the trade he hit .396 against St. Louis pitching. The '83 Mets may have finished last, but the Cardinals dropped from first to fourth after the trade. The San Francisco native would admit that he was a little intimidated by the city at first. Rusty Staub, Mets slugger turned pinch-hit savant who made the best ribs in town at his own midtown restaurant, showed Hernandez New York's glamorous side and convinced him to stay. Hernandez became the steadying hand for a team full of young players. His 5-for-5 night in the final Mets–Cardinals game of 1985 raised his career average against the Cardinals to .333. What he wanted most heading into 1986 was to beat his former team for first place.

Everyone expected another close race between the Mets and Cardinals in '86. It had taken a quarter century, but the Mets had a full-blown rivalry. That the Cardinals just so happened to be their March neighbors livened up the otherwise humdrum routine of spring training. Rivalries can run hot and cold, and this one would burn out as the veterans of the mid-1980s moved on. The teams' spring partnership was near its end as well. The Mets traded St. Petersburg—not to mention St. Louis—for St. Lucie.

Al Lang Stadium had been remodeled a decade earlier, but the Mets opted to get their own park, from scratch—for no scratch. In June of 1986 the Mets signed what the *New York Times* called "an irresistible contract" to have a stadium and training center built to their specifications—an $8 million price tag for the developer at no cost to the Mets. Thomas J. White Development Company won the day—and its name on the team's ballpark in Port St. Lucie, on the other side of the state. With just 38,000 residents when the Mets moved in, sleepy Port St. Lucie would feel like a ghost town to many a Met and visitor—"Port St. Lonesome" remains a common epithet. But it also meant no more sharing with the Cardinals. No more playing the Cardinals in the spring, for that matter, until the Cards too swapped Florida coasts in the late 1990s.

The exhibition schedule remained as insignificant as always—except for someone trying to make the team. The Mets finished 1986 spring training at 13–13, plus one tie, but on a team this stacked, the spring battles were about making the roster as extras. The Opening Day starters, plus platoons at second base and center field, were set—or at least it seemed so until an ill-fated rundown drill.

On March 5 the Mets were on a practice field in the last round of the drill. Gary Carter manned first base, Rafael Santana was shortstop, and Mookie Wilson was the runner. The script required Wilson to be picked off and get in a rundown, but when he looked back to see how close the shortstop was, Santana's throw nailed him right in the sunglasses. He went down.

Carried off the field on an electric equipment cart, Wilson was examined on the trainer's table at Payson Field by Dr. John Olichney, associate team physician, and then sent to St. Petersburg Medical Center to meet with an ophthalmologist. It took 21 stitches to close the wound above his right eye and 4 more for the cut on the side of his nose. His sight remained blurred due to the blood that filled the chamber of the eye. "His vision is impaired significantly," Dr. Olichney warned. Though it seemed like the sunglasses made things worse, the doctor explained that the glasses Wilson had started wearing a year earlier took the full blow, thus sparing him more damage. He was fortunate the blurriness went away after a few weeks, but the extended rest the doctors cautioned cost him a month and a half of the season. On the plus side, it enabled his surgically repaired right shoulder to fully recuperate.

With Mookie not on the Opening Day roster, a spot opened up for another outfielder. Adding to the degree of difficulty, owners had agreed—not colluded, mind you—that they would all voluntarily reduce rosters to 24 players, the first time major league rosters had fewer than 25 men since 1938. That put a premium on versatility—say, having one bench player with power and speed who could play several positions. Being helpful in a fight was important with these Mets, too. Enter Kevin Mitchell.

In 1980 Roger Jongewaard, who was scouting southern Californians Darryl Strawberry and Lenny Dykstra at the time, signed the undrafted Mitchell several months after he got out of Clairemont High School in San Diego. All he did was hit the ball. He hit a few other people as well, including another team's manager and top Mets prospect Darryl Strawberry during a fight on a basketball court in St. Petersburg during Instructional League in 1981. "I picked up Darryl and slammed him on his back," Mitchell said in an interview, adding that he did not know who Strawberry was, but that he had provoked the minor league confrontation by making gang symbols in Mitchell's face. "Crips and Bloods, man, I came from a Bloods area. I didn't come up here for all that. You know, I didn't think baseball was like that."

Growing up among gangs in the Logan Heights ghetto, Mitchell was hit by random bullets more than once. While playing in Tidewater he learned that his stepbrother had been killed in a gang-related shooting. His grandmother, who'd convinced him to sign with the Mets instead of playing football at San Diego State, convinced him not to quit baseball—and not for the last time. Mitchell prospered his second year in Triple-A and in spring training 1986 he was more than ready for the majors. He led all Mets with four homers and batted .353 in March while playing all over the diamond and was given the John J. Murphy Award as the club's top rookie in spring training. He earned the coveted final roster spot at the expense of other prospects, including two former first-round picks. Shawn Abner, the first overall pick in the 1984 draft, hit .438 (7-for-16) with two home runs in spring training. Stanley Jefferson, a first-round pick in 1983, batted .500 (13-for-26) and recorded four stolen bases, not to mention a home run in the first spring game broadcast back to New York in 1986. The San Diego Padres must have been watching the newest "superstation," WOR-TV, because they would trade for Mitchell, Jefferson, and Abner that fall in the Kevin McReynolds deal.

With the roster cramped, the Mets went away from the common practice of the day and opted for two catchers. That it wasn't John Gibbons was a surprise. The third first-round pick by the Mets in 1980—and the one with the unmemorable name after Darryl Strawberry and Billy Beane—Gibbons had been on the verge of becoming the team's everyday catcher until an elbow to the face in spring training 1984 derailed what many thought would be a fine career. "This kid was the real deal," Mookie Wilson said in 2015 of Gibbons as a mid-1980s prospect. "He could do it all. He could hit. He never really had a career after that [injury]. He just never recovered."

Gibbons, future manager of the Toronto Blue Jays, was both unhealthy and unimpressive during spring training 1986, enabling Barry Lyons, who hit .286, to claim the backup job out of spring training. Nonroster invitee Ed Hearn had a .231 spring average in 15 games. All three would serve as backups in New York at various points in 1986.

The staff they caught was already starting to show the kind of strength that would be the trademark of the '86 Mets. And they got their work in. Ron Darling made seven starts, covering 32 innings. Sid Fernandez was in midseason form with no wins but an ERA under 2.00, a WHIP under 1.00, and 21 strikeouts in 23 innings. Bob Ojeda showed his new teammates what he could do, but the rotation was so stacked he would start the year in the bullpen with Randy Niemann, another lefty whose great control—just one walk in 19⅔ innings—won him a spot after not being on the roster when camp began. Bruce Berenyi, coming off rotator cuff surgery, showed he could still pitch out of the pen or as a starter. Another veteran righty, Ed Lynch, who had endured so many of the bad times with the club, would spend most of the good times in 1986 watching from afar—he began the season on the disabled list.

And then there was Doug Sisk, a reliever with control issues whom Mets fans loved to scapegoat even when there was no reason to scapegoat anyone. Coming off surgery to remove elbow chips, he was sent to the minors—a surprise given that he had averaged 53 games in each of the last three years in New York. He was not happy. "Nothing ever seems to come easy for me, does it?" Sisk asked after getting the news.

The Mets brain trust was most concerned about Dwight Gooden's ankle—pictures of Dr. K on crutches over the winter caused New Yorkers to suffer a collective embolism. But he would be all right. He had to be all right. The baseball world, spoiled by a never-before-seen mixture of greatness and gravitas in a 21-year-old frame, would question over and over again whether being all right would ever be good enough.

5

Comet, Computation, and Chemistry

April 1986

Throughout history, comets have been interpreted by many as portents of change—or an upcoming disaster. April 1986 saw the most famous comet of all, Halley's Comet, make its scheduled appearance. Every 75 to 76 years, humans look up in the sky for a glimpse of the passing comet, the single light of a motorcycle headlight tearing along a ridge far, far away. Mark Twain came into this world and left it within days of the two previous Halley's Comets. The legendary writer, born two weeks after the day the comet was closest to the sun, in 1835, even stated that when the comet returned, "I expect to go out with it." And he did. Twain died of a heart attack on April 21, 1910, the day after the comet passed from the far side of the sun.

First documented as occurring in 240 B.C., the comet received its name from British astronomer Edmond Halley, who asserted in the early 18th century that the comets that appeared in 1456, 1531, 1607, and 1682 were one in the same. When the comet showed up on cue in 1758, it earned his name—even though Halley was dead. Though the surname was spelled differently, William John Clifton Haley latched onto the clockwork "dirty snowball" for his legendary band's name, Bill Haley & His Comets. His million-selling hits, "Rock Around the Clock," and "Shake, Rattle, and Roll," popularized the music that made many a 1950s father holler, "Turn that racket off." Regrettably, Bill Haley died five years before the 1986 return of the comet whose moniker he shared. Well, that's rock and roll.

Halley's Comet made its closest pass to the earth just as the 1986 baseball season got underway, as predicted. Well, the comet's appearance was more than mere prediction. Predictions based on scientific method have a way of coming true again and again. Predictions based on conjecture and popular opinion are far more volatile.

Mets manager Davey Johnson was quick to dispel predictions from magazines, newspapers, radio, and television outlets. But he was not afraid to make his own. Johnson preferred individual meetings so he knew what every player was thinking, but when he gathered the '86 team together for the first time in St. Petersburg, he told his players he planned to dominate. And he didn't care who knew it. Then or now.

"First of all, if you don't think you're good, you're not good," Johnson said, still a touch of defiance in his voice almost 30 springs later. "And second of all, if you don't know what your goals are and how you're going to get there, you're not going to get there. Those were all very clear because we came close a couple of times and I felt like 'Now is our time,' because we had no weaknesses. And we didn't."

Three Rivers Stadium was as good a place as any to start. It was Pittsburgh where things had gone wrong in September of 1985. First, Keith Hernandez was put to the fire—although not on trial himself—as a witness in Pittsburgh's U.S. District Court. And then the pathetic Pirates ambushed the Mets on the field. En route to a 104-loss disaster that led to the cleaning out of the manager's office, the front office, and even a change in ownership in the wake of the public revelations of the Pirates' role in cocaine trafficking schemes, Pittsburgh had not played better than .346 ball in any month during the 1985 season. But the Bucs came to life during two September weekend series against a Mets team needing to win every game. The Pirates took two of three at Shea, putting the Mets three games out with 13 games remaining. The Mets won two of three the following weekend in Pittsburgh, even handing the Pirates their 100th loss; yet by splitting those six games, the Mets found themselves in a desperate position heading into the crucial series in St. Louis that ended the road portion of the '85 schedule. The Cardinals, by contrast, didn't lose to the Pirates after June of 1985, winning the last 10 meetings. One more Mets win over the Pirates and who knows how the '85 race might have ended.

The largest crowd in Pittsburgh in six years came out on a soggy Tuesday night as Rick Reuschel faced the first batter of the 1986 season. Lenny Dykstra battled, waited, and walked, the first of the team's league-leading 631 bases on balls. The Mets would do a lot of things more often—and more successfully—than their National League counterparts. They did, after all, plan to dominate.

After Wally Backman flied out, Keith Hernandez lined a ball in the left-center field gap that reached the wall on a hop. Dykstra beat the throw home and Hernandez took the extra base, reaching third uncontested. He scored on Gary Carter's sacrifice fly. The first four batters of the opening game epitomized what the Mets offense would do all year: take what opponents gave them, push their advantage, and if the opposition showed a weak spot, the Mets would, to use one of Hernandez's favorite expressions, "step on their necks." There would be countless spike marks to the throat in the National League in 1986.

Gooden's first batter of the year, R. J. Reynolds, took him deep—an inside fastball that hung over the plate instead of backing Reynolds off it—and the mistake traveled some 400 feet. "He was mad after that," Johnson said that night. There was no faltering by the Mets in Pittsburgh. Not in '86. The Pirates got the first two batters on base in the ninth, but Jim Leyland—managing the first of 3,499 games in the major leagues—called for his first bunt with his cleanup hitter up in a 4–2 game. Sid Bream moved the runners into scoring position, but Gooden struck out Steve Kemp and induced Tony Pena to top his 104th pitch back to the mound to end the game.

Since dropping the first eight season openers in team history, the Mets had won 15 of their last 17 lid-lifters. Their 25th opener was the start of a yearlong celebration—on the arm. A diamond-shaped patch on the "racing stripe" of their left sleeve would remind the Mets all year that 1986 marked their 25th season—rather than taking the easier math route and honoring 25 years as a franchise in 1987, the way it was done by most ball clubs, businesses, and married couples. But the '86 Mets weren't your Aunt Lillian and Uncle Harold.

Whitey Herzog arrived at Shea Stadium more than four hours before game time with a four-game winning streak. He battled the Monday morning commuters at Grand Central to get to Shea just after 9 a.m. for a 1:35 p.m. game. His goal wasn't to beat the traffic, it was to beat Dwight Gooden, or "Mr. Gooden," as was penned in notes for Herzog's book with Harper & Row. Some managers would mail in the effort on a book, let the ghostwriter, in this case columnist Kevin Horrigan of the *St. Louis Post-Dispatch*, write up what he wanted and never look at the finished product. But Herzog didn't work that way and his record of 1986, *White Rat*, began with designs on repeating—or at least a repeat of a great divisional race. There was no reason not to expect the NL East to go down to the wire again. Yet April 14 is early. As early as Whitey Herzog liked to get to the park.

He updated his charts in the empty clubhouse hours before every game. Herzog kept the pitching charts himself, with a different color for each pitcher, if the ball traveled on the ground or in the air. The process allowed him to get a feel for his pitchers, anticipating where balls might be hit to create the best outcome for his ball club.

"He had this pencil box like a kid in grade school would have," Horrigan recalled. "He was essentially compiling the stuff that is so much easier to compile today because you've got guys in the press box pushing buttons and just giving you that data. It's sort of a shame because his charts were like works of art—colorful, rainbow lines on these pieces of paper, and now I suppose they've all been trashed. Be nice to have one. Have it framed."

"The reason I wanted those charts was because I wanted to know where the opposition hit the ball against every pitcher—and I had a different color on my chart for every pitcher," Herzog explained long after he'd put away his pencil box. "Once you get four or five games where that pitcher has pitched against a certain club, it's amazing how, if he's on his game and pitching the ball where we want him to pitch and so forth, it's amazing how they hit the ball certain places. I think the fact that I had some great defensive ball clubs, those charts really helped it. A big thing was that my pitchers bought into it, they paid a lot of attention, they were very good at keeping the book the night before because I'd get to the ballpark the next day and I'd transfer everything onto my sheets for each guy, each person that we played against."

On the other end of the dank Shea hallway, Davey Johnson was looking at the charts from the printer of the team's IBM PC-XT. Johnson didn't go for colored markers; he wanted machine-generated, black-and-white data to help him make in-game decisions. Johnson knew numbers—he had a mathematics degree from Trinity University in Texas. He also knew computers—he'd first used them as a young player in Baltimore, taking a computer class at Johns Hopkins University and creating punch cards for Orioles owner Jerold Hoffberger's machine; Johnson didn't recollect the model in a later interview, but he did recall the purpose: "Optimize the Oriole lineup."

Not that he convinced his manager, Earl Weaver, to take his suggestions to heart. Johnson learned plenty from his Hall of Fame manager, both in the minors fresh out of Texas A&M and as an All-Star second baseman in Baltimore. He did have the manager's ear, as did Hall of Fame teammate Jim Palmer. "We used to get on his ass: 'Are you nuts? What are you doing?'" Johnson laughed, recalling the tormenting of the volatile Weaver. "We were the only guys on the club who could second-guess him. He didn't make many mistakes. Sometimes he'd sit down [below the dugout] and smoke a cigarette and say, 'I can't look at this. Let me know what happened.' But he had a little problem with young players. He put too much pressure on them."

Johnson, on the other hand, showed both great patience and trust in his young players. As rookie manager of the 1984 Mets, he released well-paid veterans Mike Torrez, Craig Swan, and Dick Tidrow and stocked the rotation with three rookies: Dwight Gooden, Ron Darling, and Sid Fernandez. The Mets responded with the second-best record in franchise history. As he had tried—with limited success—in Baltimore, Johnson utilized the computer to optimize the Mets lineup. But he incorporated the information with what he had learned in 13 years in the majors—sandwiched between two years playing in Japan.

"Players aren't machines," he told the *Boston Globe*'s Lesley Visser back when typewriters were still in the middle of most desks, "but the chances of something happening in a particular situation are illustrated by the computer. I don't run my club by computer, but I use it as another tool."

Despite changes to the game, from Astroturf to polyester uniforms to the designated hitter, baseball was still a dyed-in-the-wool dinosaur in terms of revising strategy or outlook. Change came from the outside.

A Kansas pork-and-beans cannery night watchman turned baseball revolutionary helped create a generation of new thinkers in baseball with the *Bill James Abstracts*. The first edition came out in 1977, so 1986 was the *Abstract*'s 10th anniversary (using Met-sian math). Not afraid to go against accepted theory, one of Bill James's claims was that the reason the Cardinals had scored the most runs in the National League was not because of their 314 steals in 1985 (the second most since 1912) but rather because of a less obvious number: their .335 on-base percentage. Lessons like this seem common sense to most numbers-minded fans of the 21st century, but this was out-of-the-box thinking in 1986.

Davey Johnson was a fan of Earnshaw Cook, a metallurgy engineer turned baseball statistician, and author of *Percentage Baseball* in 1964. Johnson was likewise intrigued by *The Hidden Game of Baseball*, which stated that many long-held beliefs on baseball statistics and strategy were wrong. The sacrifice? A bad play. Clutch hitting? Doesn't exist. Sexy stats like batting average, RBI, and the winning pitcher? Mere window dressing compared to stats that nobody in the 1980s had heard of—save for Davey Johnson and a growing army of "baseball nerds," the term for stat-heads who didn't play in four World Series or hit 40 home runs in a season. *Hidden Game* authors John Thorn and Pete Palmer had planned to publish an encyclopedia with "exotic statistics" (as labeled by the *Boston Globe* in 1985), but they had to forego a lucrative Simon and Schuster contract because it required the unworkable task of creating a first edition from scratch in just nine months. Their baby, *Total Baseball*, a seven-pound, 2,294-page bundle of baseball joy, would be born to Warner Books in 1989. *The Hidden Game of Baseball*—from Doubleday Publishing, the day job of the Mets owner, it so happened—was a consolation prize for Thorn and Palmer in 1984, but that book helped further the understanding that there was more to the game than even the most ardent fan realized. The growing voice in the desert created a market for their analytical encyclopedia to come. "Baseball is a very conservative institution, and it was even in the '80s," explained Thorn, now the official historian of Major League Baseball. "We were thrilled when the *Times* picked up [on-base percentage], that we had champions in the sports department who thought this was a new way of looking at the game. . . . reporting on those things that may have been invisible to the naked eye."

The baseball men in their respective managers' offices at Shea Stadium for the 1986 home opener understood the concept, if not all the formulas. Kevin Horrigan considers Whitey Herzog "one of the smartest people I ever met for a guy who's got nothing but a high school diploma from New Athens [pronounced "New Aythens," in southern Illinois] High School . . . In the days before sabermetrics, he sort of understood all that stuff instinctively."

Davey Johnson knew the math and evaluated his personnel using all the information available. The most basic principle—and one that proved useful while he managed the 2003 European Championships, the 2008 Olympics, and the 2009 World Baseball Classic, with limited time to ponder a lineup—he gleaned at lunch with Earnshaw Cook while Johnson was just breaking into the major leagues as a second baseman. "If you bat everybody who has the highest on-base percentage first, and the second on-base percentage second, all the way down, more guys will come to the plate and you'll score more runs," Cook told Johnson. This was in the mid-1960s, before James, Thorn, Palmer, sabermetrics, analytics, *Moneyball*, or Ivy Leaguers setting their sights on big league diamonds instead of high finance. This was just an engineer having lunch with a ballplayer, one who saw beyond the next at bat, who could distill the useful from the impracticable.

"He said if a guy is a .250 hitter and has an 0–2 count, don't let him swing, blah, blah, blah," Johnson recalled of his lunch with Cook. "All kinds of things you couldn't do, you'd destroy players. But what I really understood from what he said: Table setters, run producers, that's how you put a lineup together."

Twenty years or so after their meeting, his lineup for the home opener reflected Cook's theory. Though four games of data is the epitome of a small sample size, Davey Johnson's lineup choices would win out over the course of '86.

April 14, 1986 Lineup

Player	On-Base % 4/14/86	On-Base % Full Season
Len Dykstra	.450	.377
Tim Teufel	.333	.324
Keith Hernandez	.455	.413
Gary Carter	.350	.337
Darryl Strawberry	.350	.358
George Foster	.333	.289
Ray Knight	.556	.351
Rafael Santana	.158	.285
Dwight Gooden	.250	.119

As game time approached for the Shea opener, both managers put down the charts and printouts, tucked away the pencil box and pocketed the antacids, concluded meetings with players and coaches, and headed to opposing dugouts for introductions before the first showdown of 1986. You didn't need colored pens or dot matrix printer paper or even the gift of sight to tell whose side the revved-up crowd of 47,752 was on.

Dwight Gooden retired the side in order in the first, though all three Cardinals put the bat on the ball, much to the dismay of the twitchy K-sign wavers throughout Shea. He made up for it by striking out the first two batters in the second.

Ricky Horton, a graduate of Franklin D. Roosevelt High School in the four-term president's hometown of Hyde Park, New York, had the ball for the Cardinals. As planned. After 1985 any game against the Mets—even in April—could have repercussions down the road, so Herzog arranged to have both his lefty starters, Horton and John Tudor, pitch in New York since the Mets platoons were weaker against lefties. What Herzog didn't expect was that a Mets rainout during the first week now pitted his fifth starter against the reigning Cy Young winner.

Horton had a 2.15 ERA against the Mets over 13 previous appearances, and it didn't hurt having plenty of family and friends from Hyde Park playing hooky for Opening Day at Shea.

"It was my favorite place to pitch because it was the big leagues to me in a way that no other stadium was," explained Horton, now a Cardinals broadcaster, but as a kid he was a Mets fan who counted Ron Swoboda as his favorite player. Still a Mets fan? "The mid-'80s changed that for me."

Horton held the Mets hitless through the first three innings, but they managed a run when the southpaw walked the bases full and newcomer Tim Teufel plated the first run of the year at Shea with a sacrifice fly. The Cardinals broke through against Gooden in the sixth on a triple by Vince Coleman, followed by a single by reigning MVP Willie McGee.

Horton pitched seven innings of two-hit ball and was in line for the victory after pinch hitter Clint Hurdle's perfect hit-and-run single against his former teammates in the eighth inning. McGee then knocked in the tiebreaking run off Gooden. Lefty reliever Ken Dayley pitched the eighth for the Cardinals, and after walking the leadoff batter in the ninth, Keith Hernandez hit a shot up the middle that in one instant looked like a hit and the next seemed destined to be a "Wizard of Oz" DiamondVision highlight for the summer. Smith had trouble getting the ball out of his glove, however. He flipped it to Tommy Herr for the force, but the second baseman's throw got by Jack Clark—if Keith Hernandez had been playing first base instead of running to first base, the double play would have been turned. As it was, Herzog called for Todd Worrell. Davey Johnson sent Wally Backman to run for Hernandez. The wheels were turning like it was October—or last Opening Day at Shea.

As happened in 1985, Gary Carter again had the chance to be Opening Day hero against the Cardinals. His game-ending home run in his Mets debut against Neil Allen almost brought the house down on April 9, 1985. But Worrell was no Neil Allen. A hard-throwing rookie from Biola University—where every member of the Southern California school's faculty, staff, and student body is a professed Christian—he had saves in each of his first two outings in 1986. Herzog already knew and trusted Worrell, bringing him into tight spots throughout the 1985 postseason, even if Worrell hadn't been on the roster long enough to qualify as a major league rookie. But in his New York debut in '86, Worrell walked Carter to foul up Herzog's strategy. The manager had hoped the righty pitcher could retire the righty hitter, so even if Backman stole second—which he did against new Cardinals catcher Mike Heath (Herzog would lament that acquisition)—Worrell could then walk Darryl Strawberry and pitch to George Foster, a much better recipe for victory. But with two men on and one out, Worrell had to pitch to Strawberry, and Darryl singled home the tying run.

The Cardinals had not blown a lead in the ninth inning in 1985—until Game 6 of the World Series. (And as Herzog put it, "We had some help there.") In 1986 the first ninth-inning lead was coughed up in the sixth game of the season. "All this great strategy shows how unimportant a manager can be to a game if his players don't get the job done," Herzog said.

The managers traded knights and rooks as the chess match went into extra innings, but the Cardinals still had the upper hand on the board—or in this case, in the bullpen. Following multiple innings of relief from Dayley and Worrell, Herzog sent in lefty Pat Perry. After Davey Johnson used both Roger McDowell and Jesse Orosco for two innings apiece, the Mets bullpen came up short on pawns. In the multi-role, multi-inning bullpens of the 1980s, Randy Niemann served as both lefty specialist and long-man. He became a sacrificial lamb to the Cardinals' speed in the 13th. Checkmate.

Willie McGee, who drove in the first two St. Louis runs and snuffed a Mets rally by running down Lenny Dykstra's drive to end the 12th, led off the 13th by legging out an infield hit. He then beat Niemann's throw to second on Tommy Herr's bunt. Bruce Berenyi, the old man in the rotation on a staff full of youngsters on the 1984 Mets, was now hanging on as a reliever with a repaired right shoulder. He wound up walking his first batter, Jack Clark, to load the bases.

For a moment it looked like the Mets might yet get out of it. Tito Landrum hit a grounder to third baseman Howard Johnson, a force-out at home, maybe a 5–2–3 double play and . . . the ball never touched HoJo's glove. It skipped between his legs as two runs scored. "I was as shocked as anybody," Johnson said after the 6–2 loss, the back cover of the next day's *Daily News* showing him pawing at the infield dirt after the damage was done, the home opener spoiled. Across the dank Shea hallway, even Whitey Herzog found himself at a loss for words after the almost four-and-a-half-hour chess match. "There isn't much to say after the game," he told Horrigan. "I sure managed great to get that ground ball to go through Johnson's legs." Sometimes the biggest games are decided that way.

After five games the Mets stood 2–3 and 2½ games back in the standings—only the two Chicago teams endured a worse first week in the majors. The last time the Mets were under .500 was April 2, 1984, the first day of the Davey Johnson regime. The '86 Cardinals, on the other hand, the defending NL champs anxious to show that they—not the Mets—were the team to beat, stood at 5–1. But what did that matter in the middle of April? After all, the '84 Mets won six straight after dropping the opener, and the '85 Mets started 8–1. Look where it got them. The Mets had four days to contemplate the meaning.

A day off on Tuesday, followed by two days of rain, meant stewing over getting just four lousy singles in 13 innings against St. Louis. With the New York Knicks out of the upcoming National Basketball Association playoffs (the New Jersey Nets would be swept in the first round), that left hockey as the main course on New York's voracious spring sports schedule. And that would never be enough. A first-round playoff win by the Rangers was good grist for the tabloids, coupled with the Islanders' troubling sweep at the hands of Washington, but that was not sufficient to satisfy the media beast in a baseball town. Sure, the Yankees were off to the same fast start as the Cardinals, but in an age before interleague play created an annual New York baseball hype machine for the contrived "subway series", the AL and NL operated in separate orbits: different schedules, different rivals, and—with the DH—even different rules. Out of sight, out of mind—and right now the Yankees were in Cleveland.

No matter how early in the year, there was a dear price to pay as the number one team in a nine-team market: being feted when you did the least little thing right, and being filleted when anything went wrong. So while April showers kept falling in New York, the press kept harping on the Mets' great promise and poor beginning to 1986. At least until Dwight Gooden gave them something else to write about.

He didn't get into trouble on the field—Gooden rarely did that in the mid-1980s—but he found trouble close to Shea: at LaGuardia Airport. Doc and his sister, Betty Jones, plus his fiancée, Carlene Pearson, were returning a rental car to Hertz the night after the home opener. There was a discrepancy about the mileage and Carlene had to go back to check in the rainy parking lot. It was a very wet month, and it only got wetter for the Hertz attendant, who had a drink thrown in her face by Gooden's sis. (The Goodens said it was soda; the Port Authority police said it was whiskey.) Dwight Gooden made matters worse by being abusive and the trio was brought to the Port Authority station. It was already the third strike of '86 for Gooden in terms of public opinion, and he hadn't even made his third start of the season. During the winter he didn't tell the Mets about his sprained ankle, and then he missed an exhibition start against the Pirates in

Bradenton for what he said at the time was an accident. In both cases there were conflicting reports about what happened. Now came the third incident, at the Hertz counter. Taken individually, it seemed like nothing. Put them together and it added fuel to the "what's wrong with Doc" stories that started popping up even on days when he won.

As *Daily News* columnist Mike Lupica wrote at the time, "He might as well understand that if he steps out of line even a little, the penalty will be a public strip search. Every time." The penalty was a press conference packed with reporters without game stories to write because of the rain, and the subject was juicier than any ballgame wrap-up. That Gooden wasn't apologetic made matters worse—or better from a tabloid viewpoint. He twice could have walked away before the incident got out of control: once when the Hertz manager asked them to leave—that's when the drink was thrown; the second time was when the Port Authority cops showed up and told Gooden the matter would be dropped if his group apologized. He then did the equivalent of walking in a run with a .125 hitter at the plate, refusing to apologize for his sister throwing the drink or for his calling the attendant a "stupid bitch." He was still on the offensive at the press conference, claiming "we didn't do anything wrong." Those sitting in the press conference, hearing it on the news, or reading it in the paper responded as one: Of course you were wrong; you threw a drink in someone's face. That action may seem dramatic in a black-and-white flick on the Channel 9 *Million Dollar Movie*, but in real life tossing a drink in someone's face will get even the best young pitcher on the planet an hour cooling his heels at the station—ironically, because of someone else's poor throw.

When Gooden told the press gathering that he should consider "bringing all my furniture and moving it into the clubhouse," it was an indication that maybe all those articles the past two years about maturity and poise hadn't done Doc any favors. He sounded like an ass. "Even if the clerk is rude, you just walk away," Lupica admonished. "Because there is no way you are getting the win."

Gooden handled the pressure far better on the mound. After the Mets ended their three-game losing streak on Friday—they would not lose three in a row again until July—Gooden took the mound on Saturday afternoon with all eyes on him. He was indeed much better at pitching than speaking. As the April 20 *Daily News* headline summarized, "Mound Is Remedy for Doc."

Starting for the third time in his team's first seven games, Gooden was his dominant self. He fanned 10 Phillies, a good thing since his outfield included Gary Carter in left field (his first start there since 1976) and Kevin Mitchell in center (his first career start there—and his debut as a leadoff hitter). Each caught a pair of fly balls with no misadventures, and since both were in their positions to take advantage of their bats, it was fitting they played key offensive roles. Mitchell's double knocked home Gooden all the way from first with the tying run in the sixth, and Mitchell scored the tiebreaking run in the eighth on Carter's single. Phillies lefty Shane Rawley had a perfect game for four innings, yet he wound up the tough-luck loser. Gooden, who went all the way for the 3–2 win, didn't have to be perfect; he just needed to pitch instead of bitch.

The next day the Mets completed their first sweep and their first blowout, 8–0, behind Sid Fernandez. The Mets would win 27 games by at least five runs in '86, and lose just nine times by that margin—both establishing franchise marks. But the mark of a good team is the ability to win close games and pull out games that seem lost. While using every player on the team to do it.

Wally Backman was an offensive catalyst. He could hit and run, for sure. But he could also field, and outthink and outhustle the opposition. His Achilles heel was that he was a switch-hitter who could not switch-hit. It wasn't by choice. "I hated hitting right-handed," the naturally left-handed-hitting Backman explained, still a little exasperated almost a quarter century after his last right-handed at bat (he struck out). Taught in the minors to be a switch-hitter, he spent 14 years in the majors and hit .294 from the left side and .165 from the right. He lobbied several times to bat left-handed against southpaws, "but was told I had to turn around and do it the other way." Backman's inability to switch-hit was a job creator, though.

In eight seasons in the Mets system, Kelvin Chapman's only extended chance in New York came during the dregs of 1979—the Mets lost 99 times that year, including 24 of the last 28 games in which Chapman appeared. But he played for Davey Johnson in Tidewater in 1983, as did Backman, and Johnson was loyal to the ballplayers who played smart and hard for him in the minors. So when Johnson was promoted, Backman and Chapman came north, too. Chapman played against lefties in 1984, batted .289, and even contributed a grand slam. When Chapman hit .174 in the first half of 1985, however, he returned to Tidewater (where he hit .185). Backman started almost every day the rest of that year in New York, but after he hit 200 points lower batting right-handed, it was clear that a new platoon was needed.

Tim Teufel had pop. The Minnesota second baseman hit 10 home runs from the eighth spot in the Twins' order in 1985. He had 16 homers in his first full year in '84 while batting second, behind another Twins rookie named Kirby Puckett. Given Backman's lack of success against lefties—not to mention Ray Knight's anemic .218 against everybody in '85—the Mets weighed their options. Assistant GM Joe McIlvaine had been watching Teufel since he was at St. Petersburg College, prior to transferring to high-profile Clemson. When asked about his defense after the January 1986 trade, McIlvaine stayed with the positive: "The thing Teufel does best is hit." The Mets sent three minor leaguers to the Twins, none of whom ever did much—as players. One, however, would make a mark on the game.

It pained Frank Cashen to trade Billy Beane, a smart if flawed ballplayer he'd considered drafting with the number one overall pick instead of Darryl Strawberry in his first Mets draft in 1980. Cashen took Beane later in that first round, but six seasons after that draft Strawberry was a perennial All-Star and Beane was a Twin. As GM of the Oakland A's, Beane would be star of the book and the film *Moneyball*—a Cashen for the new millennium, just with less money to spend, math on the brain, and open collars instead of bowties. Beane even penned the foreword for Cashen's memoirs, calling the Mets general manager the reason he became a GM. But Cashen had a serious task in the winter of '86: needing to win 99 games just to improve over the previous year's record. When margins are tight the future is something to focus on another time. Billy Beane would have made the deal, too.

Through the first eight games of '86, Teufel started five times and hit .130. Managers liked squeezing the Mets with southpaws, especially with Mookie Wilson out of the lineup, and Pittsburgh's Larry McWilliams became the latest lefty to hold the Mets spellbound. His one mistake through seven innings was a fastball Gary Carter drilled over the left field fence. Jim Leyland, whose Pirates had won six straight, sent in Cecilio Guante to protect the lefty's 4–2 lead. He retired Carter and Strawberry in the eighth before walking George Foster.

Ray Knight had been on the trading block the same time the Mets were adding Teufel in the winter, but there were no takers. With Howard Johnson not yet showing he could hit lefties and Knight batting .291 in spring training, the Mets kept Knight. Were they ever glad they did. Knight's average was .421 coming into the game against Pittsburgh, though he hadn't yet played enough against righties to show he could be the everyday third baseman in 1986. Marty Noble, the *Newsday* beat reporter for the '86 Mets, recalled Knight waiting to bat against the right-hander in the eighth, expecting to be called back at any moment by Davey Johnson. "Ray's on deck and he looks over his shoulder and he's sure HoJo's coming up because Guante's like a side-armer." The manager motioned to Knight, "Go on, go on, hit." In an interview

Ray Knight NATIONAL BASEBALL HALL OF FAME LIBRARY, COOPERSTOWN, NY

that year for the team highlight film, Knight reflected that it was "the most crucial at bat of my career." Knight expected to be called back—as had happened in the home opener against a righty. "Davey wanted to see what I was going to do in that situation and I looked to hit a home run. I was swinging home run. It was the first time in my career that I wanted to hit a home run and did." Davey Johnson played the percentages, but the math major applied chemistry.

"Let me tell you what chemistry is. Everybody's screwed up about chemistry. Chemistry is one thing . . . everybody in that locker room needs to have a job. And they need to know if they excel at their job that their role may be expanded," Johnson explained. "It's not just 9 guys, or 10 guys, or 15 guys; it's all 25 are important. . . . It's that simple. Then you have great chemistry."

Knight, seeing his role being expanded, responded by launching a Guante fastball into the bullpen to tie the game. Better living through chemistry.

"Ray just goes nuts going around the bases," Marty Noble remembered. "I don't think he was happier when he hit the home run in the World Series. He was really happy and that put Ray on fire." Knight answered the curtain call—like Carter had earlier—from what would be the smallest crowd of the season: 10,282. Where was everybody? Many of them were glued, no doubt, to the most-watched syndicated show in history: the opening of Al Capone's vault. As host Geraldo Rivera built up the potential contents and backstory for two hours on live television, the long-sealed, underground, 125-foot-long area that had once been the 1920s Chicago bootlegger's lair was dynamited open to reveal, to reveal . . . a whole lot of dirt and a couple of empty bottles. There were 30 million suckers who watched, many of whom wished they'd watched the Mets game instead—even if they hated New York.

The Pirates grabbed the lead in the top of the ninth when Joe Orsulak squeezed home ex-Met Lee Mazzilli. Dykstra led off the home ninth with a single and Kevin Mitchell sacrificed him to second. Tim Teufel, who'd hit .200 against lefties with the Twins in 1985, was just 3-for-23 to start his Mets career as the right-handed ride share at second base. But it had started to click for the 27-year-old Connecticut native. "That [season] was the first time that I actually platooned; it was an adjustment," Teufel, now a coach, explained. "I was still a young player, like two years in the league, the American League, before I got traded. So adjusting to not playing every day was something new to me. You have to figure it out pretty quick."

Teufel already had two hits on the night when he drilled a third into the left field corner against Pat Clements to tie the game. After walking Keith Hernandez, a righty came in to face Carter, but Kid drove home Teufel and sent the small crowd into ecstasy. This was the last night the Mets (6–3) owned a spot in the standings anyplace but the top. It was the first of 11 times, including October, that the '86 Mets left the opposition standing on the field at Shea, feeling as letdown as Geraldo looking into Al Capone's empty vault.

The Mets arrived in St. Louis on April 24, winners of five in a row since dropping the home opener to the Cardinals at Shea Stadium. They were tied with the Cards for first place, just where New York wanted to be almost seven months earlier when the teams last met on a Thursday night at Busch Stadium. St. Louis won that game and the division title.

But the 1986 Cardinals were suffering from a hangover, and it wasn't because they were owned by a brewery. The Cards were baseball's best team in 1985, coming as close as a team can to winning a World Series ring without getting one. The '85 Cardinals won 101 times—the most in baseball—and needed almost every victory to hold off the Mets for the division title. They then knocked off the Dodgers in the Championship Series, despite spotting L.A. the first two games and losing the fastest man in the game to a tarp moving one mile per hour.

Vince Coleman, whose 110 stolen bases as a rookie in 1985 were 30 more than perennial AL leader Rickey Henderson of the Yankees, was stretching on the field at Busch Stadium prior to Game 4 of the NLCS when it started to rain. A Cardinals groundskeeper pressed a button on the stadium's state-of-the-art automatic tarp system. The 180-foot cylinder began slowly fanning out over the Astroturf. Coleman was about to grab a bat, unaware of the creeping contraption behind him. The tarp rolled over his left foot and ankle and continued moving for 30 seconds. Reporters hundreds of feet away in the press box could hear the outfielder screaming, "Get it off! Get it off!" Coleman was soon freed, but the Cardinals' vaunted running game was grounded.

Coleman missed the rest of the postseason and the Cardinals scored just 13 runs while batting .185 in the World Series against Kansas City. The Cards stole just two bases in the seven-game Series—almost the team's per game output in 1985. Even without "Vincent Van Go" (what passed for a clever nickname in the 1980s), St. Louis was still one tragic call from its second world championship in four seasons.

With the Cardinals clinging to a 1–0 lead in the ninth inning of Game 6 in Kansas City, Jorge Orta hit a chopper to first baseman Jack Clark. Reliever Todd Worrell raced to first base and caught Clark's throw a half step ahead of Orta, but umpire Don Denkinger made the safe call. Almost three decades before instant replay in baseball—and in an era when umpires never consulted to get a call right—the decision stood. The Royals rallied to win the game, and with Denkinger behind the plate in Game 7, Kansas City won the world championship the next night.*

---

* After their inspired '85 World Series victory, the Royals went three decades before their next postseason appearance. But Kansas City would win its second world championship at the expense of the Mets in 2015.

In April 1986 the shocking turn of events from the previous year's World Series still stung the Cardinals. And then the Mets hit town. Despite the sore feelings and buildup, the '86 Busch Stadium rematch turned into quicker work than a fight sequence on the campy 1960s show *Batman*.

"Bam!" Down two runs in the bottom of the ninth of the series opener, Howard Johnson launched a game-tying home run off Cardinals closer Todd Worrell. An inning later, after Darryl Strawberry drew an intentional walk, George Foster singled in the go-ahead run in the 5–4 win. It was the eighth time in their last 20 meetings that a Mets-Cardinals game went extra innings, and the 12th time in that span that a game was decided by one run. "We play October games in April," Cards manager Whitey Herzog said after the game. "Every game with these guys seems like this."

"Bang!" The league's leading home run hitter Ray Knight clubbed two more in a 9–0 romp, seven of those runs coming in the last two innings. Dwight Gooden threw his third complete game of 1986, and his 26th in just 70 career starts.

"Boff!" After scoring four times in the first inning, the Mets did not cross home plate again on NBC's *Saturday Game of the Week*. Held in check by Sid Fernandez for eight innings, the Cardinals awoke in the ninth with four straight hits—three off reliever Roger McDowell—making it a 4–3 game. With the tying run at second and the go-ahead run on first, Jesse Orosco entered from the bullpen to turn around switch-hitter Terry Pendleton. Batting right-handed, Pendleton hit a smash that glanced off the mound, which slowed the ball just enough for Wally Backman to dive for it and start a game-ending double play. "You can't knock that guy out," Orosco said of Backman, who'd been flattened an inning earlier at second base by Ozzie Smith. "Even if he was buried six feet under, you'd see his glove sticking up."

"Bonk!" John Tudor, winner of 23 of his last 24 regular-season decisions, allowed home runs on Sunday to Kevin Mitchell and Tim Teufel, hitters who'd never faced him before. Bob Ojeda,

another new New Yorker, went the distance to win the battle of crafty southpaws, 5–3. How much was it the Mets' day—make that, weekend? Mitchell, playing his first career game at shortstop due to an injury to Rafael Santana, handled all seven chances; perennial Cardinals Gold Glove shortstop Ozzie Smith made a crucial error to help New York to its ninth straight win since losing its home opener on an error.

Game, set, Mets.

It was the Mets' first four-game sweep in St. Louis since the last weekend of 1979, but that had been against a disinterested Cardinals club playing out the string as the Mets tried to avoid 100 losses. This Mets team had its sights set on 100 wins. "This sets a tone," Keith Hernandez said after the game. "This was a wake-up call. We're beating them the way they beat us last year."

The Mets, their observers, and even their opponents left no doubt that this series—however early in the season—was the turning point.

Newsday beat man Marty Noble and Dan Castellano of the *Newark Star–Ledger* were getting on the elevator in the basement of Busch Stadium, on their way to the press box. Mets second baseman Wally Backman joined them just as the door started to close. He saw Cardinals pitcher Ricky Horton walk by, and Backman shoved his hands in front of the door so it wouldn't close. "Don't let us get too far a-head," Backman called, ending in a singsong taunt—in the words of Noble, "like a seven-year-old teasing his sister." The doors slid closed on both the basement and the Cardinals. "That's what the Mets were," Noble said. "They almost enjoyed insulting or angering the opponents, especially the Cardinals."

St. Louis went on to lose 12 of 13 games, dropping 8½ games in the standings. Whitey Herzog told Kevin Horrigan in early May, "We're out of the race." There was no song in his voice.

6

Top Gun

May 1986

One month in and the Mets were backing up the bragging. They ended April with an 11-game winning streak, matching the longest streak in team history. Their five-game lead after 16 contests equaled the leads of the other three division leaders put together. Their 13–3 mark exceeded the highest winning percentage in any month in franchise history.* Given the franchise's celebration of its 25th anniversary, it was fitting the '86 club reversed the first month as a ball club in 1962: a 3–13 opening by the mother of all expansion teams.

After blasting through St. Louis, the Mets swooped into Atlanta and won twice more before losing. The Mets then embarked on another winning streak. It was time for the rest of the National League to call out, "Mayday! Down in flames!" Just like Goose would say it.

Top Gun was the pinnacle of mid-'80s movie cool. At age 23 Syracuse-born Tom Cruise had already appeared in several popular

---

* The exceptions were a handful of Octobers that featured a smattering of games to finish out the schedule. And the '86 team would even add a denouement in October with the most wins in a month without a loss (5–0). The 2015 Mets also won 11 straight after starting the year 2–3; they too ended the year in the World Series, though on the wrong end.

movies: as a boarding school cadet (*Taps*), a greaser pump jockey (*The Outsiders*), a high school football stud (*All the Right Moves*), a teenage pimp (*Risky Business*), and whatever the hell *Legend* was about. In *Top Gun* he stepped into Hollywood legend. He starred in a movie that did not just pack theaters throughout 1986, but also, in the words of the *Washington Post*, "made America love war."

By the mid-1980s the Vietnam War had been over since most college students were in footie pajamas, and many of the struggles at home and in the deltas of Vietnam had been overlooked or oversimplified. The war had transformed from the daily consciousness to conceptualized art in the cinema. The past decade had seen film treatments ranging from Francis Ford Coppola's epic *Apocalypse Now* to Sylvester Stallone putting the pow in POW in *Rambo*. (Oliver Stone's Vietnam opus, *Platoon*, wouldn't come out until the end of 1986.) *Top Gun* wasn't about the military's past—and was in no way about American failure on the battlefield. It was quite the opposite.

Top Gun blasted through any preachiness or deeper issues at Mach speed, rocking out to Kenny Loggins and the synthesized sound of Berlin while subduing a new, dark enemy. Though the bad guys aren't named, it is implied that they come from a shady Middle Eastern government—a perfect stand-in for Libya, against whom the United States had launched air strikes in April because of terrorism backed by the regime of Muammar al-Qaddafi. Of course, Libya had not been attacked by American jets until after the movie was in the can, but when the military has script approval, details work themselves out.

Top Gun generated $344 million at the box office at a time when the average movie ticket was $2.75. In turn, the movie helped resuscitate the military's image. With special Navy recruitment tables inside many theaters showing *Top Gun*, enlistment increased after the film's release Memorial Day weekend. Recruitment officers in California reported that calls about the aviation program doubled and that about 90 percent of new applicants stated that they had seen the movie. Film producers and the military were a match made in heaven—or at least in the skies above. The Navy let the producers loose at a real "Top Gun" school in San Diego, allowing use of a small fleet of $37 million F-14 jets and charging only gas money—which still ran about $7,600 per hour at a time when filling up your Ford Escort cost 89 cents per gallon. In return, the Navy got script approval.

The Navy redlined scenes it did not think made the military look its best, like the death of Goose—played by Anthony Edwards—originally scripted to be killed in a midair collision. *Time* magazine, which called *Top Gun* "a 110-minute commercial for the Navy," reported that the Navy changed the fighter pilot's death to ejector seat failure. But Tom Cruise's character, enlivened by the world's hottest astrophysicist (Kelly McGillis), takes down the nameless bad guys in their black MiGs. A *New York Times* story in May of 1986 noted that "at movie theaters across the country, its bellicose climax is drawing explosive cheers from youthful audiences stirred by its Rambo-esque triumph over the forces of Communism." And *Top Gun* did not just make war fun again; it was a trendsetter. A 2011 *Washington Post* piece stated that after *Top Gun*, Hollywood repeatedly came calling with hat out asking for the military's help, often in return for script approval. The top-grossing movie of 1986 "was the template for a new Military-Entertainment Complex."

"Remember," Tom Skerritt as Viper—the commander and lone 1980s power mustache in the movie—tells Maverick during a requisite dressing-down. "There are no points for second place. Dismissed."

And that's where the Mets left everyone else: in second place (or worse), while they zoomed by at Mach 2. From April 18 to May 10, the Mets won 18 of 19 games, sweeping the Phillies, Pirates, Cardinals, Reds, and Astros—plus two of three against the Braves. Over that span the Mets hit 39 doubles, smacked 21 home runs, drew 72 walks, and scored 105 runs—or 3 more runs per game than their pitchers allowed (5.53 to 2.21). Mets pitchers, meanwhile, struck out 130, walked 57, and tossed four complete games.

As the Mets took the field on May 11, the moms in the crowd, who a couple of years earlier would have scoffed at the notion of spending their day at a ballpark, now clutched their giveaway Mother's Day tote bags, pointed at Gary Carter's curly locks—"Have you seen his Ivory commercial?"—and wondered how Dwight Gooden could lose. His lone mistake was allowing a rare three-run single to Pete Rose. Charlie Hustle's hit wasn't rare—he did have more hits than anyone else in history—but he was batting .125 entering the game as Cincinnati's 45-year-old player-manager. With the Reds owning baseball's worst record, having dropped 15 of 16, and trying to avoid being swept by the Mets for the second straight weekend, Rose brought in his young Brooklyn-born closer to start the eighth inning. John Franco, who, like Rose, would play until he was 45, ended New York's latest winning streak at seven, fanning two future home run champs

(Howard Johnson and Kevin Mitchell) as well as a two-time home run champ (George Foster) with two men on to collect his first career save at Shea Stadium.*

Sure, Mom was disappointed with the Mets losing on Mother's Day, and with the fact that "poor Gary Carter got bowled over by that nasty Eddie Milner." And it was hard to believe that Dwight Gooden became the first of the Mets' killer quartet of starters to lose a game in 1986. But Mom and everyone else could bask in the team's achievement through its first two dozen games.

At 20–4 the Mets had sprinted to the fastest start in franchise history, the best record and biggest lead in baseball. The Mets not only managed the best start in the National League since the 1977 Dodgers, but they also equaled the start by the 1984 Detroit Tigers, whose historic pace of 35–5 is still the mark to beat at the quarter pole.† The '86 Mets were, you might say, dominant.

Teams already lay by the wayside. Four NL East clubs were at least nine games back—including the Cardinals. The Expos were playing .600 ball to the Mets' .710 winning percentage, though Montreal had the good fortune to not yet play the Mets. But in the history of the National League, which turned 110 years old in 1986, the last team to have a .700 winning percentage was the 1909 Pirates of Honus Wagner fame. A few AL teams had managed the feat since then, but no club had reached .700 for a season since the schedule was lengthened from 154 to 162 games in the early 1960s. And just to show how hard it was to win 7 of every 10 games—winning every series, on average—the Mets immediately went into a lull.

The Mets dropped five of seven as the Expos crept within three games. And who was right there with the Mets among the division leaders in May? Their neighbors a few subway stops away.

---

* John Franco would become a Met in 1990 and rack up more saves than any reliever at Shea, more than any Met, and more than any left-hander in major league history.

† Though the Mets could not maintain the pace of the '84 Tigers over their first 40 games, they would win more games over the course of the year: 108 to 104.

Upon exiting the 161st Street subway platform, riders expected to see reminders of baseball greatness in the city. It was, after all, where you got off for Yankee Stadium. A subway stop is a great place to advertise, especially in a time before heads were burrowed in a downward slant at handheld devices, ears cocooned in headphones—though the Sony portable audio cassette player had made enough of a mark that "Walkman" entered the *Oxford English Dictionary* in 1986. At the time, the only phone available to most people on the go was a pay phone—check your pager!—and the only reading material was a newspaper, magazine, or book scrunched into a pocket or hidden in a purse or a bag. So advertisements at places where waiting was the rule could get a lot of attention. Riders at the Yankee Stadium stop would expect to be met by future Hall of Famers Rickey Henderson and Dave Winfield, or reigning MVP Don Mattingly. Instead, Yankees fans embarking on the subway in the Bronx were met by Mets.

What they glimpsed was the joy in Queens in poster form: Gary Carter and Dwight Gooden about to high-five after yet another Mets victory. Beneath was the now familiar refrain: "Baseball Like It Oughta Be," the creation of veteran adman Jerry Della Femina. His campaign of "The Magic Is Back" for the Mets in 1980 had brought chuckles from superior Yankees fans who were used to everything going their way and not needing to rely on magic or marketing. Della Femina even drew a $5,000 fine for insinuating that the Bronx wasn't safe for families to venture to. Six years later, Della Femina was pressing a knife to the throat.

"The subway is the best place to reach baseball fans, and some nights it's the best place to reach *disappointed* baseball fans," Della Femina told the *Daily News* about his ongoing war for the hearts and minds of New York baseball enthusiasts. "That [161st Street stop] is where there are going to be a lot of people wondering, 'Why did we go? I'd rather watch Dwight Gooden *losing* than any Yankee pitcher winning.'"

Like the team he represented, Della Femina swung for the fences and wasn't afraid to miss. The advertising personality's best-selling book in the 1970s was entitled *From Those Wonderful Folks Who Brought You Pearl Harbor* (hint: the same nationality as the people who brought you the Walkman); Della Femina's book is credited as a key source of inspiration for the award-winning television show *Mad Men*. Della Femina was quick to jab and frame the argument so that resistance seemed futile. "Well," he said, "they could counter by putting a photograph of George Steinbrenner near Shea Stadium. They could say, 'Baseball like it used to be.'" Check, please.

The subway stop where Yankees fans gathered on game days was half as crowded as the platform in Queens that carried Mets fans to and from games. The dollar subway token used by riders to Flushing added up to $1 million, while the Yankees fans brought the city less than half that sum, according to a study the previous year from the city comptroller. The Mets may not have been historic winners—it was 13 seasons since their last postseason appearances in 1973, a span never matched in franchise history—but their ascent brought out something in New Yorkers that the repeated waving of pennants can't still.

With Dwight Gooden as their ace, the Mets outdrew the Yankees by half a million fans in 1985, but this still did not cede to the Mets the unaffiliated masses. There was a bandwagon full of fans ready to come down on whichever side crossed the finish line first, with the promises of more wagons to follow. The Yankees were the enemy of three different groups of fans over time—the Giants, Dodgers, and Mets—so some people would not root for the Yankees under any circumstance. And vice versa. But many people just chose New York against any outside foe. Always a big game town, stadiums would be filled come October with people who rooted for the NY on the hats regardless of the color.

Yet even when a ballpark is sold out, there are always far more people watching at home, or huddling together at their favorite watering hole. The 1980s were the heyday of sports bars—many patrons longed for their bar to be the one where everybody knew their name, like *Cheers*. At NBC's fictitious Boston bar, you rooted for the Red Sox or you got booted. That might happen in a one-team town, but in real life in a shared market like New York, viewing habits were often determined by mob rule—and timing.

In 1986 the Yankees switched from their long-established 8 p.m. home start time to 7:30, which most teams—including the Mets—had already switched to. This time change meant that Yankees and Mets games generally started at the same time (if they were both playing in the eastern time zone). Even a hard-core Yankees fan bartender was loath to put his tips on the line in the face of public opinion that was skewing blue and orange. Bill Rose, a Yankees limited partner under George Steinbrenner, conceded the point. "I've learned that business comes in front of the heart," Rose told the *Daily News*. He also owned the Sporting Club, with its massive 10-foot-screen TV. "These days, if the Yanks and Mets start at the same time, the Mets get the big screen."

Mets fans who'd had to scrounge, beg, and stuff tip jars for years to get a few innings of a Mets game on the tube at the local tavern now sat back and watched natural selection at work. In New York the strong survive.

Young people in the mid-1980s seemed to gravitate toward the Mets. Yankees allegiance skewed older—including their players. While the Mets pitching staff's average age was under 24, Yankees hurlers were mostly over 30, including two pitchers over 40: Tommy John and Joe Niekro.* Lou Piniella was a rookie manager at age 42, the 14th Yankees managerial change since Steinbrenner bought the team 13 years earlier—that's especially high turnover for a team that won five division titles, four pennants,

* Joe Niekro's 46-year-old brother Phil had pitched for the Yankees in 1985, winning his 300th career game in his last start. He was cut by the Yankees in 1986 spring training, but he signed with Cleveland and made 32 starts for the Indians, beating the Yankees twice. He pitched for three teams in 1987 before finally calling it a career at age 48.

and two World Series in that span. The *Sporting News* preseason yearbook counted off George's 13 victims with an axe under each manager's name—there were four axes under Billy Martin's.

Martin endured four firings by Steinbrenner, most recently after the Yankees won 97 times in 1985.* That wasn't even a record for most wins by a manager summarily dismissed by Steinbrenner: Dick Howser, promoted after Martin was let go for the second time, was fired in 1980 after 103 victories in his only year running the team. Oh, there was always a reason for the firings—like Martin's September of '85 fight with beleaguered Yankees pitcher Ed Whitson, in which the manager's arm was broken. The constant owner-GM-manager bickering seemed exciting when the Yankees were winning championships in the late 1970s, but by the mid-1980s the strife had worn down many casual fans, the kind of fans casual enough to put on a new New York hat with a bluer hue and a different style NY. As Joe McGrath, proprietor of the Fan Fare store at the Port Authority told the *Daily News* in 1986, he couldn't keep Mets merchandise on the shelves. "We get a lot of tourists from Britain, Sweden, and France and they buy a lot of Yankees stuff because they don't know any better. To New Yorkers, it's all Mets."

The Yankees did provide New York with a second first-place team early in the 1986 season. A six-game winning streak put the Yankees at a high-water mark of 3½ games in front in the AL East on April 25, a game ahead of the Mets' lead on St. Louis at the time. After having the best record in baseball through the first 16 games, the Yankees had the 10th best mark in baseball from that point on (78–68), spending their last day in first place on May 15, feeding into yet another Steinbrennerism. He had derided All-Star Dave Winfield as "Mr. May," for putting up big numbers when it wasn't crucial, as compared to another Yankees outfielder, Reggie

---

* Six of those wins belong to Yogi Berra, unceremoniously fired 16 games into the 1985 season. Yogi held a grudge against George Steinbrenner and stayed away from the Yankees until a reconciliation in 1998.

Jackson, aka "Mr. October." Now Reggie was an Angel and the Yankees—five years removed from their last postseason appearance—were no longer a team to plan October around. The Mets, on the other hand, were ascending. And hitting a high note.

With both clubs using more canned music at their stadiums than ever before, neither was timid about blaring "Theme from New York, New York," the Frank Sinatra anthem that became the Chairman of the Board's theme song during the legend portion of his life. First sung by Liza Minnelli in a 1977 Martin Scorsese film by that name, Sinatra took over "New York, New York" when he belted it out at his 1978 Radio City Music Hall concerts. Two years later he released the song for the first time on his triple album, *Trilogy: Past Present Future*, with "New York, New York" very much being his future showstopper. The concept behind the Fred Ebb and John Kander piece is that of a singer coming to New York from a small town, trying to make it big in New York. Sinatra's native Hoboken, New Jersey, a stone's throw from Manhattan, is hardly the sticks, but the song stirs the imagination of New Yorkers old and new who have made a name in the city. Both New York teams laid claim to the song.

The Yankees held onto it tightest and still play it after home games, but the mid-1980s Mets played it as often if not more—especially after walk-off wins as the players mobbed the hitter that came through in front of the jubilant Shea crowd. As much as any song they played at Shea in 1986, "New York, New York" fit the Mets like a custom-made suit. It was brash, brassy, and steeped in the arrogance that they—and their city—were better than any place, or anybody else. "These little town blues" were what the other team would be singing, because wherever they were from, it was not New York, New York.

There was no "Theme to New York" played on the road. New York was a place hated by many on sight, or, more often without ever having seen. The city was still emerging from a period when infrastructure was old, the streets dirty, "grindhouses" one after the other showed X-rated movies around the clock in Times Square, and a reputation as America's crime capital wasn't just something out of *Fort Apache, the Bronx*—but Jerry Della Femina was the one fined for besmirching the Bronx's image! It was a good time to drive a taxi, since more than 250 felonies were committed each week on the subway system. The New York subway lost an estimated 300 million riders during the 1980s. In 1984 there were 2,300 crimes committed just in the block of 42nd Street between Seventh and Eighth Avenues, 20 percent of them deemed serious felonies, including rape and murder. Times Square was not the best place for families then.

Word got around. New York represented all that the God-fearing people in smaller cities, suburbs, or exurbs feared. That combined with the "melting pot" perception of New York as home to many cultures, religions, and nontraditional attitudes—well, who wouldn't want to come out and boo the baseball team from there, especially one as arrogant as the Mets. It was a role the Yankees had been filling in the American League for generations, though the combination of repeated work stoppages and jaw-dropping salaries had widened the gulf between the average ballplayer and the average executive, never mind Joe Six-Pack, who could purchase said six for about $3.50 in 1986 (including deposit). It was just as easy for other teams' fans to hate the Mets as it was for New Yorkers to fall for the swaggering, staggering juggernaut that dominated the first six weeks of the season.

Through 28 games the Mets had proved unstoppable both at home (10–4) and on the road (11–3). Their last road trip had been like Sherman's March to the Sea, with Atlanta managing the lone setback in the 10-game trip that included St. Louis and Cincinnati. This time the Mets were headed where they had too often been bloodied: the Astrodome, followed by the dreaded West Coast road trip.

Mookie Wilson recalled what West Coast trips were like in his formative years as a Met in the early 1980s. "A West Coast trip was like 14 days—it was 14 days of losing," he said. "At least it was warm. If you're going to lose, you might as well lose in California."

Though the Mets had put together a 7–3 road trip to California in 1985, you had to go back another decade for the last time they'd won that many games on the West Coast since the 1969 birth of the San Diego Padres turned the trip into a California trifecta. In August 1975 a California swing plus a Houston series resulted in an 8–6 mark—though that was far from pain-free. That trip featured two walk-off losses and getting no-hit at Candlestick Park by Ed Halicki, the fifth and final time in the first quarter century of Mets baseball that the team was held hitless.

The '86 Mets faced a pitcher in Houston who'd thrown five no-hitters by himself, Nolan Ryan, but the Mets beat him for the second time in just over a week. Ryan had been outpitched a week earlier by Sid Fernandez at Shea Stadium, with Darryl Strawberry homering for the first—but not the last—time against the Ryan Express. In the rematch at the Astrodome it was reserve Danny Heep with a two-run homer off Ryan. It couldn't erase him being Ryan's 4,000th strikeout victim, which Heep couldn't help but see over and over at every stadium with a video board. "I figured he owed him something," Davey Johnson said of Heep after the game.

Heep earned the start the next night in left field in Los Angeles, as George Foster rode the bench again with a right-handed starter on the mound, this time Orel Hershiser. Foster did not even pinch-hit. Jesse Orosco, who had not allowed an earned run in his first 18⅔ innings of the season, finally allowed one, and it was on a bunt—Bill Russell's walk-off suicide squeeze in the bottom of the 11th. Platoon talk seemed squashed as Foster started the next night in L.A. against a right-hander, Bob Welch, but Foster, in a 2-for-24 slump, whiffed three times as the Mets stranded 11 in a 6–2 loss. Foster was back in the lineup and back to life on Sunday in front of the national cameras.

He crushed a three-run home run to center field off lefty Jerry Reuss in the first inning and then pulled another down the line his next time up, giving him more home runs (23) than any visiting player at Dodger Stadium. "What platoon?" Al Michaels mused on *ABC Sunday Afternoon Baseball.* "When you hit two home runs your first two times up, you're a regular every day." Michaels's assertions aside, Foster did play in two of the three games in both San Francisco and San Diego. The Mets won both series to eke out a 6–5 road trip, getting a bases-loaded wild pitch and Orosco's first RBI in two years to take the final game of the trip in San Diego in 11 innings. Given the franchise's past West Coast horrors, the Mets were happy to arrive in New York with the same four-game lead they left with.

"To finish all of our road schedule that we've had the first six weeks and to be 27–11 and now having a home schedule until the All-Star break" was a key advantage, Keith Hernandez said in a pregame interview about the Mets having 33 of their next 47 games at Shea Stadium. "We've got to be real pleased. . . . I think that our fans definitely have an effect on our play." Fans at Shea could respond to that tribute by standing and taking a bow, though in the mid-1980s that would simply have started the wave.

With Darryl Strawberry nursing an injured thumb, Danny Heep started in right field and batted fifth. George Foster, hitting sixth in left field, did not fare much better in the early going against Bob Welch than he had in L.A. a week earlier. And he was getting booed at home, as was so often the case with the well-compensated but struggling slugger. Since his two-homer game he'd gone just 1-for-15, including strikeouts his first two times up against Welch, the fourth time in five at bats he'd fanned against the big right-hander. Yet Welch was handcuffing the whole Mets lineup that night, as he often did. He'd won six straight decisions against the Mets, and he had a two-hitter through five innings in a 1–1 game. But just like that it fell apart.

Five straight Mets got hits to take a 3–1 lead to open the sixth. Tommy Lasorda, the longest-serving manager in one spot in the major leagues at the time, went old school—old school even for 1986. With the bases loaded and Foster up, Lasorda brought his top reliever into a game he trailed by two runs in the sixth inning. Tom Niedenfuer had fanned Foster with a man on in a tie game in Welch's last start at Dodger Stadium. This time Foster was ready. He pulled a fastball down the line that cleared the fence and cleared the bases. Jogging George toured the bases at a snail's pace, as if pondering each of his 14 career grand slams, which tied him with brooding former Mets teammate Dave Kingman for the most among active sluggers.

Niedenfuer seethed. The burly Dodgers reliever had suffered the humiliation of allowing ninth-inning home runs to the Cardinals in the last two games of the previous year's NLCS. Niedenfuer, who had never allowed a run in seven previous postseason appearances as a Dodger, was the goat of the series. Mindful of that scenario—and "that some pitchers regard it as an affront when a batter takes such a bow"—Channel 9 producer-director Bill Webb kept the camera trained on the Dodgers reliever as the climax built toward the inevitable curtain call.

It was only the day after Memorial Day, but it was evident that everyone around the league loathed the way the Mets milked the crowd and answered every encore request. As if fans in other cities didn't cheer like mad when the home team hit home runs—now it was expected, the fans not sitting down until the player tipped his cap, waved his arm, or, à la Gary Carter, pumped a jubilant fist at the crowd. Foster knew the Shea tradition, and he relished the moment and the fickleness of the crowd, perfectly captured by *Daily News* cartoonist Bill Gallo's transforming the familiar "Boooo" into "Boooom" for Foster's resurgent power. After a few seconds Foster stepped out of the dugout and waved to the crowd. It was like waving a red cape in front of a bull.

"I tell you, one look is worth more than a thousand words right there as Niedenfuer [is] standing in dejection," Mets announcer Steve Zabriskie told the audience. "And you might have thought that was a freeze-frame videotape, as he did not move for a full minute." The bull let loose.

Niedenfuer's next fastball drilled Knight on the left elbow. Knight did not hesitate, flinging down the bat, getting a three-step jump on the umpire and catcher on a full sprint to the mound. Niedenfuer tossed his glove behind him, tossed his cap aside, and braced for impact. Toro!

In the melee that followed, Niedenfuer used, in Zabriskie's words, "the double leg takedown," with Knight pummeling the pitcher in the head with short, sharp punches even as they went down and were engulfed in bodies from both benches. It was the first, but by no means last, fight in 1986 caused by an opponent incensed by the Mets' cock-of-the-walk air and playing to the crowd. They hadn't made friends, but they'd made a point. The Mets were the only team in baseball playing .700 ball, and didn't they know it.

Somehow neither of the main combatants was ejected. Niedenfuer stayed on the mound with the small crescent moon of a black eye Knight had given him, though he exited the game after another hit and his own error on a bunt by pitcher Ron Darling—the ninth straight Met to reach base (still with nobody out). Knight later told the press that he knew the pitcher meant to hit him, but unlike matadors and bulls, these two actually sat down to dinner after the Mets won the next night and buried the hatchet. The night after that the Mets buried the hatchet in the Dodgers' back by sweeping the series.

The Mets-Giants matchup in San Francisco had been a battle of first-place teams. Ten days later at Shea, the Mets were six games in front while the Giants had tumbled to fourth. A less humble club might have heeded the sin of hubris in others or the locker room bromide of "It's a long season." But the Mets? Foster came out for a curtain call in the third inning.

It was a back-and-forth game, as Bruce Berenyi, who'd taken over in the rotation for slumping Rick Aguilera, knocked himself out of the rotation by joining Aggie in the 6.00 ERA club. The bullpen duo of Roger McDowell and Jesse Orosco had been excellent so far in '86, but this time McDowell allowed the tying run in the eighth and Messy Jesse served up just the second major league home run of Robby Thompson's career to lead off the 10th.

The Mets were not done, however. Keith Hernandez singled to start the home 10th against lefty Mark Davis. With one out, Kevin Mitchell singled and Howard Johnson walked. Ex-Mets farmhand Juan Berenguer threw Ray Knight "probably the best fastball I've seen all year," Knight admitted on *Kiner's Korner* after the game, but he still hit it far enough for the runner to tag up. Hernandez, who had collided with Dodgers catcher Mike Scioscia the night before, tumbled over home plate again, crawling back to slap home plate before Giants catcher Bob Brenly could touch him. Hernandez had dirt all over his uniform, on his face, and in his hair, but it was 7–7.

Even before Hernandez could splash water on his face, Rafael Santana popped the ball up on the infield around second base. He threw his bat down in disgust, but Thompson and shortstop Jose Uribe came together and the ball mystically landed on the ground. Mitchell scored and the Mets had their sixth straight win, their 29th victory in 36 games, and the record for the quickest any Mets club has ever gotten to 31 wins (only 42 games). It would certainly not be the last time the '86 Mets won on someone else's egregious error.

As Ralph Kiner put it that night on his Channel 9 postgame staple, "It's a tainted win, but they'll take it." Cue Soft Cell's 1980s anthem "Tainted Love": *Sometimes I feel I've got to* (bump, bump) *run away . . .*

7

Not Your Father's Mets

June 1986

No matter how great a team is, no one runs away before June—and certainly not in the era of two-division leagues. Unless . . . unless they just keep winning. But as many teams have found, a season can quickly turn on its ear, and a great start can turn into a disappointing campaign. One prime example of what could happen to a team that sputtered after a tremendous start was the Mets—the 1972 Mets.

That '72 team kept coming up in '86 whenever the records were checked for the best start in Mets history. They seemed a very unlikely measuring rod for greatest start in club annals. After all, coach Yogi Berra was thrust into the manager's office days before the 1972 season began due to the shocking death of Gil Hodges. Not only was Berra the antithesis of the strict but beloved Hodges, but the Mets also had traded Nolan Ryan and shipped out their top three hitting prospects (including Ken Singleton) to Montreal for Rusty Staub. The '86 Mets could claim the best mark in club history after 20 games (16–4), yet the '72 Mets used their own 11-game win streak to catapult to the top spot in team history at 23–7 after 30 games, 25–10 after 35 games, and, following the best May in club history, 29–11 after 40 games. The '86 Mets matched that 40-game start, but the lesson is that fast starts are just that: starts. Finishing is what matters, what lasts.

After Jim McAndrew's 6–1 win over the Phillies on June 1, 1972, the 30–11 Mets stood five games ahead in the National League East. At 30–11, the 1986 Mets held a six-game lead in the NL East. After 41 games the '72 Mets, beset by injuries, bad luck, and a return to the norm, went just 53–61 despite a staff that struck out more batters than any team in baseball and boasted Tom Seaver in his prime, NL Rookie of the Year Jon Matlack, a not–yet-30-year-old Jerry Koosman, and Tug McGraw, whose 27 saves more than doubled the previous team record. That's nice, a lesson from the age of bell-bottoms and Pong. But in the era of acid-washed jeans and the Sega Master System, past stumbles by the franchise were a passing thought to ballplayers who had been in high school and even grade school in that year before anyone had heard of Watergate. Dwight Gooden was all of eight years old at the time. Just two players from that 1972 team were still active in the majors in 1986: Nolan Ryan, now an Astro, and Tom Seaver, who'd won his 300th game in a White Sox uniform the previous year in New York's *other* ballpark, much to the consternation of Mets fans and the front office that let him get away.

June of 1986 opened with consecutive 7–3 losses to the Giants. No big deal, but the Mets also lost two potent bats: Darryl Strawberry and Howard Johnson.

Johnson had already lost playing time to Ray Knight, now among the league's leading hitters, but HoJo did reach base in 35 of his first 100 times up. Though he had just one home run, it was perhaps the biggest long ball of the season: the game-tying homer in the ninth inning that spurred the sweep that left St. Louis in tatters. With Knight playing so well, Davey Johnson pushed the envelope and had started Howard Johnson at shortstop 20 times since his home run in St. Louis. Johnson had made only six career starts at short before 1986—five of them the previous year—and he was still inexperienced at the position at the major league level.

"Early in the season I will lean toward offense and give a lot of people the chance to play," Davey Johnson philosophized in a *Newsday* interview. "Early in the season, early in the game, I will put a lot of offensive players out there. I see who is going to have a good year for me."

Putting offense ahead of defense is a gamble, though. And in front of 49,000 at Shea, the Mets lived up to the sponsor's name on Butterfinger Cap Day, committing five errors. But the most unsettling play was not ruled an error. HoJo and Dykstra collided chasing a pop fly into short left-center in the second inning. It turned out to cause a hairline fracture of the right wrist, costing Johnson three weeks—and the shortstop job. Having now lost the third baseman's job and his shot at shortstop, he joined announcer Tim McCarver in complaining about Dykstra playing too deep in center, which he believed made infielders vulnerable to collision when chasing a short pop. "I hate to criticize a player for the way he plays," HoJo said after being placed on the disabled list, "but I think something should be looked at, maybe they should do something to try to work it out so that, you know, no more key injuries."

The outfielders didn't change how they played, but Davey Johnson did change his mind. Supersub Kevin Mitchell continued to play shortstop on occasion—usually when "fly ball pitcher" Sid Fernandez started. Howard Johnson did not. When he returned from the DL at the end of June, the manager started HoJo at shortstop just a handful of times the rest of the year, and had him take over on occasion at short late in games after he'd pinch-hit for superior defender Rafael Santana. Santana's .218 average was the lowest of any Met position player with at least 33 at bats in '86, but zone ranking techniques that came along later confirm that he was among the league's top fielding shortstops. And Davey Johnson's computer and experience verified that defense late in games or late in the year was essential.

An injury to Strawberry, on the other hand, didn't simply tweak the lineup; it altered the entire batting order and caused concern throughout the tristate area. Though his balky left thumb was deemed just a contusion, his making just one start over a two-week span brought back frightening visions of 1985, when the lanky slugger missed seven weeks due to a torn ligament in his right thumb. After an 18–8 start, the '85 Mets lost 4½ games in the standings without their most imposing slugger. In the words of longtime beat writer Jack Lang, Strawberry's '85 absence "probably cost the Mets the pennant."

Straw was never a high-average hitter, but other teams were scared enough of his power to pitch ever so carefully to him. Through the first two months of the 1986 season, his 22 walks put his on-base average at .355, his 17 extra-base hits pushed his slugging to .468, and his 27 RBI were second on the team to Gary Carter's 31.

Bad thumb and all, Strawberry could still hold a drink—though he could not hold his liquor. Among the many sins confessed in a post-career memoir, he stated that '86 was the year his intake of alcohol and speed reached epidemic proportions. "Greenies," or amphetamines, were available to ballplayers dating back to the 1950s. The grueling schedule requires teams to play at least six games a week, and the 1980s still had its fair share of doubleheaders. (The '86 Mets played nine twin bills.) Amphetamines provided quicker reaction time and helped ballplayers get up for games when they otherwise would have been dog tired from playing, traveling, or partying. Most players in the 1980s had grown up post-1960s, a time when drugs became part of the culture. Many turned a blind eye; others jumped right in. Even players who would never think of indulging in hard drugs took greenies.*

The notoriety that came with being a young superstar in New York wore on Strawberry, and he tried to cope with it by partying. Moving from the projects in Los Angeles to New York as one of

* Though using amphetamines without a prescription had been a federal crime since 1970, it was not tested for by Major League Baseball until 2006—three years after major leaguers were first tested for steroids.

the game's most heralded prospects came at a price as he tried to blend in with older players. "I got caught up in it to fit in and act like a man around them," the slugger confessed in *Straw*. "By '86 my consumption of speed was really out of hand. . . . Drinking helped put some temporary insulation back on my speed-frayed nerves and slow down my buzzing brain. A drunk speed freak is bad news. He'll say a whole lot of things he wouldn't say otherwise." Strawberry clung to the back of buses and airplanes with the "Scum Bunch," a group that consisted of Jesse Orosco, Doug Sisk, Danny Heep, and Dwight Gooden and that specialized in cruel and obnoxious behavior. "Even some of the guys on our own team hated the Scum Bunch," Strawberry explained, "because we'd pick on them, crack a lot of jokes about them, and we got pretty harsh sometimes."

Besides smoking, drinking, and speed, Strawberry also indulged in cocaine, which was just as accessible to ballplayers as it had been before the 1985 Pittsburgh drug trials. You could blame it on the '80s, just as players from previous decades could blame their sins on their decade. The hard partying helped some players bond, cope, or cut loose. Whatever they were doing, no one wanted the '86 Mets to change a thing. They were winning, winning big.

The Mets went 6–3 in Strawberry's absence before he returned for a D-Day doubleheader in Pittsburgh on June 6—marking 42 years since the Allied invasion of Normandy in World War II. The heavy artillery was out that night at Three Rivers Stadium.

The Mets were stymied in the first game by Rick Rhoden. In the fifth inning, with the Bucs leading 4–1, Gary Carter—acting on advice from first-base coach Bill Robinson—called for the baseball to be checked. Home plate umpire Billy Williams thought the ball looked suspicious and inspected Rhoden on the mound. Finding nothing on the pitcher, Williams let the at bat resume and Carter struck out. As Rhoden left the field, Robinson—a teammate of Rhoden in the early 1980s—crossed in front of the pitcher and told him, "You don't have to cheat." That was followed by more words and some shoving, and in the blink of an eye the Mets were in the midst of their second brawl of the season.

Pirates manager Jim Leyland pinned Mets pitcher Ed Lynch, whose knee was already bad enough that he was missing his start in Pittsburgh. Leyland had to be restrained by umpire Joe West. No one could stop Kevin Mitchell. Scrawny Pirates shortstop Sam Khalifa was foolish enough to try to take a run at Robinson within view of Kevin Mitchell.

"Bill Robinson, he was my mentor on that team and he really taught me the ropes and how to prepare myself," Mitchell recalled. "And I got into a lot of trouble for that day. It was Sammy Khalifa. I went after him and ended up putting him in a chokehold and wouldn't let him go."

After scuffing Khalifa's face along the Three Rivers Stadium turf, Mitchell eased up on his chokehold at the pleading of his Mets teammates. The Mets lost the game, but won the fight—about the only victory they had all year against the scuff ball.

The Mets rolled the Pirates in the nightcap, 10–4, with Strawberry, 4-for-7 in the doubleheader, hitting his first home run in a month. For good measure the Mets took four of five in that series—and did not lose any of their final 13 games against Pittsburgh in 1986. The Mets clobbered everyone—with bats as well as fists. Despite Strawberry sitting for almost two weeks, Howard Johnson missing most of the month, Ed Lynch unable to pitch, and Rick Aguilera not winning his first game until June 15, the Mets continued to roll, their lead growing taller and taller like Jack's beanstalk.

They took four more from the Pirates the following weekend at Shea—including a sweep of the Banner Day doubleheader on Father's Day with a parade of some 2,500 handwritten, handheld signs. The Mets landed in Montreal on June 16 with a 10½-game lead, the largest lead at any point in the team's 25 seasons of existence and on pace to win 117 games, one victory better than the Cubs' 80-year-old record.

Despite their dominance, the Mets had not had the chance to inflict any carnage on their closest competitor. Appearing on the schedule for the first time in mid-June, the second-place Expos were just hanging on. And that was with a roster fortified by four homegrown Mets sent northward in the Gary Carter trade 18 months earlier: shortstop Hubie Brooks, center fielder Herm Winningham, catcher Mike Fitzgerald, and pitcher Floyd Youmans.

Ron Darling (7–2), the last Mets starter to surrender his perfect record in '86, pitched the series opener against another former Mets prospect, Jay Tibbs. A second-round pick in Frank Cashen's first draft as Mets GM in 1980, Tibbs was traded to the Reds for veteran Bruce Berenyi during the 1984 season; Cincinnati then flipped him to Montreal in a six-player deal for pitcher Bill Gullickson. Though wild, Tibbs held the Mets at bay for seven innings, shutting them out until first baseman Andres Galarraga dropped the throw on Darling's two-out squeeze bunt to plate the contest's first run. Darling proved game, if erratic. Having lost almost 20 pounds due to the flu, he endured two rain delays and six walks on a night when the temperature dropped from 85 to 54 degrees by the time the game finally ended at 1:17 a.m. As if those delays weren't enough—not to mention the loss of the video feed on SportsChannel—home plate umpire/fashion policeman Bob Engel sent reliever Roger McDowell to the locker room in the eighth to change his tattered undershirt. When McDowell came back in a new shirt, a walk and two singles tied the game. No matter, the Mets won their seventh in a row on Strawberry's RBI and Lenny Dykstra's two-run single against former Met Jeff Reardon in the 10th.

After 60 games, the 44–16 Mets had more wins than the 1962 Mets had after 160 games. Though that's like comparing the constantly rising Home Run Apple and oranges. The '86 team seemed unbeatable wherever they played—they had as many wins at home as on the road, they had no peer in team annals or anywhere in the major leagues . . . yet people still worried about Dwight Gooden. The public—and most of his teammates—were not aware of his escalating cocaine habit, but everyone was taking turns speculating about what was wrong with him. While there had been such talk throughout the first third of the 1986 season, there was little justification for it on the surface. Through his first 13 starts Gooden was at almost the same place he'd been in 1985: 8–2 after 102 innings. His 2.21 ERA was more than half a run higher than at the same juncture a year earlier, but his six complete games were more than he'd had to open '85. And though his strikeouts were down, Gooden said all the right things about that—even if his syntax was off: "I think I'm more of a smarter pitcher this year." As Gooden took the mound in Montreal in the rubber game of that series, he was coming off a season-best 13-K performance against the Pirates, and only a Friday the 13th meltdown by Jesse Orosco had denied Doc his ninth win of the year.

In Montreal Gooden faced Floyd Youmans, who'd been the ace on Gooden's high school team in Tampa until he moved to California to live with his father as a senior. Youmans, six months older than Gooden, was drafted by the Mets in 1982 in the second round, one round after his lifelong friend. Doc—or "Bugsy," as "Fruit" Youmans had called him since age seven—took the slightly faster track to the majors. Youmans was just 21 when he debuted for the Expos in 1985.

Youmans was the crown jewel of the Carter trade, as far as the Expos were concerned. He wasn't Doc (or even Bugsy), but he was young, cheap, and strong. And Youmans outpitched his buddy in their first matchup. Montreal lit up Gooden for seven runs, with Doc striking out just one Expo. He allowed six hits and walked six. Tim Wallach, who came in 1-for-19 in his career against Gooden, became the first player to ever homer twice off him in one game. Gooden wasn't much better when he faced Youmans and the

Expos in a rematch in his next start, but he was bailed out at Shea by a three-run fifth, scoring the tying run himself on a wild pitch by Youmans. The Mets lost that game in 10 innings and wound up dropping four of six to the Expos in June. Buoyed by taking four of five from the Cubs, however, the Mets ended the month leading the NL East by 9½ games. Their 19–9 June matched the team record held by the 1969 world champion Mets. That was the kind of company the '86 Mets wanted to keep.

Legend has branded the '86 Mets as a collection of partiers, addicts, and assholes. William Hayward Wilson was none of the above.

One of a dozen children growing up on a farm with a tin-roof house and no running water, Mookie belonged to a family that had sharecropped in South Carolina for generations. He liked baseball as a break from their hard rural life, yet he never played any type of organized baseball until reaching Bamberg-Ehrhardt High School—a recently integrated school. A local judge arranged for Mookie to play American Legion ball, hooking him up with rides in the back of a local police car and finding him a part-time job to help support his family. Then he enrolled Wilson at two-year Spartanburg Methodist College on a baseball scholarship. "Why would this white man go out of his way for a black kid from the South?" Wilson wrote in his 2014 book, *Mookie*. "It was extremely important for me, as a young athlete, to know that some total stranger thought more highly of me than I did of myself."

From there Mookie integrated the University of South Carolina baseball team, where he got to know future Mets teammate Ed Lynch. He met his future Mets roommate, Hubie Brooks, during the 1977 College World Series when the Gamecocks lost to Arizona State in the championship game, 2–1 (though Mookie made the All-Tournament team and Hubie did not). Mookie had turned down the Dodgers a year earlier when they drafted him in the fourth round. Just as the '77 College World Series got underway,

Mookie Wilson NATIONAL BASEBALL HALL OF FAME LIBRARY, COOPERSTOWN, NY

Wilson was drafted by the Mets in the second round, one round after New York chose Wally Backman. Though his family wanted him to finish school, Mookie negotiated a $22,000 signing bonus, which he turned over to his parents, and received their blessing. He was the type of person who would complete his degree on his own, anyway.

The $500 per month salary (before taxes) and $4 daily meal money would have been a hardship for most, but it was better than Wilson made at home. At Class AA Jackson he was married in an on-field ceremony, unconventional in more ways than one because he wed his brother's ex-wife and adopted their four-year-old son, Preston, a future All-Star center fielder. He learned how to switch-hit on his own in Triple-A, becoming an even more valuable commodity. It was time to head to New York.

Wilson arrived at the Mets' nadir. They were trying to focus on young players, the main drawback of that plan being that most of their young players weren't any good. Mookie was an exception, but he was blocked in center field by Lee Mazzilli, the 1980 team's lone drawing card. The Mets moved Maz to left field in 1981, putting Mookie in center, and just before the '82 season traded Mazzilli to Texas for Ron Darling and Walt Terrell.* Wilson was stealing 50 bases and scoring 90 runs a year for a punchless team. Twice in four days in the summer of '83 he ended games by scoring from second base on balls that didn't even leave the infield. The one thing he could not do was get on base more often, walking just 18 times in a major league–high 683 at bats in 1983. You'd think that someone who grew up in a home with one outhouse for 14 people would have come to the plate with more patience.

Mookie could see a positive change in the team. "In '83 we really thought we were developing something that was going to be special," he said. "We didn't know how special because we were

* The Mets traded Walt Terrell to Detroit for Howard Johnson in the 1984 off-season, adding dividends on what was already one of the franchise's best trades.

still unknowns. There was a difference in the clubhouse. Guys were eager to come to the ballpark, they weren't in a hurry to leave. So we started to see the whole dynamic and mental aspect of the team change."

Mookie Wilson was front and center as the team made the long, slow transformation from godawful to goddamned good. That's when it started to come apart for him. After a solid '84 season, Wilson got off to a tremendous start in 1985. He was batting .297 at the end of May and already had 16 steals, but his right shoulder was aching. That prompted the call-up of Len Dykstra, who became an immediate favorite in New York for his gutsy play, headlong dives, and unflappable demeanor. Life at Shea would never be the same for Mookie. Shoulder surgery cost him more than two months as Dykstra shined and the Mets battled for first place. Wilson did take over for Dykstra in September and batted .307 with a surprising 12 extra-base hits and even more astonishing 14 walks over his final 31 games. The Mets came up short of the Cardinals, and Mookie came up short in the Mets' eyes.

The Mets planned to platoon in center field with Wilson and Dykstra, even before Mookie was hit in the eye during the spring training rundown drill. Wilson's season finally started with a pinch-hit at bat on May 9, 1986. After beginning just 2-for-17, he batted .337 (34-for-101) over the next month, scored 22 runs in 26 games, clubbed four home runs, and stole 11 bases without being caught. Dykstra likewise was hot, creating the daily challenge of who batted first and who played where.

While Mookie was frustrated that he played more against lefties than righties—he had over time become a better hitter from the left side than the right side—he never took it out on the new guy. He went out of his way to compliment the man who had taken a nice chunk of his playing time. "I will not even say any more that he is trying to establish himself as a major league leadoff hitter," Wilson said of Dykstra in June of '86. "I say he has established himself." Dykstra, not surprisingly, confessed he would not be as accommodating as Wilson if he were the veteran in this situation, but not everyone can be Mookie.

Mookie would grow frustrated over time as the platoon persisted. In the summer of '86, however, he rode the wave as the Mets kept winning. His work ethic, perseverance, and understanding would be rewarded on the team everybody outside of New York loved to hate.

8

Sledgehammer

July 1986

Some contend that hip-hop didn't kick off until the summer of '86 with Run-DMC's reimagining of Aerosmith's "Walk This Way." Jerry Garcia of the Grateful Dead slipped into a diabetic coma for five days in July, then slipped back out of it to tour for another decade. It was the summer of big hair and Poison—well, the debuting glam metal group of that name—plus unnecessary umlauts for the excesses of Mötley Crüe, whose drummer, Tommie Lee, married Heather Locklear, the 24-year-old feather-haired beauty who found time for love and metal while starring in two ABC dramas: as a gold digger on *Dynasty* and as a policewoman in the William Shatner vehicle *T.J. Hooker*. July also saw tit for tat on the other end of the musical scale: one week after Genesis had its first number one hit with "Invisible Touch," Peter Gabriel knocked his old bandmates out of the top spot with "Sledgehammer." Boom box, Blaupunkt car stereo, Walkman, or even a state-of-the-art $600 compact disc player—the summer of '86 wasn't subtle on the ears. Likewise, the '86 Mets weren't subtle on the eyes.

The Mets were televised all over the country. It was not just the ABC and NBC national games, which seemed to feature the Mets every week. The Mets had their own superstation.

WOR had covered the Mets since their 1962 birth—in addition to airing the Islanders, Rangers, Knicks, Nets, and pro wrestling at various times. But the station always seemed kind of rinky-dink, even a little naughty with the bawdy *Benny Hill Show*, as well as other accented, imported fare not seen elsewhere. Now it was national.

You could thank—or in the case of the other major league owners, blame—Atlanta Braves owner Ted Turner. "The Mouth of the South" had talked his way into the National League and into living rooms across the country. In 1970 Turner purchased Atlanta station WJRJ—channel 17 on the UHF dial—and two years later he put the first Braves game on the rebranded channel. In 1976 he created the first superstation by beaming his signal via satellite to different cable systems around the nation. It was basic cable and it was good—if you liked old black-and-white movies. Within a year he had bought his chief programming: the Braves and the NBA's Atlanta Hawks. In 1980 came Cable News Network, or CNN; 1981 struck "Turner Time"—starting TBS programming at five after the hour and half hour, leading to separate, distinct, and unpaid listings in *TV Guide*; in 1985 "Turner Time" never stopped as the station went 24 hours; and by '86 he'd added even more old movies with a $1.4 billion purchase of the MGM film library, the eventual foundation of Turner Network Television (TNT).

WOR had no such interesting milestones. It wasn't even in the same league as Chicago's superstation, WGN, which had tripled its audience in the past three years and was armed with a solid lineup of reruns, multiple sports teams, and Harry Caray screaming and singing from Wrigley Field as daily counterprogramming to soap operas. But WOR had the Big Apple—even if the station was located in Secaucus, New Jersey. It also had the Mets. The majority of Mets games were on "free" TV on WOR, as opposed to its cable provider, SportsChannel. The Mets made $17 million per year from Cablevision mogul Charles Dolan—more than double the Yankees' take at that point—but much of New York was still not wired for cable. Twenty years after Manhattan received the service as an experiment to circumvent interference from tall buildings, cable TV finally started appearing in test markets in the other boroughs in 1986. After years of litigation, wrangling, and industry disinterest, the other four boroughs in the country's number one market could pay $13–$16 per month for the kind of viewing choices that people in places like Grand Island, Nebraska, had been enjoying for years. It was as if a door had been opened and people could step outside and run free—except it was TV, so it was pretty much the opposite. And it wasn't free. *Still the Beaver,* anybody?

The television landscape was fertile ground for expansion. The big three networks still showed movies two nights a week, and with reality TV far in the future, network programmers showed no fear in bending reality with pap like *MacGyver*, *Max Headroom*, *Highway to Heaven*, *ALF* (short for "Alien Life Form"), *Starman*, and don't forget *Dallas*, where Bobby Ewing—played by Patrick Duffy—had been dead all season but showed up in the shower in the last 10 seconds of the show's 1986 finale. The whole season was a dream, get it? The start of FOX as the fourth network in the fall of '86 did little to boost the overall quality of scripted programming.

WOR, known to generations of New Yorkers as Channel 9, didn't seem a savior in terms of content with its reruns of *My Favorite Martian*, *Bewitched, Hart to Hart*, *The Partridge Family*, and, well, at least there was *Benny Hill*. If you made a batting order of local stations, based on merit, Channel 9 would have been like the pitcher at the bottom of the lineup behind Channels 2 (CBS), 4 (NBC), 5 (FOX), 7 (ABC), 11 (WPIX), and 13 (PBS). But WOR set station records for ratings in 1986—when the Mets were on. Thirty years later, with the VCR long since put to pasture by the DVR and other services, the same mantra applies as it did then in terms of programming: Live events rule.

In the 1980s the video cassette recorder freed people who'd previously been trapped by the start times of their favorite shows to instead watch at their leisure—if they could get the VCR clock to stop blinking "12:00." But taped sporting events were—and remain—like fruit that can spoil with a phone ring, a beep, or an update, and your enjoyment of last night's recorded Mets-Cardinals game changes the moment the outcome is known. This was a common enough '80s experience that the first time viewers would see Jerry's apartment in the pilot for *Seinfeld* (in 1989), he is watching TV, the phone rings, he picks it up and says, "If you know what happened in the Mets game, don't say anything, I taped it. Hello?" It's a wrong number. But a moment later the door bursts open and Kramer is introduced to the entertainment universe with the words, "Boy, the Mets really blew it tonight, huh?" Yeah, New York was a Mets town. For a fleeting moment you might have even believed it could become a Mets country. And in case the Mets advertisements at the Yankee Stadium subway stop were too subtle, only first names were needed for the TV commercials beamed out around the country.

> *Announcer: What's baseball like it oughta be?*
> *Ron: Baseball's great when nine people go out there and they throw the ball hard, hit it hard, and catch it hard. That's baseball.*
> *Keith: It's a gratifying feeling when you get a bases-loaded hit in the ninth inning.*
> *Len: I think it's the way I play: hard, aggressive, and try to come out on top.*
> *Gary: Cheering for the home team.*
> *HoJo: Hard work, sweat, a lot of dirt.*
> *Roger: Baseball oughta be winning.*
> *Davey: Baseball like it oughta be, you should have a championship in New York.*
> *Announcer: The 1986 Mets. Baseball like it oughta be.*

"Do the Mets feel invincible?"

In case anyone wondered why the rest of country wasn't so fond of New York, or the Mets, or Gary Carter, the perennial All-Star catcher looked directly into the camera in St. Louis and answered the question plainly for the *ABC Monday Night Baseball* audience: "I think more than anything it's a feeling of confidence. You know, being invincible is a pretty big word. But I'd say this ball club, if we get down one, two, even three runs, and we feel we can come back. We've got the kind of talent on this ball club that we feel that we can score a lot of runs. And we've got a great pitching staff as well. We've got two guys with nine wins, two guys with eight wins, and Roger McDowell with seven wins, so we've just got a good bunch of guys, great chemistry on the ball club, and we just feel like we can win every game." Then he smiled at the end, as if he was just stating facts.

His detractors called him "Camera Carter" because of how he seemed to milk those moments—and shook his wet perm in his Ivory Soap commercial—but he had the numbers right, and it was not just the $99\frac{44}{100}\%$ pure of Ivory. In a time when wins meant everything to pitchers, the press, and the public, the Mets rotation entered July looking like this:

Sid Fernandez: 9–2
Dwight Gooden: 9–3
Bob Ojeda: 9–2
Ron Darling: 8–2*

With no other NL team having *any* pitcher with more than eight wins, the front four of the Mets had all reached that mark with a cumulative mark of 35–9 in 57 starts, not to mention an ERA under 3.00 and averaging more than seven innings per start. And reliever Roger McDowell, the *Daily News* Met of the Month for June, was 7–0 and averaging almost two innings per relief outing.

---

* Gary Carter was right. Bob Ojeda came into *Monday Night Baseball* with eight wins, and he got his ninth in St. Louis a few hours after Carter's pregame interview.

Sid Fernandez began July by beating the Cardinals, 2–1, becoming the National League's first 10-game winner for a team that was 30 games over .500. A day later they left St. Louis 31 games over .500 and 11½ games ahead. And it wasn't yet July 4. They would not skimp on the fireworks, though.

Fireworks Night at Shea Stadium was always a special night, a carnival atmosphere crowded with a mix of young couples on dates, single young people getting drunk, those who graduated from dates and drunks to parents, older people coming for a night out, and kids up way past their bedtimes, fidgeting through the game and gnawing on the nib that once held cotton candy. And even with the promise of a long walk to their cars and an epic traffic jam, most everyone stayed for the whole game.* No matter the score, people stayed to see "America's First Family of Fireworks," the Grucci family, who had emigrated from southern Italy to Long Island in the 1850s. In the formative years of the Gruccis' association with the Mets, starting in 1979, the team was usually out of contention by July 4. The '86 Mets, on the other hand, were so far ahead in the standings by Fireworks Night they were in a different stratosphere.

The Mets seemed to spot the Astros two runs in the first inning to provide drama for the largest Shea gathering of the regular season. And when the teams were tied after nine superb innings by Ron Darling, they had to spot the Astros two more runs in extra innings. The Astros were determined to hold onto the win, as rookie manager Hal Lanier made five defensive changes in the bottom of the 10th—all undone by reliever Frank DiPino's leadoff walk to Len Dykstra. As WOR producer Bill Webb focused on the fidgeting and frustrated Astros manager, Lanier had little choice but to leave in the lefty to face Darryl Strawberry. When Straw crushed his fourth hit, and second home

* The fireworks were set off in the Shea Stadium parking lot, so several thousand parking spots were unavailable on Fireworks Night. The ensuing gridlock, as well as parking spaces far from the stadium, meant many fans did not get inside the park until well into the game.

run of the game—a no doubter to dead center—Lanier kicked the floor of the dugout. But he left in DiPino, who left a ball over the plate that Ray Knight launched into the Picnic Area, the lone empty area of the park because it was in the line of fire for the fireworks. The rest of the stadium, as packed as a ballpark can be for an extra-inning game, detonated on cue as the Mets won their seventh straight. Knight, who'd struck out his first four times, came out for the curtain call as the "Theme from New York, New York" blared.

"Frank Sinatra is saying start spreading the news and the Mets are doing exactly that," Tim McCarver shouted on WOR over the noise at Shea. "They are spreading the news that they are right now the dominant team in this game. In either league." The Mets led by 12½, the second-largest Fourth of July lead in National League history after the 1912 New York Giants. You didn't even need a superstation to spread that kind of news.

The torturing of ex-Yankee Hal Lanier continued the next afternoon as the Mets won their eighth straight, 2–1, for Dwight Gooden's 10th victory of the year. Despite all the complaining about the diminished Doc, at 21 he was still one of the ten youngest players in the major leagues, he was named to start the 57th All-Star Game. Cardinals manager Whitey Herzog had heard enough about the Mets already, but he did not want to lose the All-Star Game. Again. In 1983 he managed the National League and the league lost for the first time in a dozen years. The All-Star Game was an exhibition, sure, but with separate league presidents, umpires, schedules, and attitudes of superiority exuding from both sides, no added incentive was needed. Most would have scoffed at the concept of "making it count" by attaching World Series home-field advantage as an enticement to take the All-Star Game more seriously, as happened in the 2000s. "Wild horses couldn't drag me to it—no interest," Keith Hernandez said of the new All-Star order. "They've made it into a circus, like the NBA All-Star Game." Plus, in 1986 it was a very good thing World Series home-field advantage was still determined by league rotation, because the Mets would need every edge come October.

But in July, much to the dismay of Whitey, Doc, and the NL, it was the AL's turn to start a midsummer winning streak. Its 3–2 victory at the Astrodome began a run that would see the AL win 19 of the next 23 All-Star Games, plus notch one very awkward tie.* Boston's Roger Clemens, who did not lose a game until July and whose 15 wins at the break were the most in a decade, threw three perfect innings on two days' rest. Gooden was less than perfect in his three frames, surrendering a Lou Whitaker two-run home run in the second inning to take the loss.

If blame was needed for the defeat, it was rather tempting to look at the blue and orange racing stripes clogging the NL dugout. The Mets' five representatives—and four starters—were the most in team history. Doc allowed the big hit in the game while the heart of the NL order—Keith Hernandez, Gary Carter, and Darryl Strawberry—went a combined 1-for-10, though Straw (the leading vote getter among fans) did hammer half the NL's home runs to help win the Home Run Derby, one shot hitting a roof speaker. (The derby was so casual and removed from the spectacle of today that no camera caught Straw's titanic blast.) Sid Fernandez, the NL's leader in wins with 12, struck out the side in a scoreless eighth inning despite two walks and a double steal. If you wanted to get technical, there were seven Mets in Houston, with Davey Johnson serving as first-base coach and Rusty Staub as honorary captain. Though Staub sported a Colt .45 uniform like the one he wore as a rookie (a few sizes bigger now), Rusty was very much a Met—and he was having a hell of a week. Staub, who retired in 1985 with the seventh-most games played in major league history (2,951), was feted at Shea the day before the

* If later All-Star managers showed the restraint of Whitey Herzog in keeping plenty of pitchers in reserve, the 2002 All-Star Game would never have ended in a tie. Herzog kept five pitchers on his roster idle while AL manager Dick Howser held back three hurlers in the one-run 1986 game.

break, with the whole team coming out to surprise him in orange wigs with their uniforms stuffed to simulate Le Grande Orange's physique.

Exhibition loss aside, the Mets stood at the head of the class at the height of summer in '86. The always critical *New York Post* even handed out six As on the team's midseason report card, including one to Davey Johnson. The *Post* also distributed two A-minuses and five B-pluses. When it came to deportment, however, the '86 Mets would be kept after school.

Three fights in 12 days. Records are not kept for fighting frequency, but when it comes to rough-and-tumble clubs, the '86 Mets were in their own league.

Flash back before the All-Star Game to the first of those fights—or the team's third fight of the year, for those keeping a judge's scorecard at home—which was shown coast-to-coast by NBC cameras on hand for a special *Game of the Week* on the last Friday before the break. Len Dykstra led off the home first with a walk. Wally Backman followed with a drag bunt and dove headlong into first ahead of Bob Horner's lunging tag. After the runners moved up a base on a groundout, Braves pitcher David Palmer faced Gary Carter, his catcher when both were Expos. Palmer tossed him a meatball and kicked the air as soon as Carter swung. Kid circled the bases, and his exuberant curtain call infuriated Palmer.

The next pitch drilled Darryl Strawberry in the back. Strawberry threw his helmet and headed right for Palmer, the Brave suddenly not so brave as he threw his glove at the fast-approaching slugger and then ducked away. Braves catcher Ozzie Virgil slowed Strawberry's progress from behind, but Keith Hernandez was among those who did reach the pitcher. The fight ended soon, but the nightmare continued for Palmer. He was not ejected but suffered the indignity of facing Carter again in the second inning . . . and allowing a grand slam . . . and another curtain call.

"They act as though they won the seventh game of the World Series," prescient Palmer said after the game. "I told Keith Hernandez when we were scuffling around: 'I don't mind if you hit 15 home runs, but don't show me up.'"

Carter's second home run—his 10th career grand slam—gave him 16 homers for the year. The seven RBI were a career high and gave him 65 to take the league lead from Mike Schmidt. Carter also caught Sid Fernandez's first career complete-game shutout, which may have been the best overall start of the pitcher's career—El Sid had three hits at the plate while allowing just two on the mound.

NBC, following the Mets across the country like Deadheads (Jerry Garcia *was* in the hospital and off tour for the first summer since 1980), broadcast a Mets game for the seventh time already in 1986 on Saturday. Pregame host Marv Albert, who worked in the home market as well, was not afraid to have fun with the team and asked Strawberry, "Darryl, did you realize that under New York state boxing regulations, this was a mismatch? You're listed at 6'6", he's at 6'1". In fact, NBC's fight doctor Ferdie Pacheco had you leading on his unofficial scorecard."

Strawberry, having domestic issues that would culminate with him breaking his wife Lisa's nose during a postseason altercation, skirted Albert's lead-in and brought the subject back to how the Mets wanted to be treated by others: "You have to gain some type of respect that they just can't do that because a guy hit a home run and celebrated."

After the Mets outscored Atlanta in the four-game sweep, 28–2, taking a 13½-game lead into the break, they did not miss a beat in the second half opener. They pummeled Nolan Ryan and the Houston bullpen to the point that shortstop Craig Reynolds tossed the last frame for the Astros in the 13–2 rout. Ah, but the baseball gods are fickle. Unable to humble the '86 Mets on the field, the team would be tripped up in their favorite off-field setting: a bar.

The place was called Cooter's, and the Houston dance club was where six Mets headed to celebrate the birth of Tim Teufel's first child. Darryl Strawberry and Ed Hearn took off after a little while and the other four—Ron Darling, Bob Ojeda, Rick Aguilera, and Teufel—soon wished they'd left as well. Teufel, among the least likely Mets to end up in such a situation, walked out holding a drink and was confronted and handcuffed by off-duty police serving as security. Darling, who'd taken the loss earlier in the night, took another one when he came to the aid of his teammate and was pushed up against a glass door, which shattered. Ojeda and Aguilera tried to persuade the officers to take it easy but found themselves arrested as well. Hauled in at 2 a.m., the four were not released from their holding cell until the next afternoon. Darling and Teufel posted bond of $8,000 each, Ojeda and Aguilera $800 apiece. It was $1 million worth of free publicity for the bar and just added to the team's bad boy reputation. "It was typical Mets," the mild-mannered Hearn said years later of Cooter's-gate, still thankful he left early that night.

Each of the four players' lockers had black strips (white athletic tape with black shoe polish) to imitate jail bars, stools outfitted with an empty can of Budweiser, a cup marked "tequila," as well as a bagel, a bar of soap, a razor, one cigarette, and a book of matches. The media had a field day with the story, the *New York Times* even calling it the Mets' Copacabana—not the 1970s Barry Manilow song but the New York club where a 1957 fight with patrons led to the Yankees trading second baseman Billy Martin, whose birthday they had been celebrating. The Mets would not trade their second baseman for five years and Teufel later returned to the Mets as a minor league manager and instructor. Three decades removed from the incident and serving as third-base coach on a Mets team where many of the players weren't even born when Cooter's last made news, Teufel looked off toward a wall when reminded of the incident. "It's one of those things that happened," he said with a wan smile. "I'm 57 years old. That's something that's way beyond

Tim Teufel DAN CARUBIA

me." Charges would be dropped and the incident forgotten, but not in 1986.

The Mets stumbled off the field the last two days in the Astrodome as fans hooted—or perhaps "Cooted" in honor of their new favorite local dance club. If there was a silver lining to the Mets' lost weekend in Houston, it was that both walk-off defeats came after the Mets beat up on the Astros bullpen in the ninth inning. The night after the Cooter's affair, the Mets rallied against Mike Scott and Dave Smith, but light-hitting shortstop Craig Reynolds, who'd pitched mop-up relief in the top of the ninth just two nights before, circled the bases after hitting a game-winning home run in the bottom of the ninth on Saturday. The Mets rallied again the next afternoon to forge a tie, and the game dragged on until a bang-bang play at the plate ended the game in the 15th—Hernandez, Carter, and Davey Johnson all jaw-to-jaw with umpire Greg Bonin five and a half hours after the first pitch. The game was the longest the Mets would play all season—the regular season.

The last entry on the Mets' fight docket shouldn't have happened. Well, all the fights *shouldn't* have happened, but in this case the game should have been over before any punch was thrown. The Reds, who a few weeks earlier became the first team in 1986 to sweep the Mets—and the lone club to do so at Shea—held a 3–1 lead with two outs in the ninth at Riverfront Stadium on July 22. Reds rookie Scott Terry could almost taste his first major league victory. Then Ron Robinson walked Len Dykstra and missed the plate by an inch on a two-strike pitch to Tim Teufel. Two pitches later Robinson allowed a ground-rule double to Teufel, his third hit in as many tries since his run-in with Houston's finest. Lefty John Franco—no facial hair yet—was summoned to retire the mustachioed Hernandez. Franco did his job, inducing Mex* to hit a fly to three-time Gold Glove winner Dave Parker on the edge of the warning track in right field. Reds TV announcer Marty

* Despite his teammates' playful nickname, Keith Hernandez was not of Mexican descent. His father's ancestors were from Spain and his mother's were Scots-Irish.

Brennaman was ready to pronounce this a win: "Parker, and this one . . . No! He drops the ball! The Mets tie it up as Parker coughs up a routine fly ball to right field." CLANG!

Franco was furious, bouncing the ball off the mound as he cursed. The groans from Riverfront became boos when the next batter, Gary Carter, hit a high fly to right-center and Parker cut in front of Eddie Milner at the last second and caught the ball—with one hand. The game should have been over. Instead, it raged on for another two hours, but two hours of some of the most entertaining baseball in the summer of 1986.

In the bottom of the 10th inning Pete Rose, the Reds manager and all-time hits leader, called on himself to bat for Franco and collected career hit number 4,247.* Eric Davis, sitting on the bench with 45 stolen bases because of a sore hand, came in to pinch-run. The one area the Mets had trouble with was opponents' base stealing, and Davis stole second with ease, the 106th steal in 133 tries against New York catchers. And then Davis tried to steal third.

As Davis slid in ahead of Gary Carter's throw, Ray Knight shoved Davis as if to push him off the base and tag him. Davis shoved Knight hard and—well, Davis must not have been following the Mets closely in '86. Knight coldcocked him and an instant later Carter tackled Davis, catching the base stealer at last. Kevin Mitchell and Reds pitcher/martial arts practitioner John Denny went at it. Eddie Milner took out Jesse Orosco, who'd just struck him out on the pitch that helped start it all. Dave Parker, the biggest guy on the field and still stewing over his error an inning earlier, tossed bodies around. When order was restored, the umpires did the tossing. Knight and Davis were gone—pitcher Tom Browning had to pinch-run for a pinch runner. Mitchell, who'd come in after Strawberry's ejection for arguing in the sixth

* Pete Rose would collect nine more hits in his record-setting career before playing his final game less than a month later. Rose remained as Reds manager until he was barred from the game in 1989 for gambling on baseball.

inning, was thumbed after the fight, as was hot-tempered Reds pitcher Mario Soto.

With the limits of the 24-man roster, the Mets had just one position player left and two spots to fill. Davey Johnson was livid that the Mets lost two position players while the Reds lost a player who couldn't bat and a starting pitcher unlikely to play. Johnson, who fell into the camp of managers who did not use both catchers in a game except in an emergency, had a doozy of an emergency in Cincinnati. Ed Hearn, his last position player, put on the catching gear; his All-Star catcher, Carter, became the 80th third baseman in Mets history; his last relief pitcher, Roger McDowell, came in to face Wade Rowdon; and Orosco, his pitcher when the fight started, moved to right field. Campy, you might call the situation—and sort of familiar.

The Mets' 19-inning, 16–13 win in Atlanta the previous Fourth of July—when abysmal-hitting Braves reliever Rick Camp tied the game with a home run—came to mind. Against the Braves Johnson had let nothing get in the way of winning: even if the Mets blew saves in the 8th, 13th, and 18th innings, even if he needed to use a reliever for six innings, even if he had to bust up his rotation and use a starter to finish at 4 a.m. The July 22, 1986, game would end much earlier, but it was memorable in many ways, starting with Carter.

Carter, who'd caught all 19 innings in Atlanta a year prior, had all of one inning of major league experience at third base—as a rookie in 1975, without any chances. He morphed into Mike Schmidt on the Riverfront Astroturf. He was baptized with a bunt, fielding the sacrifice and throwing to first in the 11th. He was challenged on the next play: grabbing a hard-hit ball, looking the runner back to second, and gunning it to first. There were others out of position as well.

After an inning in right field, Orosco came back in to pitch. McDowell—huge grin on his face—grabbed a mitt more suited to the task and headed to right field. Orosco got through the inning, but McDowell did not start the 12th against righty Buddy Bell because lefty Parker was on deck. As Pete Rose and the rest of the Reds dugout thumbing through the rule book could tell you, Rule 3.03 stipulates a pitcher-to-position change can be made just once per inning. "The rules allowed it, so I did it," Johnson explained three decades later. "Helped us win a game."

It wasn't so easy. Facing Orosco, Bell hit a smash to third that Carter dove for, but his throw was just late. McDowell was directed to swap spots in left field with Mookie Wilson as Dave Parker stepped up. The Cobra bounced a single to right and with the experienced Wilson out there, Bell held at second. As Reds pitcher Carl Willis squared to sacrifice, Hernandez attacked in the style that made him the scourge of bunters throughout the National League: pouncing on the bunt to the left of the mound, throwing on the run to third, and then Carter gunning across the diamond to Teufel at first to complete the 3–5–4 double play. For the fourth straight inning the Reds left the winning run in scoring position. Reds owner Marge Schott left for the night, but most of the 23,707 that showed up stuck around. Why wouldn't they?

In the top of the 13th Willis stranded two Mets, and in the bottom of the inning McDowell returned to the mound and Orosco went back to right field, where he caught a line drive from future Hall of Famer Tony Perez. "I said to Jesse that hopefully I was going to get him a fly ball," Cincinnati native McDowell, who saw Dykstra cut in front of him to make the catch with the winning run on second in the 12th, explained the next day. "I would have liked to have the putout, but I'd rather have the win."

And that's what McDowell got when Howard Johnson crushed a Ted Power 2–2 curveball into the second deck with two men on in the 14th. Orosco, who went 0-for-1 with a walk in his outfield debut, scored with Ed Hearn on HoJo's home run. McDowell got three ground balls in the 14th for the win, his first after four straight losses—including the successive walk-off setbacks to the Astros. The lost weekend in Houston? Forgotten. The swagger was back—if it had ever left—as HoJo affirmed in the clubhouse. "We're probably the cockiest team in the league," he proclaimed. "I think other teams feel that way and they come after us. But we enjoy fighting. If that's what it takes, we'll fight every team. You can't push us around." No one else was trying anymore.

9

Just Routine, Ma'am

August 1986

On the first of August, Montreal capitulated. Manager Buck Rodgers, whose second-place Expos came into Shea Stadium trailing by 15½ games, conceded the obvious after the Mets' 3–1 win as Dwight Gooden beat his childhood friend Floyd Youmans on the third try. Montreal lost not only the game, but also former Mets Hubie Brooks and Mike Fitzgerald to injuries, topping the pile of already injured 'Spos. The Mets needed an opponent to concede about as much as Ronald Reagan needed a concession speech to inform him he'd won the 1984 election over Walter Mondale. Dutch won 49 of 50 states over Fritz, the former vice president of Jimmy Carter, who'd won all of six states against Reagan in 1980. Whether it was presidential elections, Super Bowls, or pennant races, a blowout was always a possibility in the 1980s.

Rodgers's concession made it less awkward when Montreal dropped the next two games to push New York's lead to 17½. By the time the Expos walked off the field Sunday—trying not to watch as the Mets mobbed Ray Knight following his game-ending single in the 10th inning—Montreal wasn't even in second place anymore. Philadelphia was now closest in a race that wasn't even close. The Mets were thinking about October, not

August, and they busied themselves constructing a roster for that inevitability.

Frank Cashen was not afraid to bring ex-Mets home to Flushing. Dave Kingman, Rusty Staub, and Tom Seaver were Mets stars sent away by the previous regime in extremely unpopular—and unwise—trades. Cashen brought each back in the early part of his Mets tenure, if for no other reason than to keep fans interested during the wholesale rebuilding. One of the general manager's best trades had been acquiring Ron Darling and Walt Terrell just before the 1982 season. By the summer of 1986 the Mets had Darling in the rotation, as well as a crucial part of the future and the current bench in Howard Johnson—the return from Detroit for Terrell. Cashen even had back the man he'd sent to Texas in that '82 heist: Lee Mazzilli.

Maz was popular, one of the few bright spots in the late 1970s on a team that had traded the aforementioned Kingman, Staub, and Seaver. The first Met to ever have his own poster giveaway at Shea, Maz brought 14,000 to Shea in July 1979 for the only Mets season when attendance averaged fewer than 10,000 souls per game. In a rare national piece about a Met at the time, *Sports Illustrated* described Mazzilli as "olive-skinned, dark-eyed, high-cheekboned—very Kiss-Me-I'm-Italian."

The team's top draft pick in 1973, he was the lone player out of 35 rounds in that draft who ever played more than a handful of games at Shea. Maz could hit and even throw both ways—though not strong with either arm. He was an accomplished speed skater, but he quit when it became a conflict with his first love, baseball. He was an All-America ballplayer at Abraham Lincoln High School in Brooklyn, where heartthrob alums included Neil Diamond. M. Donald Grant—using the nose-to-the-grindstone scouting methods that had made Whitey Herzog such a fan of the Mets chairman's baseball expertise—first heard of Mazzilli from a cashier at his brokerage firm. But the cashier was right: Maz was a legitimate prospect. After signing for $50,000, he stole seven bases

Lee Mazzilli back in the Mets dugout DAN CARUBIA

in a seven-inning minor league game. He dove headfirst, he sent female hearts a-flutter with his tight uniform, and he made basket catches like his idol, Willie Mays. Jane Jarvis, who'd seen many Mets come and go as Shea's organist during the stadium's first 16 seasons, wasn't as impressed by the "Italian Stallion"—she played "You're So Vain" as he signed autographs.

Maz went to the 1979 All-Star Game as a reserve after hitting .320 in the first half. He was the National League's hitting hero in Seattle, homering left-handed to tie the game, and then drawing a walk from the right side with the bases loaded against Yankee Ron Guidry to drive in the go-ahead run. He lost the All-Star MVP to Dave Parker's defense—funny as it seems considering that Parker's '86 fielding gaffe in Cincinnati set the stage for the Orosco-McDowell outfield switcheroo.

With the team scraping bottom and under new management in 1980, no Met's place was secure. Mazzilli lost his position in center field, shifting to first base as the Mets prepared an opening for Mookie Wilson. Maz moved to left field in 1981, and the Mets moved him to Texas in the spring of 1982 because the Mets outfield was full with the arrival of George Foster. Maz was crushed. So were Mets fans, who gave Frank Cashen such a hard time about the trade that the general manager took off his signature bow tie when riding the No. 7 train to make it tougher for fans to recognize him and say things like, "Why in the name of God did you ever trade Lee Mazzilli?" But in the summer of 1986, for God's sake, Cashen brought back Maz.

Cashen signed the 31-year-old Mazzilli to a minor league deal a little over a week after the miserable Pirates released him on July 23. He was the kind of player needed for a major league team's postseason roster, not to help win games for Tidewater—though his home run in his first at bat with the Tides was not lost on New York, thanks to the daily progress reports in the city papers. In a complete turnaround from 1982, George Foster—now in the last year of his megacontract—found his place precarious in Flushing.

Beyond a 16-game stretch in May and June when Foster hit .333 with eight homers and 20 RBI, he was inconsistent, to be kind. Mazzilli was just a better fit for the Mets in '86. He was six years younger, a career .262 switch-hitter, still able to run well, more versatile in the field, an experienced pinch hitter, and he cost the Mets a mere $20,000. The Pirates were responsible for his contract for the rest of '86 and the $650,000 owed him in '87. Most important, Mazzilli was neither tardy nor did he insult management's integrity.

"He showed up twice late at Wrigley in August," Marty Noble, Mets beat writer at *Newsday* for more than 20 years, recalled of Foster. "I—not innocently—went into Davey and said, 'What's the fine for showing up late?' And he said, 'You mean George?' I said, 'No, I just want to know what the fine is.'" Noble figured out the fine and wrote a brief story, which resulted in a couple of reporters from other papers going to Foster the next day and paying him more attention than an outfielder hitting .173 with three homers over the past two months should get. That's when Foster dropped a bombshell.

"I'm not saying it's a racial thing, but that seems to be the case in sports these days," Foster said. "When a ball club can, they replace a George Foster or a Mookie Wilson with a more popular player."

What? Nothing will get a person in trouble in New York quicker than saying that a situation is racial—especially when logic proves otherwise. The general manager was incensed, the manager responded, "Performance dictates," and the writers started working on George Foster's baseball obituary. Marty Noble, who'd missed Foster's initial quote since he'd already written about the fine for being late, noticed an unusual buzz in the Wrigley Field press box. Noble went to Foster after the game—an 0-for-3 performance in an 8–5 loss to the Cubs. Noble told Foster, "I don't know exactly what you said before the game, but if it's about race, you better get this straightened out because if you don't, you're going to be released by 9 o'clock tomorrow morning." Foster replied, "No, no, no. I got it all straight." Foster talked to several other reporters and the outfielder was in the Mets dugout the next day, striking out as a pinch hitter in a 4–2 loss to the Cubs, the fourth straight time over the past week the Mets had lost to the fifth-place Cubs. The *next* day Foster was released.

Foster had been a divisive figure during his five years as a Met. Anyone who comes to a perennial doormat making baseball's second-highest salary (five years for $10 million), as Foster did when he arrived in a trade-and-sign with the Reds before the 1982 season, will be under scrutiny. He hit .252 with 99 homers as a Met; his top production year in New York was 28 home runs and 90 RBI in 1983, after averaging 33 home runs, 112 RBI, and a .297 batting average over his last six years in Cincinnati. During his 1977 MVP season he hit 52 homers, the sole major leaguer between 1966 and 1989 to reach that plateau.

Religious and somewhat quiet, Foster still managed to baffle and alienate teammates. One called him "a joke," and he'd angered teammates in the past by saying things like "We outhit you," meaning the black players on the Mets had more hits in a game than the white players. Still, Foster did not think his comments in the Wrigley locker room were racial. He noted the obvious: Kevin Mitchell, who now received the bulk of the playing time in left, was—like Foster—black.

While the Mets were still in Chicago, WNBC-TV's Len Berman interviewed the released slugger on the waterfront near his home in Greenwich, Connecticut. "It's become like a nightmare," Foster said. "My whole career came down to one day. I was judged on what's misquoted in the newspaper." When asked to sum up his Mets career, he looked straight at the camera and said, "A dream that didn't come true." The dream he told Berman about, of playing five more years and reaching 500 home runs, was also unrealized. Foster was picked up by the White Sox, played 15 games, and even homered in his Chicago debut, but it was his 348th and final career home run. He was released the first week of September.

Davey Johnson, on another TV station, sympathized with his former left fielder and lamented the way things turned out. Yet as manager of baseball's dominant team, he stood firm: "For this to come up, it's a shock and saddening to me, but it's something I can't condone and I can't have."

With the Foster matter over, the Mets won the last three of the five-game series at Wrigley. After the Chicago finale, a 12–3 lambasting that put the Mets back up by 17 games, a graphic appeared in the *Daily News* featuring a cartoon Davey Johnson pulling a smiling rabbit out of a Mets hat. The graphic said "Magic Number," and the card held by the rabbit read "41." Six years after a Madison Avenue madman had made the promise, this was the magic the fans wanted back. The countdown to the clinching was on—on August 8, almost two months before the last game on the schedule.

The story had a happy ending for Lee Mazzilli. He did not just vault 30 games in the standings by moving from Pittsburgh to Shea; he was going home. "It's hard to put into words," Mazzilli said after donning a Mets uniform for the first time in five seasons. "It's probably the greatest feeling of my career to come back and play in New York." Maz played happy, hitting 50 points higher as a Met than he had as a Pirate, with more extra-base hits, despite almost 50 fewer plate appearances. And he got right to it, hitting a two-run homer in his first start as a Met since 1981, the ball sailing over the Pirates emblem into the right field seats at Veterans Stadium.

Mookie Wilson, already part of a crowded outfield mix of six, still applauds the decision to bring back the former Shea heartthrob turned role player. "Mazzilli helped because he was a switch-hitter who could play first or the outfield and that gave us more versatility," Wilson said. "The only knock on Mazzilli was that he couldn't throw in the outfield."

But he could start a rally. Down five runs to the Expos in the eighth on Saturday night in front of a big crowd at the Big O, Mazzilli drew a walk as a pinch hitter after Howard Johnson had led off with a pinch-hit double. The Mets scored seven times—the capper a three-run home run by Wilson against right-hander Tim

Burke. A potential double-play ball was thrown away by HoJo, who took over at shortstop after pinch-hitting for Rafael Santana. The error helped the Expos tie the game and the 33,000 on hand didn't care that their manager had already given up the race. The next inning they found out why Buck Rodgers had capitulated.

After Mazzilli led off with another walk, he scored the go-ahead run when Gary Carter lined a two-run single off Jeff Reardon, and New York had a 10–8 win. When the Mets took the rubber game behind Sid Fernandez's 13th win, ESPN's Bob Ley noted on *SportsCenter*, "Their lead in the NL East might be considered restraint of trade." The Mets were in front by 19 games on August 11, the largest lead by a National League team on that date in the 20th century. It was a half game better than the 1944 Cardinals, back when there was a war on and Americans were more interested in filling troopships than major league rosters.

Forty-two years later, the Cardinals were neither setting records nor fighting. The Cards had given up on '86 long before the Expos had, and now they had six—count 'em—six games to play in a long weekend at Shea. Two rainouts during the first home stand of the year left the Mets and Cardinals bookending doubleheaders onto what had been a four-game series. The concept of a day-night doubleheader was blissfully foreign to baseball at the time, so both twin bills were played one game right after the other: one admission, two games. Fans were not turned off by this plethora of baseball. Even with no promotions that weekend, and with the National League still registering attendance as fannies in seats (as opposed to the American League practice of counting tickets sold), the Mets set an attendance record for a four-date series with 185,445 and reached the two million mark at the earliest time in club history. What the fans saw was far from pretty.

It began on a happy note with Kevin Mitchell, team barber and jack-of-all-trades, emerging from a slump and a haze after being beaned in Montreal, which had required two stitches and resulted in blurred vision. He saw southpaw Tim Conroy's pitch well enough to launch a two-run home run into the packed Picnic Area to give the Mets the lead in the seventh inning of the opener. Mitchell came through his next time up with a game-ending single off fellow Rookie of the Year candidate Todd Worrell, moments after Rafael Santana had been thrown out at the plate. It was the Mets' eighth straight win against nemesis St. Louis. Starting with the nightcap, however, the Mets scored just five times over the next four games and held their breath as the bodies piled up.

Gary Carter was supposed to be "resting" by playing first base on Saturday, a day game after a night game. But while diving for Mike LaValliere's hard grounder, Carter injured his left thumb; he didn't help his finger when he dove for Ozzie Smith's bunt for the third out. He went to Roosevelt Hospital for X-rays. The diagnosis sounded grim: partial tear of the radial lateral ligament. Carter, who burned for another shot at the postseason, kept thinking that with his team coasting to a division title he might miss the play-offs if he sat for six weeks, as he had the first time he injured that thumb a decade earlier in Montreal after a collision with Pepe Mangual—again playing out of position, in right field. The 1986 National League RBI leader (with 87) was placed on the 15-day disabled list, but the prognosis was hopeful.

For Ed Hearn, though, it was the chance of a lifetime. Playing behind a Hall of Famer, catching had become a once-a-week job. This was his chance. "There was a quote, it may have even been in the headline, where I said, 'It's my team now,'" Hearn recalled. "That wasn't cocky . . . I was crapping in my drawers, too. That's how I handled it. That's how I needed to handle it for the best shot I had of getting in there and filling in and us continuing to do what we had done up to that point. Fortunately it worked out. I think there was another quote where I said something to the effect of 'I can't be Gary Carter. Nobody can be Gary Carter. I got to be Ed Hearn.'" With Hearn instead of Carter, the Mets went 11–4—though three of those wins belonged to Hearn's new understudy, John Gibbons.

The injuries kept coming. On Sunday, as the finish line for this never-ending series approached, Rick Aguilera, rounding into form after a first half that looked like he was from another planet compared to the four Mets aces, limped off the mound with an inflamed right knee in the opening game of the doubleheader. Then Lee Mazzilli, who had provided the one-up moment the previous day with a game-tying home run with two outs in the ninth (his first home run batting right-handed since 1982 and his first Shea Stadium homer since '81), tried to thrill the crowd with a sprawling catch in left field. The glove bent back as he hit the ground, losing the ball and bruising his wrist in the process. If anyone should have been in the hospital it was Randy Niemann, since his wife was in labor five weeks early. But he had been summoned from Tidewater to start the final game of the series. Niemann ended the Mets' longest losing streak of 1986—four games!—and won a starting assignment for the first time in seven years.

"My job was to come in if needed," Niemann said on his role as last man on the staff in 1986, "but also to pitch enough innings that the other guys would be fresh tomorrow." Niemann stuck around New York for the birth of his third child; his teammates were back on the road.

After 20 games in 17 days, including three doubleheaders, four extra-inning games, a suspended game, a disabled All-Star, a jettisoned slugger, and a prodigal son returned, the Mets' lead was the same as it had been when it all began: 16½ games. And even after this lackluster stretch—going 8–9 after sweeping the first series in the proverbial dog days of August—the magic number was an even 30.

The Mets landed in Los Angeles, bleary-eyed, in a different time zone, and playing two hours earlier than normal on the West Coast to accommodate ABC's *Monday Night Baseball*. The Mets were ready for prime time. It was their eighth appearance on ABC—the network's sporadic baseball broadcasts featured the Mets two-thirds of the time. It seemed fitting that the network blazers worn by announcers Al Michaels, Jim Palmer, and Tim McCarver were a Mets blue hue. The Mets finished 6–2 during the season on ABC, culminating with Bob Ojeda's 13th win in Los Angeles. It was the Dodgers looking like the ones who'd endured injury, humidity, and doubleheaders before being dragged across the country and forced to play on national TV.

Two botched hit-and-run plays resulted in Ed Hearn throwing out flummoxed Dodgers, and a bunt by Mike Scioscia turned into a double play when Enos Cabell got caught in a rundown and Howard Johnson nailed Scioscia straying too far from first. In ABC's constant close-ups of Tommy Lasorda, the usually animated Dodgers manager looked so despondent you wondered if someone had replaced the ricotta cheese in his cannoli with cottage cheese.

The Mets revived on the coast. Aguilera and Mazzilli bounced back and the team became its dominant self once more. The Mets swept the Dodgers, took two of three from the Giants, and won two humdrum games against last-place San Diego, though the 11–6 Tuesday night win was not without its drama. Rafael Santana hit his first home run in 14 months, his 370-foot drive so unnerving uptight Padres manager Larry Bowa that he removed top starter Dave Dravecky in the second inning with Mets pitcher Sid Fernandez coming up. A giveaway that series to Padres fans was a flip-book of pitching tips from Dravecky, plus Smokey Bear's tips on preventing fires. Reliever Gene Walter was no Smokey, as he got burned when El Sid doubled to spur a four-run rally in the fourth. The Mets piled up 21 hits, but Davey Johnson still found cause to be angry. Pitching with a 10–1 lead, Fernandez allowed a walk, two singles, and home runs off the not-so-potent bats of Jerry Royster and Bruce Bochy, a future World Series–winning manager but a career .239 hitter and member of the backup catcher's guild.

Johnson lit into Fernandez to the press after the game about his weight. He said Fernandez had put on 10–15 pounds since the start of the season. The magic number down to the teens and the point gotten, Johnson was interviewed by Marv Albert before NBC's *Game of the Week* a few days later—with footage of Fernandez exercising in the sun wearing a sweat-inducing rubber jacket. Johnson did not just declare the issue resolved but called himself out as well. "I know about excess weight, so I'm trying to work mine off and Sid has been doing it all year," Johnson said.

Thirty years later, that 8–1 August road trip is still the gold standard for the Mets on the West Coast. They may better that mark on some future California tour, but it could not have a better ending than this trip. It's still a staple on SNY's *Mets Classics*.

Doc and Darryl should have been the heroes. Gooden tossed 94 pitches over seven innings, allowing just one run on seven hits and a walk with seven strikeouts before slight tightness in his shoulder brought an end to his night. Strawberry drove in four runs his first two times up with a bases-loaded single and a home run with a man aboard—his 100th career long ball. The Mets shelled Ed Whitson, mercifully traded back to the Padres in '86 after he developed a complex about pitching at Yankee Stadium (and the fans developed one about watching him). The Mets held a 5–1 lead on San Diego heading into the bottom of the eighth with the reliable Roger McDowell on the mound. Appearing for the 61st time and already having thrown 106 innings, he had saves in each of his last six appearances, but this was not a save opportunity. The first three Padres reached base and all still could have turned out right as McDowell got Steve Garvey to hit the ball on the ground—until Wally Backman's error let two runs score. Davey Johnson brought in Orosco, who struck out Bruce Bochy. Pinch hitter Carmelo Martinez followed with an RBI single, and a looper off the bat of Garry Templeton tied the game. Orosco retired the next two lefties, but the damage was done.

Rich Gossage, in his third inning of relief, let the two-headed Back-stra get to him in the 11th. Lenny Dykstra and Wally Backman were an opponent's—and clubhouse attendant's—nightmare: diving, sliding, spitting . . . and hitting. With the Mets and Padres tied up, Lenny singled and took third on a base hit by Wally. Keith Hernandez hit a long fly to Kevin McReynolds in center field to score Dykstra and give the Mets a 6–5 lead.

Doug Sisk, no Mets fan's idea of a sure thing closing a game, could at least take comfort that he wasn't at Shea, so the cheering in San Diego was better than the booing he would have gotten at home after allowing a leadoff double to Garry Templeton. With one out, Tim Flannery's single to center seemed sure to score the speedy Templeton and tie the game. But Dykstra chucked it home and catcher John Gibbons caught the ball on a hop on his knees, not seeing Templeton at all until the collision an instant later. Bowled over but still holding the ball, Gibbons heard Sisk yelling in his ear to throw to third. Flannery, future third-base coach of three world championship teams for Bochy, should have known better. Going from hero to goat in a blink, Flannery was tagged out by third baseman Howard Johnson to complete the game-ending, 8–2–5 double play. As Dykstra high-fived everyone in sight and then embraced Gibbons, his buddy from the minor leagues, Tim McCarver shouted clear across the country on WOR, "Just your routine double play." Just your routine road trip. Just your routine 20-game lead. Just your routine season.

10

Everybody Wang Chung Tonight

September to October 5, 1986

After winning 21 of 32 games in August, it was going to be a September to remember for the Mets. In case anyone doubted it, A SEPTEMBER TO REMEMBER was displayed in large letters on the wall in front of the bullpens in left and right field. And if you somehow missed the signs pointing out how good the '86 Mets were, you could hear them sing about it.

Many fans—and quite a few players—enjoyed "The Curly Shuffle," the Jump 'N the Saddle novelty song with a compilation video of old Three Stooges bits that played each night on DiamondVision at Shea, often slowing Keith Hernandez's infield warmup throws as he chuckled at Larry, Mo, and Curly from first base. But the '86 Mets were too popular to not be capitalized on musically. Two team-related songs were released that summer. The first was produced on the season's first off day—and it had to be an off day in the control room to create the congealed mess that was "Get Metsmerized." The idea was cooked up by George Foster, and the worst part of that idea was to have nine Mets sing—rap, you could call it, though a more apt description would be a word rhyming with *rap*. *Bleacher Report* later deemed "Get Metsmerized" the worst song ever recorded by athletes, a list that includes musical forays by Shaquille O'Neal and Deion Sanders, who each made the list twice, and five spots ahead of—behind?—the Chicago Bears' "Super Bowl Shuffle," which "Get Metsmerized" was purported to rip off, er, emulate.

"Get Metsmerized" was unauthorized. The team ignored numerous requests for an endorsement, delaying production and paving the way for the team's entry into the bad baseball song pantheon. "Let's Go Mets" was better produced, had the full backing of the team, featured a professional video, and, most important, included *no* player singing. It was a stylistic dud, but it did have a memorably hokey opening line: "We've got the teamwork to make the dream work." And "Let's go Mets," a cheer as old as the team itself, was given an extra "go" in the chorus. After the video played on DiamondVision the first 100 times, many fans wished it would just go away. But there was about as much chance of that as there was of the Mets letting a team in the race.

The reviews of the day were not kind. After a segment on NBC-TV on the making of the video, featuring off-key singing by the players (mercifully not heard on the final version of the song or video), Marv Albert deadpanned, "Those fellows should not quit the day job." Michelle Marsh, anchor gabbing on set, was gentler on CBS-TV: "I love them so much I can't say anything bad. I hope they dance better than they sing." Well, Michelle, at least they could pitch.

While Keith Hernandez and Ron Darling were on the covers of *GQ* magazine three months apart in 1986, Roger McDowell and Lenny Dykstra landed in MTV's studio, pitching the new video in a sit-down with Martha Quinn in September. She said that for a while it looked like a Subway Series might be possible, "but in fact the Mets are the ones who came through." A Yankees fan—with cable—could only mumble, "Et tu, Martha?" The Albany-raised Quinn had gone overnight from struggling NYU grad to first-generation VJ (aka video jockey), and by 1986 she had been the channel's most popular VJ longer than Dykstra and

Lenny Dykstra looking fresh faced before he made the Mets for good in 1985 NATIONAL BASEBALL HALL OF FAME LIBRARY, COOPERSTOWN, NY

McDowell's combined tenures in the big leagues. She threw softballs at the Mets, though she got a nugget from McDowell about growing up a fan of Tug McGraw, the life-loving reliever who pitched the Mets to pennants in 1969 and 1973; Dykstra was a Rod Carew man. When she asked which band they'd like to be in, McDowell revealed himself a fan of Mike and the Mechanics as well as British pop-rock group Level 42, sharing an interest in soft '80s synthesized sound and a uniform number. Dykstra's tastes ran to Huey Lewis and the News. "I like the Rolling Stones, too," the married outfielder said to Quinn, pausing, then charging on, "but I like you better." Nailed it.

When asked to predict the playoffs, McDowell said the Mets would sweep Houston, while Dykstra presciently predicted the Mets in six. "You guys are America's heroes. Baseball is America's game," proclaimed America's Sweetheart, holding the bat Dykstra and McDowell presented her, doffing her brand-new Mets hat and shirt under her denim jacket. If you missed that call to load up the bandwagon, there'd be more.

"Now playing third base, Don Mattingly." The Yankees could not knock the Mets off the back pages, but they did steal the prize for most unusual short-term third baseman in 1986. The Mets had used Gary Carter in an extra-inning emergency in Cincinnati after multiple ejections forced the Mets to put an All-Star Gold Glove catcher at third base. The Yankees trumped them by putting an All-Star Gold Glove first baseman at the hot corner due to an injury to Mike Pagliarulo. The transition to third base would seem less difficult for an accomplished first baseman than for a catcher, but there was a big difference: Mattingly was left-handed.

Lefties don't play third base. Unless they backhand the ball, they always throw off the wrong foot or take extra steps before throwing toward first. Lou Piniella didn't care. The Yankees rookie manager was down a third baseman, and since it was the last weekend of August, he had to wait until September 1 for the rosters to expand so fresh bodies could be recalled from the minor leagues. Mattingly was flawless in his third-base debut, handling all six chances and starting a double play, his extra moves and spins like watching Gene Kelly dance across the Kingdome Astroturf. The Yankees rallied from a 12–5 deficit to waltz past the Mariners. He made just one error in three games at third.

Mattingly was not the first left-handed thrower to man third, though until the mid-1980s, no lefty had played there since 1926. Mike "Spanky" Squires, southpaw supersub who also caught (another against-the-book use of left-handers), played third base 13 times for Tony La Russa's White Sox in 1984. Future manager Terry Francona played third base for Montreal in the who-cares 1985 season finale at Shea after the Mets had been eliminated. But as September appeared on the 1986 calendar, the Yankees were desperate to stay alive—and stay relevant—against their two greatest tormentors: the Red Sox and the Mets. The Red Sox and Yankees had been rivals since before they were known as the Red Sox and Yankees, dating back to 1904 when the Boston Americans slipped past the New York Highlanders in a down-to-the-wire pennant race won by Beantown. The Yankees' rivalry with the Mets was more recent, less rational, and ego infused. And by the final month of the '86 season, the Red Sox and Mets consumed the Yankees' volatile owner.

Like two allies encircling a common foe, the Mets and Red Sox even met at Fenway Park in September for an exhibition. "A meeting between two teams that have a shared heritage of frustration and romance over the past quarter century, and a surprising number of mutual fans," Joe Klein wrote in a Mets profile that month in *New York* magazine. And George Steinbrenner caused the Mets-Sox summit.

The Mets and Yankees had played an annual Mayor's Trophy Game to support New York sandlot baseball almost every year from 1963 to 1983.* Started long before interleague play, the Mayor's Trophy was a marquee event. Original Mets manager Casey Stengel, dismissed by the Yankees in 1960, used his top pitchers to both start and relieve in the early contests, but by the late 1970s the most interesting moment concerned whether Yankees Gold Glover Graig Nettles threw a ball away on purpose to get the 1978 game over with. (He had to meet with commissioner Bowie Kuhn to deny erring on purpose; the Yankees won the '78 game, anyway, in 13 interminable innings.) If the games were supposed to be fun, it was lost on Steinbrenner. He put far too much meaning into meaningless exhibitions between the New York teams, throwing tantrums for every loss to the Mets in spring games in Florida, and obsessing over the Mets' popularity to the point where he fudged Yankees attendance figures upward despite it costing him money on the road teams' share.

The Yankees didn't like being second to anyone, but public opinion stated otherwise. "For six years the Mets had a better record than the Yankees," former *Newsday* columnist Steve Jacobson said of the period from 1984 to 1990.† "In that time the Mets outdrew the Yankees every year. That '86 team was in the middle of it."

Len Berman, whose job as sports anchor at NBC-TV in the 1980s was to figure out airtime for New York's plethora of teams, left no doubt who was number one. "I can't emphasize enough how the Mets owned the town," he said. "I know nobody is going to believe it, but the Mets were bigger than the Yankees, and they were bigger than the Giants winning the Super Bowl." It may indeed seem hard to believe three decades and many Mets disappointments later, but in the mid-1980s it was simply the truth—the Mets were *the* team in New York, and it ate at Steinbrenner. His loathing was no secret. Writing in *Sports Illustrated*, Peter

* The Yankees held a 10–8–1 advantage in Mayor's Trophy Games.

† The Mets had a better record than the Yankees in 1991 as well.

Gammons stated plainly that the Yankees owner "had effectively ended the Mayor's Trophy game in New York."

For his part, Mets general manager Frank Cashen didn't like Steinbrenner, either. "A supreme egoist, he loved only his own team," Cashen wrote of Steinbrenner in a posthumously published memoir, *Winning in Both Leagues*. "Most of all, he loved throwing his baseball wealth in your face." In the mid-1980s, with the Mets able to throw wealth and success back in George's face, the Mayor's Trophy was a casualty of the crosstown feud.

So the Mets made arrangements to play a 1986 exhibition against the Red Sox at Fenway Park, with the proceeds benefiting sandlot baseball in New York and the Jimmy Fund in Boston. The single date that worked for both clubs was in September. The Mets won the game but lost the bus, which broke down in the Sumner Tunnel in traffic, and several Mets hitched rides to Fenway. The angle of the game as a potential World Series preview was played up—Channel 9 even ran a computer World Series simulation in which the Mets beat Boston in seven games—but in reality the main benefit was familiarizing National Leaguers with the Green Monster. Just in case. "You field some balls off the wall, feel the proximity of the crowd," Davey Johnson said after the exhibition. "The next time you come in you're not looking around in wonderment."

It was a rare loss for the Red Sox, who continued to stretch their lead over the Yankees. The Yankees would somehow win 90 games despite injuries, age, a rookie manager, and a meddlesome owner. Steinbrenner's adoration of pricey veteran ballplayers—more than half the men who played for the '86 Yankees were 30 or older—had almost kept Don Mattingly on the bench in 1984, but he played and won the batting title. He was gunning for another batting crown two years later.* Steinbrenner played up Yankees tradition as much as he could, naming Willie Randolph and Ron Guidry cocaptains

* Mattingly hit a career-high .352 in 1986 but finished second to Boston's Wade Boggs at .357.

that year and retiring Billy Martin's number 1, which was wise to keep reserved because the Yankees would hire him to manage a fifth time before the decade was out. Yet none of it could change the inevitability of the AL East race in 1986. On September 12, when the Yankees concluded the four-city trip that began in Seattle, the Red Sox were waiting for them in the Bronx with a 10-game lead. That same night the Mets were down the turnpike in Philadelphia, needing one win to clinch the NL East title.

It was a noteworthy sports weekend. Tom Kelly, who would win world championships in Minnesota in 1987 and 1991, was hired to replace Ray Miller as manager of the Twins. In Kelly's second game as skipper, future Hall of Famer Bert Blyleven set an American League record by allowing his 44th home run on the year, as Bobby Valentine's Texas Rangers went deep five times against him in a 14–1 rout. (Four starts later Blyleven would establish a still-standing major league mark with 50 homers allowed.) Bo Jackson, the number one pick in the nation in football who spurned Tampa Bay after the Buccaneers owner flew him in his private jet (making him ineligible to play baseball at Auburn due to NCAA rules), opted for professional baseball and hit his first major league home run—a 475-foot shot for the Royals that weekend against the Mariners. The Buccaneers, meanwhile, were smoked at home by the Vikings en route to a 2–14 season. The New York Giants, after losing their opener in Dallas on Monday night, beat San Diego at Giants Stadium in a 14–2 season that ended with their first Super Bowl. The Jets, now sharing a home with the Giants instead of the Mets, lost to New England in a rare Thursday night game, but Joe Walton's club would win its next nine, lose its last five, and make the playoffs, giving six of New York's nine teams a postseason appearance in 1986.

But as the second weekend of September commenced, the one sports story everyone expected was the Mets finally clinching the

NL East. Mets fans were not shy about throwing their weight around in the City of Brotherly Love. Five of the six biggest crowds at Veterans Stadium in 1986 were Mets games, and two years earlier a Mets contingent recorded the first documented TKO of the Philly Phanatic during an upper-deck fracas at the Vet. This time the Mets were knocked off their pegs.

The Phillies unceremoniously swept the Mets—the only time it happened on the road all year. So the champagne was packed up and taken to St. Louis. OK, so this was more fitting, anyway: clinching the NL East title in the same place where it was essentially lost a year earlier. And almost a year after a classic scoreless duel between Ron Darling and John Tudor, the pair did it again, though this time Tudor's shoulder stiffened and lefty Ricky Horton served as stand-in, keeping the Mets scoreless for seven innings of relief. The only run in 13 innings scored on a close pitch from Roger McDowell to Curt Ford that was deemed ball four with the bases loaded.

The next night the Mets broke their longest scoreless streak since the Joe Torre regime (25 innings). Mookie Wilson, who played for that 1980 team, scored the run that broke the schneid. You also had to go back to 1980 for Wally Backman's last triple batting right-handed, and he scored an insurance run in the 4–2 victory that clinched at least a tie. There were a few shaving cream pies tossed in the visiting clubhouse, but it was just preliminaries. Keith Hernandez warned, "Tomorrow night it won't be shaving cream, it will be champagne."

Long before they met in the playoffs for the first time in 2015, Mets/Cubs was a curious rivalry. When the Mets came into being in 1962, the Cubs were enduring their College of Coaches era, an ill-advised concept by Cubs owner P. K. Wrigley of rotating coaches to run the team rather than a single manager. In almost nine decades as a professional franchise, the Cubs never lost 100 games until 1962. Yet thanks to the 120-loss Mets of that year the Cubs still finished 16½ games out of last place.

Linked by ineptitude, the National League's New York and Chicago franchises slowly rose. After becoming the first team to ever finish behind the Mets, in 1966, the Cubs had their highest win total (87) since their last pennant in 1945. Though the Cubs were a distant third to the Cardinals the next two years, it was coming together for Chicago in 1969.

The Cubs rode a stirring Opening Day comeback to an 11–1 start and did not let up as the weather warmed up. By mid-June 1969 the Cubs were 22 games over .500 and owned a nine-game lead on the Mets, who, for the first time in their seven-year existence, had a winning record. Two months later Chicago's lead was still nine games, with the Cardinals in second place. The third-place Mets were 10 games out. Then came something Amazin'—capital *A*, no *g*.

The Mets dominated down the stretch with their novel five-man rotation of Tom Seaver, Jerry Koosman, Gary Gentry, Don Cardwell, and Jim McAndrew—Cardwell the lone starter older than 26. The starting five was so solid that future strikeout king Nolan Ryan was a swingman, starting just 10 games and relieving in 15 others for the 1969 Mets. A 39–11 finish put them eight games ahead of the grief-stricken Cubs, who collapsed due to, take your pick:

A. Manager Leo Durocher never resting his veterans;

B. All day games in the only major league park without lights;

C. The mediocre Cubs bullpen;

D. All of the above.

It was D. As in disaster. Chicago heartbreak became even more acute when New York swept Atlanta in the first National League Championship Series and then knocked off heavy favorite Baltimore in the World Series. The '69 Mets were declared a baseball miracle. For the Cubs it was more of a curse. Many felt Chicago's moment had been stolen by undeserving upstarts. Cubs fans never forgot. Or forgave.

The Cubs did the rallying in August 1984 to knock off the resurgent Mets for the National League East title, but the Cubs reverted to mediocrity following their disastrous loss to the San Diego Padres in the '84 NLCS. By mid-September 1986 the Cubs were on their third manager of the year and had already clinched a losing record. So despite the '86 Mets' recent outbreak of clinch anxiety, the silver lining was a chance to seal the deal at home . . . against the Cubs.

The fifth-place Cubs were 22 games under .500 and 33 games behind the Mets. Their pitching staff had already allowed 717 runs, 73 more than any other National League team. The Cubs had been counting down the days even more than the impatient Mets. The difference was that the Cubs just wanted to call it a year. The Mets were calling this their year.

The Mets had clinched the 1969 division title, pennant, and World Series at Shea Stadium—and fans tore the place apart each time. Yet '69 seemed like a love-in compared to the riotous atmosphere when the Mets upset the Reds to win the 1973 NLCS. The wives and families of the Reds players and officials had to be escorted from the field before the deciding game was over due to pushing, shoving, and taunts from Mets fans. When Tug McGraw recorded the last out minutes later, fans poured out of the stands, creating dust clouds like stampeding cattle and acting as such. Two riotous Yankees clinchings in the Bronx later in the decade provided further evidence that New Yorkers liked their pillaging almost as much as a one-sided pennant race. Yet on September 17, 1986, Mets general manager Frank Cashen and the team's security contingent were wholly unprepared for the fan reaction to the team's first clinching in 13 years.

With the Mets leading in the ninth, thanks to three hits and two RBI by call-up Dave Magadan (starting at first base in place of an ill Keith Hernandez), the fans crowded onto the Field Level by the thousands. The anticipation and intensity of the horde grew as the Mets were set down in the eighth inning. Dwight Gooden, who'd help reinvigorate Shea crowds with his rapid ascendancy to stardom as New York's favorite teen in 1984, had his audience's confidence. Even as he allowed the second career home run by Rafael Palmeiro to cut the lead in half, the fans and the manager maintained full faith that Doc would get the job done. Allowing the tying runs to reach base in the ninth heightened the crowd's increasing fervor. When Gooden caught Jerry Mumphrey looking for the second out, the crowd chanted "We're number one!" Policemen atop the dugout prepared for an onslaught.

Chico Walker looked at a ball and then fouled off two pitches. As had been the case since the summer of '84 in anticipation of a Gooden strikeout, the crowd grew even louder as the clinching reached one-strike-away status. As the riotous eagerness intensified, fans eyed the same entry routes onto the field as their predecessors had taken in 1969 and 1973. Tonight was their turn. It felt like a century since '73.

At 10:15 p.m., with five days of summer still on the calendar, the Mets officially wrapped up the title that had been their destiny since the spring of '86, an attack plan they had been working on since winter. Like their manager had told them to do in spring training, the Mets dominated.

Walker hit a grounder toward second base. Wally Backman had challenged fans at Shea to be in peak form for this game. "I remember telling the media that the fans should celebrate with the players on the field," Backman reminisced decades later. "When the ground ball was hit to me, there were like 10,000 people jumping over that rail. If I'd have missed that ground ball, they'd have just kept running and killed me." Backman's throw to first base came within a few feet of the fans running in fair territory.

Sick or not, Keith Hernandez insisted he be on the field for the final innings. He caught Backman's throw and ran toward the mound, though the mob was gaining on him. "One of the fans tried to pull [the glove] off my hands when we were on the mound—I had to squeeze my hand and he wasn't able to," Hernandez recalled. Other players weren't so lucky. But they had more hats, gloves, and equipment in the locker room. Their main priority was reaching sanctuary in one piece.

The capacity crowd enveloped the field, the dugouts, the bullpens—every inch of space expressly forbidden in the accepted fan-team relationship. All was for the taking. Fans didn't just tear up the grass, they made off with the stacks of fresh sod the Mets had stored in the bullpens in the event repairs to the field were needed. The bullpen car was hijacked and discarded on the field, the two-seater tested by countless derrieres.

Yankee Stadium was far more sedate at that moment. The Yankees, losing to the sixth-place Orioles, displayed the news on their scoreboard: "Yankees congratulate the New York Mets 1986 National League East Champs." There was a mix of cheers and boos, as well as plenty of envy from the 18,000 in the Bronx on the only night of the year both teams were home. At Fenway Park, Don Baylor, dispatched by the Yanks to Boston just before the start of the season, hit his 30th home run in a win over Milwaukee. The Yankees fell 10 games back with 16 to play.

Shea, meanwhile, dealt with the cost of winning. In the locker room champagne covered everything and everyone. Shaving cream doused anyone conducting an on-camera interview. Even Hall of Famers weren't immune. During a special *Kiner's Korner* from the victorious locker room, 63-year-old icon Ralph Kiner was doused with shaving cream and champagne. Hernandez, his Gold Glove mitt safe from pillagers, did not watch his back and had so much ice dumped down it on camera that he almost spilled his Michelob. Almost. "It's such a great feeling, Ralph," Hernandez said, his voice hoarse from the combination of the flu and all the interviews. "The club had been down for so long when I was in St. Louis, and to have a turnaround like this within three years is just so great. And winning at home—I never thought it was going to feel better than winning the first time in St. Louis, but it feels so much better."

Outside, the 300 police officers *sans* riot gear, horses, or dogs—a product of the Mets front office's belief that fans would behave—regrouped and formed a cordon to keep the fans out of the dugouts. They fanned out, pushing the fans little by little off the field and through the gates at the 410 mark in center field—the inverse of Banner Day. Yet for all the mayhem, the 5,000 or so people on the field caused about a dollar's worth of damage per head—or half the cost of an overpriced Bud in a Harry M. Stevens cup at Shea. To Frank Cashen, however, the situation was an affront to decency, tradition, and the game itself. Cashen had been at Shea as Baltimore's GM when the fans eviscerated the field after defeating the Orioles in 1969. But that had been in another lifetime. Now he took it personally.

"Every son of a gun that picked up a piece of sod and threw it up in the air may have deprived me and my team a chance to win a playoff or a World Series," the GM said the day after the clinching. "If you're asking, 'Does this put a pall over winning this thing?' the answer to that is, 'Yeah, at the present time.'"

Groundskeeper Pete Flynn and his crew were responsible for getting the field back into playing shape. The clincher was the opener of a seven-game home stand. The replacement for the extra sod cannibalized by the fans did not arrive until 7 a.m.; the grounds crew had already put in four hours of repairs by then. *Daily News* cartoonist Bill Gallo recreated the crew's yeoman repair work in a drawing, dubbing Flynn "MVG": Most Valuable Groundskeeper. Asked about his toughest job decades later, Flynn considered for a moment all the repairs to the Shea surface he'd handled following each of its sackings, the hundreds of doubleheaders, the in-season concerts, the double duty as the Yankees and Mets shared Shea in 1974, and quadruple duty when the Yankees, Mets, Jets, and Giants called it home in '75. Through his Irish brogue, he pronounced his verdict: 1986. "There was a day game the next day."

Aye. The day after a capacity crowd came, saw, and conquered Shea Stadium, an intimate gathering of 13,726, the second-smallest crowd of the year to that point, came to see Mets farmhand Rick Anderson face 20-year-old Greg Maddux. Making the third major league start of what would be a Hall of Fame career, Maddux sported a thin mustache in a vain attempt to make himself, the youngest player in the National League, seem older. He faced none of the bleary-eyed starters from the previous night's game (except for Magadan), but the cobbled-together lineup—and turf—did the Cubs no favors. Palmeiro and Maddux, who would collect 21 Gold Gloves between them, each committed an error. And late-season Mets call-up Kevin Elster was credited with a hit when the new grass did not produce the hop Cubs third baseman Keith Moreland expected on a routine grounder.

"I can give that hit to the fans of New York," the 22-year-old Elster cooed after the game. "Tell them, 'Thanks very much.' They can tear up the field anytime."

The Mets won the game. Of course.

The Mets already had as many wins, 96, as any other major league team would have in 1986. And they just kept rolling during their victory lap through the NL East, obliterating opponents and records until the final pitch.

The Phillies won three from the Mets that weekend against a mixture of Mets starters, backups, and call-ups. The Phillies finished the year 10–8 against the Mets, the lone team with a winning record against them, and Philadelphia's Mike Schmidt would win his third NL MVP in 1986, with Carter and Hernandez finishing third and fourth, respectively. (Knight, McDowell, Dykstra, and Ojeda also received votes.) It was a last hurrah for Schmidt, who turned 37 the last week of the season. He led the NL in slugging percentage for the last time and also won his final Silver Slugger, Gold Glove, home run, and RBI crowns.*

The everyday Mets lineup was on display for the Cardinals, as was the just-installed dugout sign—with letters almost big enough to be seen by passing planes—declaring the Mets "1986 N.L. Eastern Division Champions." Worthy of a T-shirt.

New York hit five home runs in the short (but sweet) two-game series, giving them as many homers against St. Louis (19) as any team. Darryl Strawberry, hearing cheers after a prolonged Shea slump, homered in both wins. Wally Backman hit his only home run of the year—on his 27th birthday. Keith Hernandez, who didn't play an inning against the Phillies because of the flu, started both games against St. Louis and added a home run in a 9–1 rout, sneaking a peak into the Cardinals dugout as he rounded the bases. The Mets went 12–6 against the Cards, their first winning record against St. Louis since their last division title in 1973.

The Mets also went 12–6 against the Cubs, reaching 100 wins at the same address where they'd hit that mark in 1969. Kevin Mitchell's titanic blast across Waveland Avenue was the 140th Mets home run, breaking the 1962 mark set by a team that was as bad as the '86 club was good. Brooklyn-born Ed Lynch, who debuted as a Met the week before Mookie Wilson and Wally Backman in 1980, had been traded to the Cubs in June and endured the celebration at Shea from the visiting dugout. He was the loser in Mets victory number 100.

The Expos threw in the towel early, but they played the Mets tough and had a chance to win the season series when rookie Bob

* On-Base Plus Slugging was just starting to be mentioned in 1986, thanks to John Thorn and Pete Palmer's book, *The Hidden Game of Baseball*. Mike Schmidt led the majors in both OPS (.937) and adjusted OPS (154). A later system to rank players, Wins Above Replacement (WAR), would retroactively place Schmidt fifth in 1986, behind Mike Scott, Rick Rhoden, Tony Gwynn, and Fernando Valenzuela. Keith Hernandez (eighth) was the only Met in the top 10. Hernandez's ninth consecutive Gold Glove was the lone award received by a Met for the 1986 regular season.

Sebra became just the third pitcher to shut out the Mets in 1986. A great effort by Ron Darling was wasted by what the Mets even admitted was a lack of effort in front of 6,000 at Olympic Stadium. Someone was even asleep in the mail room, too, as 64,000 World Series tickets were sent to the Pacific Conservancy of Performing Arts in California instead of the tickets the school had ordered for a play. The printer, the school, and the Mets got it together. And the ball club won out the schedule.

An extra-inning victory in Montreal was followed by Gooden winning the rubber match against childhood friend Floyd Youmans. A rainout at Shea versus Pittsburgh set up a doubleheader—with Rusty Staub and Bud Harrelson the first players inducted into the Mets Hall of Fame between games. The Mets swept the Pirates, and almost swept the entire season from the Bucs. An unmatched franchise mark of 17–1 was marred only by the game in which the Mets accused Pirate Rick Rhoden of scuffing the ball—they lost the game but won the ensuing brawl, remember. First-year manager Jim Leyland went 61–81 against the rest of the league, a respectable showing given the franchise hitting rock bottom in '85, plus the drug trials. But the Mets' repeated thumping left the Pirates the worst team in baseball with 98 losses and helped push the Mets into a tie with the 1975 Reds for the most wins in the National League in the expansion era (since 1962). The last team to surpass 108 wins in the NL was the 1909 Pirates, with 110. The Mets' 21½-game margin of victory was the league's largest since the 1902 Pirates.

"When you win 108 games," stated Davey Johnson, an integral part of three teams to win at least that many games, "I think it should be pretty clear that you don't have a whole lot of weaknesses; 108 is a pretty good number." But in the postseason, all it takes is a couple of days—or a couple of innings—where things don't go your way. Or an opponent on an epic roll, oblivious to any history made in the regular season.

There was immense pressure for the 1986 Mets not to blow it. Three teams that won more games than the '86 Mets failed to win the World Series: the 1906 Cubs (116 wins), the 1954 Indians (111), and a 109-win Orioles team, with Davey Johnson at second base, that was laid low by the Miracle Mets in the 1969 World Series.

In a race that had been over before it ever started, the real work was about to begin. The last day on the '86 schedule, though, was a celebration. The Mets scored nine times to make up to Ron Darling for sleepwalking through his previous start in Montreal. Gary Carter mashed a three-run homer in the first inning to match Rusty Staub's club RBI record of 105, and later Darryl Strawberry unloaded a grand slam for his 27th home run to nudge over 90 RBI—both Carter and Strawberry's feats had added significance given the games both missed due to injury. As a record crowd watched—the 2.767 million in attendance* was the most to that point by a New York team, was second in '86 to the Dodgers, and was a smidge better than the franchise mark the Mets had set the previous year—the last milestone came on the final pitch of the '86 regular season. A Sid Fernandez roundhouse curve caught Pirates rookie Bobby Bonilla looking, notching his first career save and his 200th strikeout. The Mets poured out of the dugout to mob El Sid. Carter and Hernandez were already in street clothes.

A special video montage of '86 highlights played on DiamondVision with Willie Nelson singing "Wind Beneath My Wings." The images of the season put to music—it doesn't sound schmaltzy when Willie sings it—can leave a lump in a Mets fan's throat, especially those who experienced the lean years before 1984. Perhaps a more apt (and upbeat) accompanying song for the partiers, curtain callers, and night crawlers on the team and in the stands would have been "Everybody Have Fun Tonight," released that September by Wang Chung, a band at the height of its tenuous fame. "Everybody Have Fun Tonight," with its memorable

* The Mets sold more than three million tickets in 1986, but at that time the National League did not count no-shows as part of attendance. In 1993 the NL adopted the AL policy of counting tickets sold to determine attendance.

and eponymous command, "Everybody Wang Chung tonight," would get enough airplay to reach number two on the *Billboard* charts before 1986 was over—stopped at the top by the female band The Bangles and "Walk Like an Egyptian." Then again, after Wang Chunging the National League, maybe a song that only got to number two wouldn't have sufficed. The '86 Mets had their sights trained on number one. Or bust.

Part II.
Destiny

11

Scuff Enough

October 8–15, 1986

Cheating was in. It was in the movies. Rodney Dangerfield became the world's oldest freshman in *Back to School*—Rodney was 65 in '86—cheating every which way he could, even hiring Kurt Vonnegut to write his Kurt Vonnegut term paper (and getting an F). Ferris Bueller took the day off, with Matthew Broderick breaking more truancy rules than the Little Rascals. And what year would be complete without a Woody Allen story about Mia Farrow being cheated on? This immorality was by Michael Caine with Barbara Hershey in *Hannah and Her Sisters*. Their cheating hearts remained Woody's biggest box office hit until 2011.

Ivan Boesky told the graduating class at the University of California–Berkeley in May of '86, "Greed is all right, by the way. I think greed is healthy. You can be greedy and feel good about yourself." Sounds a lot like the "greed is good" speech by Michael Douglas as avarice incarnate in Oliver Stone's *Wall Street* the following year. By the time the film came out, Boesky had been prosecuted by U.S. Attorney Rudy Giuliani and sentenced to three years for insider trading, and he was on the hook for $100 million in a civil settlement. Boesky's trial would lead to bringing down "Junk Bond King" Michael Milken. But that paled next to the courtroom proceedings of New York crime boss John Gotti, who twice went on trial in 1986 and got off both times. Scot-free.

Mike Scott seemed to have mountains of evidence against him, but nothing happened. (John Gotti would not be as lucky in the years to come.)* Though accused of cheating by many—including San Francisco manager Roger Craig, who'd taught the Houston pitcher the career-altering split-finger fastball two years earlier—Scott was never caught scuffing a baseball. He was cast as a villain in the New York press: a former Met now succeeding with the enemy while utilizing unfair practices. "The Scott scuff-ball" perplexed National League foes all season. He faced the Mets once during the 1986 regular season, receiving a no decision, and was 2–5 in 10 starts with a 4.02 ERA against the Mets since his 1982 trade to Houston for Danny Heep. After he learned the split in 1984 as a last chance to salvage a middling career, his fortunes had reversed. And 20 of the 25 career earned runs allowed to the Mets were B.S. (Before Split).

Mike Scott as villain only worked from the New York view of the world, however. Seen from the eyes of Texas, or the rest of the country, Scott was the hero, the guy who'd turned his career around and threw a no-hitter to clinch a division title against the Giants. The peaceable 'Stros fans hadn't seen fit to tear up the field, though they would have needed X-Acto knives to get up the turf. No, the villain in their eyes was anyone marching around with "NY" on their hat. New York in the mid-1980s conjured up images of streetwalkers, junkies, vagrants, midday muggings—institutionalized urban decay that needed a Charles Bronson vigilante cleansing like in the *Death Wish* movies. In a case of life imitating art (or at least Charles Bronson), Bernhard Goetz shot four would-be assailants on the subway and was awaiting trial in the fall of 1986. Though the city had come a long way in the past decade, to many it still represented a writhing mess of lawlessness, un-Americanized

* John Gotti was convicted in 1992 by a sequestered jury—jury tampering having played a major part in his good fortune in past trials. He died in prison 10 years later at age 61.

Mike Scott, former Met, resident villain NATIONAL BASEBALL HALL OF FAME LIBRARY, COOPERSTOWN, NY

immigrants, and fast-talking swindlers. From that view, anyone with the chance to beat New York was no villain.

The Mets had 100 ways to get under the skins of opponents and fans from other cities, even if it was just as the starting point of annoying rituals that would soon take hold in parks all over the country: the wave, the curtain call, and the rally cap—a quirky dugout ritual to stave off defeat turned synchronized performance art by a team that lost only 54 times all year (three NL East teams had 50 losses by the All-Star break). And the Mets were just Yankees as far as most Texans were concerned. Damned Yankees at that. Never mind that the Astros had just three native Texans on their 1986 playoff roster. Or that 10 players on the Mets' postseason roster hailed from California, along with 3 from Florida and the rest scattered all over the country from Georgia to Hawaii, plus Dominican shortstop Rafael Santana. There were as many New York natives on the Mets roster (Brooklyn-born Lee Mazzilli) as there were Texans (El Paso's own Danny Heep). And that doesn't include manager Davey Johnson, who had attended high school and two colleges in the Lone Star State. It was not so much *where* the individuals came from as much as it was *what* the Mets represented that was abhorrent to the opposition. And the arrest of four Mets at Cooter's in July just made them that much easier to hate.

Houston was the one city where things did not go the Mets' way in 1986. The Mets set still-standing franchise marks for best record on the road (53–28), during the day (42–19), and at night (66–35); they dominated the NL East at a record pace (59–31) and notched a mark against the West (49–23) that may stand forever, as will the 26–10 record against the West Coast teams.* Only Philadelphia, where the Mets went 2–7, was a worse stop for the '86 Mets than Houston (2–4). And then the network screwed them, along with the NFL.

---

* The 1986 Mets set a franchise mark for best record at home at 55–26, but they exceeded it two years later. The 2000 Mets also matched the 1986 Mets win for win at Shea.

At the time, the host city in the League Championship Series was determined by annual rotation, not by best record. And 1986 was the NL East's turn to host the first two and last two games of a best-of-seven NLCS. Unfortunately for the Mets, the Astrodome was already booked. Since many prognosticators picked the Astros to finish fifth or lower, plus rumors swirled of the team moving to Washington, why wouldn't a football game be scheduled for the Astrodome on the same Sunday as Game 5 of the baseball playoffs? Maybe the NFL could have finagled its schedule, or pushed the Bears-Oilers to a second Monday night game (as later became the NFL's emergency practice), but Major League Baseball—with maybe a little network prodding from ABC—swapped New York's home games for Houston's, handing the Astros home-field advantage.*

"How we didn't have Games 1 and 2 and 6 and 7 at our ballpark is beyond me," Keith Hernandez wondered. When reminded that it had been done to appease leagues and television rights, he understood. "Ah, so television," he cooed. "It just made it better for us that we were able to overcome the Astros in their backyard."

"The Eighth Blunder of the World" was what *Washington Post* writer Tom Boswell deemed the Astrodome. "Just as belligerent Yankee Stadium can daunt foes, so the Astrodome can depress visitors." The lights were dim, the dimensions cavernous, and even in a league where half the teams played on artificial surfaces, the Astroturf the Astros played on was deemed to be the worst. And the Mets had never played well at the Astrodome. The Mets lost their first seven games indoors the year the place opened in 1965, but Mets announcer Lindsey Nelson emerged intact after broadcasting a game from a gondola suspended from the roof, gaudy jacket and all. In the building's first 22 seasons of operation, the

* Two years later the Mets again failed to get home-field advantage because the rotation was changed in 1986. In '88 the Mets would not be as fortunate in October.

Mets had winning records at the Astrodome in just four seasons—even the 1969 world champions went 0–6 there.* One other thing the place had going for it as the Astros took the field on October 8, 1986: It was loud.

From the first pitch the dome was in an uproar. In case anyone might have been lulled to sleep by batter after batter being sent down, the Mets' constant arguing with God kept the fans on their toes.

It started in the first, when Gary Carter turned around to umpire Doug Harvey to ask him to look at the ball that dove out of the strike zone just as he swung. Harvey was known as "God" because, as he stated on the first page of his book (written with Peter Golenbock), *They Called Me God: The Best Umpire Who Ever Lived*, in 4,673 games umpired over 30 years, "I don't believe I ever made a wrong call." The Mets severely tested his theory in Game 1 of the NLCS.

Harvey threw the ball back to Scott and Carter struck out on the next pitch to end the first inning. Keith Hernandez got into a heated exchange with Harvey after he struck out in the sixth. And the game ended with Ray Knight barking at Harvey as the tying run died at second base. There were so many Mets yelling at the umpire, it was easy to forget that Dwight Gooden pitched a superb game of his own, allowing the game's sole run on a second-inning home run by Glenn Davis. As soon as Scott threw his 125th pitch and Knight became Scott's NLCS-record tying 14th strikeout victim, manager Davey Johnson held a rare team meeting. When the media came in a few minutes later, the players were like kids apologizing for being rude to a neighbor, even though they felt deep down they'd done nothing wrong. Playing off the arrest of the four Mets in July, a T-shirt designed by Houston police officers was in full force for the playoffs. It said, "Houston

* The Mets would have a winning season just once more at the Astrodome, the year the place closed in 1999. In all the Mets' record in the Astrodome was 85–133, including the postseason.

Police 4, New York Mets 0." You didn't even have to be a cop to come up with a shirt that read, "Mike Scott 1, New York Mets 0."

Bob Ojeda took care of matters the next night. The Mets got him a couple of early runs on a Gary Carter double and a Darryl Strawberry sacrifice fly, but Ojeda's busted sacrifice almost killed a rally in the fifth. Yet Bobby O. found the speed he thought he'd left behind in a part-time job in Visalia, California. Ojeda's fondness for vanilla milkshakes sprinkled with popcorn at the ice cream shop where he worked in high school had added 30 pounds and cost him his speed. Realizing his bunt went right to Astros third baseman Phil Garner, Ojeda turned on the afterburners not seen since Redwood High to beat second baseman Bill Doran's relay throw and avoid a double play. After Astros pitcher Nolan Ryan came up and in on Lenny Dykstra, "Nails"—as in "tough as"—singled the other way to move the jacketed Ojeda to second. When Wally Backman singled up the middle, Ojeda's Redwood Rangers speed was again on display. Center fielder Billy Hatcher's eyes got so big at the opportunity to nail the pitcher that he threw the ball away. Keith Hernandez then tripled past the diving Hatcher and the Mets led, 5–0. Eleven Astros reached base from the second through the seventh innings against Ojeda, but Houston could do nothing with runners aboard against the pitcher with the highest winning percentage in the league—in fact, the first four pitchers in that category were Mets.

Unless you count a Jets playoff game that ended with a Richard Todd interception at the 1-yard line in 1981, Shea Stadium had not seen the postseason since 1973. Jerry Koosman won that game, beating the Oakland A's and putting the '73 Mets one win from a World Series championship. That win never came, but Kooz was in the house to throw out the first pitch as the October bunting was back up at Shea in 1986. Even though the home team had won 108 games, the crowd was cold and a bit pensive after seeing the transformation of Mike Scott from the Met who cringed when Shea fans banged in unison on seat cushion night in 1981 to the man who was unhittable, unrestrained, and—when it came to scuffing the baseball—uncatchable in 1986. Scott wasn't due to pitch until Game 4, so the Mets needed Game 3. But in a year in which the Mets had plenty of luck, they hadn't had much against Bob Knepper. The tall, deeply religious, slow-throwing southpaw started four times against the Mets and relieved once in a 15-inning game in 1986. The Astros won four of those five games, with the Mets scoring just 1.67 runs per nine innings off Knepper.

The 17-game winner was even better when staked to a lead. With the Saturday game starting just after noon, thanks to football—college football altering the NLCS schedule this time—the Mets looked as if they'd just rolled out of bed. Ron Darling allowed two runs, three hits, a hit batter, and a wild pitch in the top of the first, bailing himself out by picking off Glenn Davis to end the inning. It was not the end of his trouble, though. Bill Doran hit a two-run homer in the second to put Houston up, 4–0, just 10 batters into the game. In 16 previous NLCS, no team had ever trailed by four runs and come back to win a game.

By the sixth inning Darling was done, the score still stood at 4–0, and it looked like the two-on, none-out rally might go by the boards as Gary Carter hit a slow roller to shortstop Craig Reynolds. But the ball rolled under his glove, Kevin Mitchell scored, and the tying run was at the plate. Strawberry crushed the next pitch over the *Newsday* sign in right field to clear the bases and the scoreboard. A hitless August at home—an 0-for-45 skein that zeroed the boo birds on Strawberry—was far away now. Strawberry the hero was summoned for a curtain call.

No sooner had fans chugged the remains of their beer to coat their already hoarse throats on this October afternoon than the momentum shifted. Rick Aguilera, in his second inning of relief, walked Bill Doran to start the seventh. Billy Hatcher dropped down a bunt that Ray Knight grabbed, but it stuck in his glove.

His ill-advised throw got away and Doran raced to third. The Astros broke the tie without a hit as an infield out brought home Doran. Knight felt he'd blown the game.

The bottom of the ninth began with the fans on their feet and the rhythmic "dum-dum-dum" of "We Will Rock You." Even though Charlie Kerfeld pitched a solid eighth inning, manager Hal Lanier went with Dave Smith for the ninth. Why? "When you have a pitcher with 33 saves, you use him. That's what he's here for."

Smith had trouble with the Mets. During the Mets' weekend from hell in Houston in July, he blew a win for Mike Scott the night after the Cooter's arrests. The following afternoon Smith was handed a three-run lead and let three runners reach base before departing and letting someone else blow the save. The Astros won both games, but Smith's ERA against the '86 Mets coming into Game 3 was 15.00 and he'd been responsible for the tying or go-ahead run scoring in all three of his outings against New York. Lefties, however, only hit .167 against him for the year. And Davey Johnson was sending up lefties in the ninth.

The first was Wally Backman, the switch-hitter who hated to switch-hit. He'd gone in to play second base for Tim Teufel in the top of the ninth. It's what made the Mets bench so dangerous. Even when a left-hander started and Backman and Dykstra—aka Back-stra—were on the bench, as in Game 3, they became a weapon that could be utilized when the manager needed them late in the game, after the relievers came in. It was Davey Johnson's turn to affect the outcome.

"The manager really only manages from the sixth or seventh inning on," Johnson explained. "It's basically my bullpen against their bench. And then their bullpen against my bench. And that's when you really manage. Anybody can put a regular lineup out there against a starting pitcher. But when you really manage is late in the game. And that's why you need a good bench and a good bullpen."

Speed didn't hurt, either. On a 1–1 pitch Backman laid down a drag bunt. First baseman Glenn Davis fielded it and made a move to tag the runner, but he wasn't there. Backman was on the other side of the baseline, staying far away from Davis—far enough away where he could have had on his blinker for the Whitestone Bridge. Backman then lunged for the bag, touching it with his outstretched left hand. Umpire Dutch Rennert called him safe, ruling that he didn't think the fielder had a play, so Backman could establish his own baseline. Even Hal Lanier, who argued for several minutes, admitted after the game that it was the right call.

The next lefty was pinch hitter Danny Heep. Johnson asked his pinch hitter to do something both of them were loath to do: bunt. Heep had but two sacrifices in his career to that point, and he fouled off the first bunt attempt. On the second try he pulled the bat back, screening Alan Ashby, and the ball popped off the catcher's mitt and toward the screen. Backman went to second and Heep could swing away. He did, hitting a fly to center, but it did not advance the runner.

So up stepped Dykstra, who'd fanned against Knepper as a pinch hitter and was up for the second time. He'd faced Smith twice before, with two hits off him—including a game-winning double on July 4 at Shea. Down a run with the fastest Met in scoring position, a single would do just fine. Dykstra fouled off a fastball, which convinced him Smith would come with the forkball. It was his best pitch, and as Lanier said in the clubhouse as Shea Stadium still pulsed above him, "You go with your best." Smith's best went a long way.

Dykstra hit the pitch with one hand, but he hit it perfectly and right fielder Kevin Bass tracked the ball until it disappeared into the Mets bullpen. Dykstra leaped and leaped around the bases. His wife, Terri, hugged and hugged—the longest coming from Nancy Lopez, wife of Ray Knight, now free of the goat horns.

Nine home runs in two years and Dykstra had gone deep at the most opportune time—one of the half dozen greatest endings ever at Shea Stadium, a list that may even include the legendary 1965 Beatles concert at Shea closing with "I'm Down." Shea was anything but down. Thirteen Octobers without baseball, but Flushing was back with a bang, and a boom.

What to do for an encore? Nothing. The come-from-behind win on Saturday proved even more important because Mike Scott was unhittable on Sunday. He was supported by home runs by Alan Ashby and Dickie Thon—Ashby's coming after Rafael Santana called for a foul pop-up and watched it land in the first row of temporary seats in left field. Scott set down Mets and set playoff records: his 19 strikeouts in two games broke Tom Seaver's NLCS record of 17 for the 1973 Mets and surpassed the LCS mark of 18 set a year earlier in three starts by Toronto's Dave Stieb. The Mets were no-hit into the fifth and shut out until the eighth, breaking the LCS shutout record set in 1974 by noted scuffer Don Sutton. The Mets had just three singles, with Danny Heep's sacrifice fly the lone ball hit out of the infield. The Mets were lucky 3–1 was just the score of the game; it easily could have been the score of the series.

Since the Mets couldn't hit Scott's signature pitch, they collected baseballs with his signature mark—a scuff the size of a 50-cent piece. Every time a Met hit a foul ball, it was examined and put aside in the dugout amid nods of agreement. This time they didn't bother asking the umpires, and instead went to the league president. Charles "Chub" Feeney, the longtime Giants executive who considered preventing the National League from adopting the designated hitter to be his greatest achievement, examined the evidence. With Yale president Bart Giamatti set to replace the retiring Feeney, he was not going to let his 17-year run end by invalidating his league's best pitcher during a Championship Series, no matter how many beat up balls he received. Feeney vowed to keep an eye on Scott in his next start.

So the new strategy was to make sure there was no next start for Scott. This task was made more difficult when a Monday rainout allowed Hal Lanier to replace rookie Jim Deshaies with future Hall of Famer Nolan Ryan. Seventeen years ago to the day, Ryan had come out of the bullpen against Baltimore in a bases-loaded jam during Shea's first-ever World Series game. His first batter, Paul Blair, scalded a drive into the right-center gap that Tommie Agee caught with a belly-flop on the warning track, his second sensational catch on that Tuesday afternoon. On this Tuesday afternoon, October 14, 1986, Agee and Ron Swoboda, who had made a game-saving catch of his own in the '69 Series, threw out first pitches. Agee and Swoboda had been retired since the Mets were last in the playoffs, in 1973. Now with Tom Seaver injured and at the end of his career, Ryan would be the last Miracle Met playing in the majors. And he pitched like it was 1969. Only better.

New York was not a fit for Nolan Ryan. He was wild—Ron Darling, Mike Torrez, and yes, Oliver Perez at their wildest could not touch Ryan's club-record 116 walks in 1971, his last year before the disastrous deal that sent him to the Angels and put Mets fans on a decades-long bender of what might have been. Relapses could still flare up in 1986. *Imagine if Gooden and Ryan were on the same pitching staff.* Well, how about if they were on the same mound for one spectacular October afternoon?

The hitters had no chance. For all the "What's up with Doc?" talk in '86, the big question about Gooden during the NLCS was "What does this guy have to do to get a win?" The run he allowed came on a double play not turned—but Gooden caught a break when the Mets got a double play call that prevented a run in the second inning.

Ryan, who already owned the major league record for no-hitters—and strikeouts—retired the first 13 Mets, fanning 8. He went nine innings in Game 5, throwing 134 pitches while striking out 12 and allowing just two hits and one walk. And Ryan did all this, it was revealed later, after suffering a stress fracture in his ankle while breaking up the double play that scored Houston's lone run. In the visiting clubhouse after the game, *Newsday* reporter Marty Noble ran after Ryan, who was exhausted, injured, and angry.

"Nolan, I've really got to talk to you."

"Oh, Jesus, come on."

"One question: That pitch you threw Straw . . ."

"I've thrown that pitch I don't know how many times, a thousand, two thousand, three thousand times. No one has ever hit that pitch that far in that direction. His talent beat my talent."

Darryl Strawberry's line drive down the right field line just stayed fair and was just high enough over the fence for the first run—and first hit—off Ryan. The crowd went wild, though it was not the 54,986 seen in box scores. Because of the rainout Monday followed by rain all Tuesday morning, the turnstile count for the playoff matinee was just 33,377, the lowest number of people, by far, to ever witness a postseason game at Shea Stadium. Ed Randall, covering the ALCS for Canadian sports network TSN, had a unique vantage point as he returned to New York from California. "I was on the right side of an Eastern Airlines shuttle," Randall recalled. "Back then you remember they used to fly right over the stadium, so I could see it from my window and I said, 'Wow, there's nobody there.' It was crazy given the importance of it."

The run was all Ryan allowed, managing to surrender just two hits—and three baserunners—in the first 11 innings. Nine hits and a run in 10 innings—the longest outing of his career—was all Houston managed against Gooden. Then Orosco threw two perfect frames. Wally Backman led off the bottom of the 12th with a one-hop shot the opposite way that bounced off third baseman Denny Walling's glove for an infield hit. With Keith Hernandez at the plate, Charlie Kerfeld's errant pickoff throw sent Backman to second. The strategy was obvious: Walk Hernandez and pitch to Carter. He was 1-for-21 in the series. The Astros had twice walked Hernandez to pitch to Carter in Game 2, even though he'd doubled in a run earlier in the game. He'd come up dry both times and was hitless in his last 15 at bats as he stepped to the plate in the 12th inning of Game 5.

Even Carter acknowledged it was the right move. But Astro Bill Doran told Backman on second base, "The way he's started to swing the bat, he's the last person I want coming up there in a spot like right now." Carter received plenty of encouragement from the crowd and the on-deck circle. "Don't let them do this to you, Kid," Darryl Strawberry called to him as Houston completed the intentional walk to Hernandez. "Don't let them do it." Carter didn't.

Kerfeld fell behind 3–0 and threw a strike, and then Carter fouled off three straight pitches. He hit the next pitch on the bat's sweet spot and sent it back up the middle. In Game 3 Kerfeld had snagged Carter's hard grounder behind his back and pointed at him before throwing to first. This line drive was hit to the same area, but it sped through the infield before Kerfeld could move his glove. "I don't think he was going to play that one behind his back," a jubilant Carter said after the game.

Backman slid in ahead of the throw as the Mets poured out of the dugout. Kerfeld trudged off the mound and sat in the dugout. It had been a rough trip to New York. The Mets never led yet won twice in their last at bat. And death threats were made to manager Hal Lanier, reliever Dave Smith, and Kerfeld at the team hotel. The manager called them "cranks" and Smith said "they're probably nuts," but Kerfeld acted the John Rocker part back when Rocker was still in middle school.* Kerfeld's career reached its apex that week—he'd be back in the minors the following summer due to a ballooning waistline, and ERA—and he spared no feelings about New York during the 1986 playoffs: "I'm ready to get away from this zoo. I'm ready to get back to where some real people are."

---

* Braves reliever John Rocker taunted Mets fans during the 1999 NLCS at Shea Stadium, later letting his bigoted feelings vent to *Sports Illustrated* writer Jeff Pearlman in an article that resulted in a 14-game suspension.

People—real and loud—were still cheering at Shea: "Gar-ee! Gar-ee! Gar-ee!" The catcher hugged anyone within arm's reach. The slump was broken, the Mets led the series, and they could take the pennant without facing Mike Scott again. All they had to do was win Game 6.

Two years earlier, the pennant would have already been won—in both leagues. The League Championship Series was a best-of-five affair for its first 15 years, but it was changed to a best-of-seven by owners and players during 1985 negotiations for a labor deal. That fall's world champion Royals would have been eliminated by Toronto if the ALCS had still been a best-of-five. In 1986 the Angels would have clinched their first pennant in four games under the old setup, but they were fighting for their lives with a seventh game in Boston. The Mets too would have won a best-of-five on Carter's hit. Those what-might-have-beens were the stuff for sleepless off-season nights. There were more pressing what-might-have-beens now.

Houston was still up in arms over umpire Fred Brocklander's call the day before in Game 5, as replays and photographs showed Craig Reynolds beating the throw to first base in the second inning. That would have allowed a run to score in a game decided in extra innings. Keith Hernandez added fuel to the fire with an interview broadcast during Game 6.

"I'm not going to sit here and say he was out because I looked at the paper this morning," Hernandez said, noting that as he stretched for the throw he noticed a "questionable look" on Brocklander's face. "I figured I'd put a little something in there and I just screamed, 'Out!' And whether it affected the call or not, who knows. We were fortunate to get the call our way."

In his rich, Tennessee baritone, ABC's Keith Jackson called Hernandez a "crafty fellow." The announcer explained that the Brocklander call overnight had become as big a controversy in

Houston as the Scott scuff ball was in New York. Houston morning disc jockeys already had a song about Brocklander and that morning's *Houston Post* featured the headline "We Wuz Robbed." God he was not, but like Doug Harvey, Fred Brocklander was convinced he was right—even looking at the replay could not change his view. So heading into the sixth game, the Mets might have had a one-game edge, but the teams were even when it came to umpires.

The field still bore the marks of the football game that cost the Mets home-field advantage—no one in New York was sad that the 1–5 Oilers lost to the Bears—and the Mets went three-and-out in the first. Hernandez dove at the 25-yard line to snag Billy Hatcher's sizzling grounder in the bottom of the first. That was the only out Bob Ojeda got from the first six Astros in the order. Three runs in, Rick Aguilera warming up in the bullpen, and Houston went for the jugular—with a bunt. With runners on the corners, Alan Ashby squared for the suicide squeeze and missed. Kevin Bass was tagged out. The camera focused on Hal Lanier in the Astros dugout, leaning against the railing, uttering a silent "Damn." Ashby lined out to shortstop to end the inning.

It was remarkable Ojeda survived the first inning. His left elbow had locked up on the way home after his Game 2 masterpiece and he was unable to get loose for his bullpen session in New York. So Ojeda flew to Washington to receive two shots from the team doctor, James Parkes, who was there for a conference. One shot was a numbing agent, the other cortisone. Ojeda then hopped on the shuttle back to New York—it's not all bad having a stadium next to an airport. In a candid 2012 piece in the *New York Times*, Ojeda recalled that warming up before Game 6 felt "like I had two sandbags stuffed in my elbow." Davey Johnson stuck with him, even though the press, the fans, and the team knew the Mets were in serious trouble if they faced Scott again. Ojeda, who had pitched with pain in his arm since age 12, kept throwing and "the sand" began, "grain by grain, to run out."

Sand, or rather, sandpaper was the word of the day in Houston. Fans throughout the stadium displayed it in tribute to Mike Scott. Even the man who threw out the first pitch, Harris County judge Jon Lindsay, held up a block of sandpaper to roars from the Astrodome. By hook or by crook, if Scott took the mound again in Game 7, many felt the Astros couldn't lose.* And given the way Bob Knepper was pitching, it looked like a seventh game was coming. Knepper, pitching on three days' rest, had a one-hitter until Tim Teufel singled in the eighth, the Mets' first hit since the third inning. The next batter, Rafael Santana, bounced into a double play.

"The biggest game we had was the sixth game in Houston, against Knepper," Davey Johnson reflected. "We were down three runs and the next day we had to face Scott. Everybody knew we needed to win this damned game."

Lenny Dykstra came off the bench to face the lefty to lead off the ninth inning of Game 6. He had pinch-hit against Knepper in Game 3 and struck out. With a 1–2 count, Knepper tried to put him away with a slider. Dykstra crushed the ball 380 feet to right center. Center fielder Billy Hatcher, playing in while the other outfielders were in a no-doubles defense, could not get to it and Dykstra legged out a triple. Knepper had two strikes on Mookie Wilson before he too hit a ball that was almost caught—it fell for a hit. The score was 3–1.

Kevin Mitchell hit a high hopper that moved up Wilson, but the Astros had the first out of the ninth. Keith Hernandez was up next, lefty on lefty. Hernandez had hit .341 to that point in his career against Knepper, though for what it's worth he'd hit .377 against Mike Scott, and that did not carry much weight in this series. Another statistic did. ABC flashed a graphic that read,

* And Mike Scott would be scuffing. After keeping up a cone of silence on the subject for 25 years, he let a cryptic tidbit go national in 2011: "They can believe whatever they want to believe. Every ball that hits the ground has something on it. . . . I've thrown balls that were scuffed but I haven't scuffed every ball that I've thrown."

"Keith Hernandez is hitting .333 with runners in scoring position over the last eight seasons." He was 1-for-3 with two RBI in that situation in the NLCS—plus three intentional walks—as he batted in the ninth. Hernandez lined Knepper's 101st pitch to right-center, scoring Wilson and making it a one-run game. Standing on second base, Hernandez clenched his fists and yelled, "Yeah!" "Damn"—and worse—was on lips again in the Houston dugout. Hal Lanier came out to take the ball from Knepper.

Before leaving Shea Stadium the previous day, Houston reliever Dave Smith had made his feelings about the Mets quite clear: "We've got to beat the Mets because I can't stand them." While that was a sentiment held by many, Smith could actually do something about it.

Smith threw close pitches to both Carter and Strawberry on 3–2 pitches. He thought he struck each hitter out. Fred Brocklander failed to raise a hand on either pitch, the ump giving the Mets a run for their money as most hated uniformed personnel in Houston. With the bases full, Smith got ahead 0–2 on Ray Knight. Smith missed twice, but he thought the third try was perfect. Ball three. Ashby dragged his catcher's mitt on the dirt and Smith screamed at Brocklander over the Astrodome's cacophonous din. Lanier came out to argue with the umpire, but the biggest shock was Knight yelling at both the catcher and the pitcher, then the shortstop. Dickie Thon seemed madder than anyone—except maybe Knight—and after some gesturing, Lanier and Ashby urged Thon back to his position. "He's very emotional," Thon said of Knight. "I'm emotional, too." Knight, the ex-Astro who still had a house in the area he was trying to unload, wasn't asking any of his former teammates to an open house. He was yelling at them to stop umpiring; they yelled back what he could do with his opinion. The game—and the pennant—hung in the balance: bases loaded, full count, a one-run lead. A double play could even the series and a double could end it. Now if they would just stop arguing with each other and play.

"If I'm Ray Knight right now, I'm swinging at anything," ABC announcer Tim McCarver said. "He may call anything that Smith throws up there a strike now." Knight swung and hit a fly ball to deep right. Kevin Bass caught it as Hernandez tagged up and scored, a triumphant hop in the air as he crossed the plate to tie the game. It's safe to say Knight won the argument.

Houston's 46th and final pitch of the ninth fanned Danny Heep with the bases loaded. But Smith had failed against the Mets. Again. No wonder he hated them so much.

As Roger McDowell came into the game, many others jumped aboard as well. They weren't players, though the Mets did have a new double-play team in Backman and Kevin Elster, while Dykstra took over in center and Mookie moved to left. The workday was over in the East. People in offices were leaving, kids were home from school, people who seldom watched sports stopped what they were doing to focus their attention on the Mets. Unless they had Hebrew school.

Reporter Mark Simon, who now specializes in New York baseball for ESPN.com, was an 11-year-old in Manhattan in 1986 who lost his battle with his mother to skip Hebrew school the day of Game 6. "She made me go," Simon said, still sounding disappointed three decades later. "So we're doing whatever it is we're doing, and the teacher says to us at 5:30 . . . 'We're going to bring in the other class.'" East 79th Street in Manhattan, where Temple Shaaray Tefila still stands, has been prime Yankees territory since the mid-1990s, but it was awash in orange and blue in the mid-1980s. So was Simon's elementary school, Little League team, and just about everywhere he frequented during that age where sports can be the most important thing in a child's life. Even the few Yankees fans he came into contact with were on a career path in that direction. Mark Feinsand, longtime Yankees beat writer and former chairman of the Baseball Writers Association of America's New York chapter, was in the other class that came in for a "special project" that October afternoon. The other teacher came in with a transistor radio. "The special project was to listen to the ninth inning," Simon said.

As Simon walked home after Hebrew school let out in the 10th inning, he saw people lined up on the street outside store windows with TVs, or clustered around radios—strangers linked by a local baseball team, *the* local baseball team at the time. "People were jumping up and down," he said. "We were getting pretty excited." The Mets were pretty excited in Texas, too.

Roger McDowell, who had pitched just once in the NLCS, was summoned to keep the game tied. The rainout in New York eliminated the usual off day between locales, and Jesse Orosco had pitched two innings the day before, so McDowell was rested. He pitched the game of his life.

Davey Johnson had a tremendous bullpen, but he trusted only half of it. McDowell and Orosco combined for 22 wins, 43 saves, 133 appearances, and 209 innings and allowed just 10 home runs between them. Johnson used Rick Aguilera, a trusted starter and one of six 10-game winners on the staff, for two long relief outings (including three innings in Game 6), and Doug Sisk threw one inning (in Game 4). Randy Niemann did not pitch.

"He was going to go to the whip with Aguilera and Roger and Jesse," Hernandez said of his manager's bullpen order. "He just didn't factor in a 16-inning game." The longer the game went, the more critical it became that the Mets win. Beyond Mike Scott looming as Houston's Game 7 starter, the Mets bullpen would be toast if there was a seventh game. The Astros would ride Scott as long as possible, and after his first two performances against the Mets, why would anyone take him out? Especially when the alternative was the Astros bullpen.

Dave Smith did something in the 10th inning he had not done since 1985: He got the Mets out without the tying or winning run scoring. Lanier then handed off to Larry Andersen—like McDowell a born prankster but dead serious on the mound. Andersen's legacy would be as the man traded to Boston for Jeff

Bagwell, but in Game 6 Andersen retired nine of the ten men he faced. McDowell was even better, throwing 50 pitches in five innings and allowing one hit to Kevin Bass, who was thrown out stealing in the 12th.

McDowell might have continued pitching, but his spot in the order came up during a rally. Aurelio Lopez replaced Andersen in the 14th and the first two Mets reached base. Davey Johnson hated the bunt, but he tried it with the man who had tied the game. Ray Knight had two successful sacrifices in 1986—including two on turf in September, dress rehearsals for such a moment. When the moment came he flubbed it. The pitcher grabbed Knight's bunt and threw Carter out at third. Backman followed with a single to right and Bud Harrelson sent Strawberry homeward. The gamble paid off and the Mets were up, 4–3. Unlike their last two wins, when their first lead occurred on the final play of the game, this time the Mets had to hold it.

Orosco came out of the pen to wrap up the pennant. It looked good after he struck out Bill Doran to start the inning. Then Billy Hatcher came up. He crushed the first-pitch fastball he was waiting on, but it veered into the crowd to the left of the tall screen that served as the foul pole at the Astrodome. On 2–2, the Mets felt the sting of Fred Brocklander, who called ball three when Orosco clearly thought his slider was strike three. Hatcher then swung so hard at the full-count fastball that his momentum knocked him back toward the dugout. The ball hit the foul screen (fair ball!) and bounced to the turf. Hatcher told author Mike Sowell that relatives staying in his apartment a few blocks away from the Astrodome could hear the cheering from the indoor stadium after his home run.

With the exception of Houston's starting pitching (2.47 ERA), almost everything had worked in the Mets' favor in this series. Houston had given up four leads; now the Mets had surrendered one. When Orosco retired the next two batters, Game 6 became the longest game in terms of innings and time in postseason history. Gary Carter, who had caught 26 innings in just over 24 hours, took off for second on a ball in the dirt and was thrown out. He strapped on the gear and the Astros were retired in their half of the 15th.

Hatcher, who'd been too shallow when Dykstra knocked the ball over his head in the ninth, was too deep when Strawberry skied a ball to short center to start the 16th. Hatcher was standing in the end zone still marked on the field and charged like a punt returner racing to catch a kick with a lot of hang time; Bill Doran raced into the outfield like a receiver. Neither caught the ball and the big bounce allowed Strawberry to reach second. Knight, who'd tied the game in the 9th and bunted poorly in the 14th, got the hit sign and singled to right to give the Mets the lead. That was all for Lopez, but Lanier did not bring in Charlie Kerfeld, who had warmed up several times, or Danny Darwin, owning a 2.21 ERA since being acquired from Milwaukee in August, or rookie left-hander Jim Deshaies, bumped from a Game 5 start by the rainout and the lone NL pitcher with a .700 winning percentage who wasn't a Met. The Astros manager opted for Jeff Calhoun. The lefty had spent much of the season in the minors and hadn't pitched in two weeks.

Calhoun threw two wild pitches—one with Backman batting right-handed and the other with the pitcher up. Backman, hitting .144 as a righty, wound up walking; Orosco watched Knight score as the ball got by Ashby. Orosco bunted Backman to third and Back-stra came through again—Dykstra's hit made it 7–4.

Orosco took the mound with a three-run lead, but he was running on fumes. He fanned Craig Reynolds, an even worse hitter against lefties than Backman. The next three Astros all reached base, with Hatcher's second hit off Orosco making it a 7–5 game. Orosco retired another left-handed batter, Denny Walling, with Keith Hernandez throwing to second for a close force play to keep the tying run out of scoring position. That proved huge when Glenn Davis followed with an RBI single.

This was already the longest postseason game in history in terms of both innings and time—past four-and-a-half hours—and now the tying run stood at second base. Really? This game needed to end. Jesse Orosco, Gary Carter, and Keith Hernandez converged on the Astrodome mound, an island of noise. The task was to do whatever possible to get one more out. Now. Hernandez didn't like the look of Orosco's fastball. He told him so: "If you throw another fastball, I'll kill you." The years have taken away one of the participants along with the certainty of what was said, and to whom. Carter denied Hernandez made a threat or called pitches during the multiple mound conferences in the bottom of the 16th, stating in his final memoir that his plan was to call sliders for the last out and his only words were those of encouragement. Orosco pled the fifth in a recent interview: "It was so loud I didn't hear a thing, and I stepped away to try to regroup myself on the mound. I threw whatever pitches Gary called." Hernandez said he was kidding. "Jesse was just exhausted—he was gagged and he was gassed," said Hernandez, switching to announcer mode, a role that's lasted twice as long as his Mets playing career.

"He's throwing fastballs and that's fine; you've got eight gloves out there," Hernandez went on. "I just came in more for just comic relief. It wasn't a threat. It was more to get a smile from Jesse because it was loud in that dome. And all the pressure is on the pitcher and I always felt that you crack a joke and break the tension. Anyway, Jesse's big pitch is his slider and he didn't have his fastball anymore and it got to the point where [Houston] could have the game tied again. . . . OK, no longer can you just throw a fastball; you've got to start mixing it up, which he did. Kevin Bass was the perfect final out because it was a good matchup for Jesse. He's a much better left-hand hitter, Bass, and not a good downstairs hitter and he didn't like a good down-breaking pitch right-handed, and that was what Jesse's ace pitch was. And Jesse threw him nothing but those sliders and struck him out."

"Swing and a miss! Swing and a miss! Struck him out! Struck him out! The Mets win it! The Mets have won it! They're in the World Series, Saturday night at Shea! Oh, and they are mobbing Jesse Orosco!" WHN carried Bob Murphy's voice on commuter trains, on elevated platforms, in homes, and in countless vehicles on city streets and parkways struggling not to flip over from excitement. Murph couldn't help but shout; he and his employer were going to their first World Series since 1973.

After the more subdued call on ABC, the cameras focused on the Astros filing out of the dugout as much as on the Mets celebrating near the mound. The camera panned to Houston second baseman Bill Doran watching the Mets hug on the field, pondering how close his team had come to that moment. Doran's right arm bent on the dugout railing, propping up his head, his blue eyes twinkling sadly, the gate next to him swinging shut as the solemn grounds crew went about its duties. The game had been over for one minute. "So," Keith Jackson said in what was his last baseball game in a long career known for football, "the struggle is done. Sadness, disappointment, fatigue, you name an element and it exists. On one side or the other."

Two days in a row, the Mets had been held to two hits through 8 innings—11 innings in Game 5—and yet they won both. The Mets became the first team since divisional play began to win a Championship Series while hitting under .200. They batted .189 overall, while going, in the words of *Daily News* columnist Mike Lupica, "0-for-Scott"—the Mets hit .130 off him to be exact, but they won the most important battle: They did not have to face Scott a third time, in a winner-take-all Game 7. That forever remains in the "what if" column. Into the "so what" column went Scott as Championship Series MVP, the first time the award went to a player from the losing NL team. Arguments could be made for players from the winning team: Lenny Dykstra (New York's leading hitter, .304, and in the middle of every big rally), Jesse Orosco (the first reliever in postseason history to win three games a series), or Darryl Strawberry (two game-tying home runs). But like Scott's 1986 Cy Young Award—or his subsequent Wiffle ball endorsement (the plastic ball is known to move even more when scuffed)—the Mets were plenty content to pour the champagne all over the visiting clubhouse in the Astrodome.

The celebration continued on the airplane home, where it famously got out of hand. Frank Cashen blamed himself for giving in to the players' request to bring the wives along on the charter. But like the bill for fixing the field after the fans destroyed it, the actual damage figure for the plane—Cashen said it was more than $7,000, while others have claimed above and below that sum—seemed a small price for winning the pennant and a game for the ages. Phil Pepe's *Daily News* column the next day was entitled "Greatest Game Ever," and *Newark-Star Ledger* columnist Jerry Izenberg wrote a book just about Game 6 with almost that same title. Three decades later, there is not a lot of argument against it.

More than a dozen LCS have gone the full seven games since 1986, but the drama of this six-game series remains unparalleled. Even the Game 7 that wasn't played is a better story than most of the Game 7s that were. "I think we would have beaten [Scott]," Ray Knight said in the victorious locker room. "But I'm glad we don't have to try."

12

So Far Away, So Good

October 18–23, 1986

All-Northeast World Series have become exceedingly rare. That has not always been the case. Once upon a time, before relocation and expansion, it was rare when a World Series was not played in the Northeast, defined by the Census Bureau as the six New England states, plus New Jersey, New York, and Pennsylvania. The Northeast is the richest section of the country and also considers itself the smartest, what with the Ivy League, the Little Ivies, and scads of exclusive prep schools, all the way down to elite nursery schools seen as ground zero for the right connections to ensure the perfect northeastern life. When it comes to recreation, the Northeast loves its baseball. And nothing feeds that sense of history or heightens regional rivalries like winning a championship against people you can laud it over.

Between 1908 and 1934, there were 10 World Series between Northeast teams. The lone Series not involving at least one northeastern team in that span was 1919—the year eight White Sox players went for the fix against the Reds. The 1921 World Series marked the first of 14 Subway Series between New York teams until the Dodgers and Giants left for California after the 1957 season. Before 1986 the last all-Northeast World Series had been in 1960, when Bill Mazeroski's Game 7 blast disappeared into the Pittsburgh haze, stunning the Yankees and costing Casey Stengel and George Weiss their jobs (freeing them, it turned out, to run the fledgling Mets). When the Mets and Red Sox emerged from tortuous Championship Series battles to reach the '86 World Series, NBC jumped for joy.* Many viewers jumped for cover. Yankees fans tried to yawn through their worst nightmare come true, and others, tired of the Northeast's sense of entitlement, pretended not to notice. The ratings stated otherwise.

The 28.6 rating for the 1986 World Series was almost as high as Boston's epic seven-game World Series loss to the Reds in 1975. And with the Mets the overwhelming World Series favorites at 2½–1, the Red Sox made for an interesting pick. The 1986 rating was comparable to the Mets World Series in 1969 and 1973, in a precable era with a lot less competition on TV. The 1986 World Series was seen by an average of 36.37 million viewers per night—they were all night games now, thanks to baseball's first billion dollar TV contract. A 46 ratings share for the '86 Series remains untouched since then; it would take adding together four World Series broadcasts since 2010 to surpass it.

Some tuned in to see New York lose, given how much the Mets were disliked outside (and inside) the Northeast. "We played hard," Kevin Mitchell said, recalling the '86 Mets mantra. "However we can win. If we had to cheat—we want to win. . . . Whatever it took to win, we tried to do it. Even if we had to fight." Three decades later, a little of the attitude that rubbed quite a few people the wrong way can still ooze out. To the Mets alums of 1986 it's not being cocky, it's just being true.

The '86 Red Sox were true underdogs. Down three games to one to the Angels in the ALCS and trailing 5–2 in the ninth with fans ready to pour onto the field in Anaheim, the Red Sox scored four times in the ninth. A two-run homer by Don Baylor made

* Since 1986 there have been two all-Northeast World Series: the Mets and Yankees in 2000 and the Phillies and Yankees in 2009.

it a one-run game and, after removing starter Mike Witt, reliever Donnie Moore surrendered a two-run shot to Dave Henderson, subbing for injured Tony Armas. The Red Sox won Game 5 in extra innings, jetted back to Boston, and gutted the Angels like a fish that gave up a fight it thought it had won.

Game 1 of the World Series felt like a night for ice fishing. The game-time temperature was listed at 50 degrees with a 9-mile-per-hour wind, but by game's end it seemed like it had dropped to 9 degrees with a 50-mile-per-hour wind. Heaters were installed in the dugout roofs and bats were wrapped in warm towels. The only two Mets starters without long-sleeve shirts under their uniforms during player introductions were Keith Hernandez and Tim Teufel, and by the second inning Teufel had thrown on a sweatshirt underneath. You could say it was a cold day in hell when New York and Boston met in the World Series.

Of course, the Yankees and Red Sox had been rivals forever, but New York and Boston had not matched up in the World Series since 1912, when, in brand-new Fenway Park, the Giants had the lead in the 10th inning of the deciding game until an error on a routine play fueled a rally for the home team. Christy Mathewson was the pitcher that fateful day for the Giants. Tris Speaker was the hero for the Red Sox. A kid named George Ruth was still sewing shirts at St. Mary's Industrial School for Boys in Baltimore.

Except for the lights and the music blaring, Game 1 of the 1986 World Series resembled a game from the Deadball Era. Even a baseball purist might think it dull.

"I remember the extraordinary tedium of Game 1—the most boring 1–0 game ever," said John Thorn, now official historian of Major League Baseball. In '86 as coauthor of the influential *Hidden Game of Baseball*, he was sitting in former Astros GM Tal Smith's seats.

Neither team got a runner as far as third base for the first six innings. Bruce Hurst was superb. Ron Darling was just as good. He allowed only three hits through six innings, but Darling

Ron Darling at Fenway Park the night after he won Game 4 of the 1986 World Series DAN CARUBIA

began the seventh with a walk to Jim Rice. After a wild pitch he retired Dwight Evans on a comebacker. Up came Rich Gedman, whom Darling knew from high school competition in Worcester, Massachusetts. In a big spot in the World Series—and with a base open—Darling got Gedman to hit a grounder at the second baseman. And then the ball was in right field, right through Tim Teufel's legs as Rice crossed home plate.

The night seemed to get even colder for the Mets after that. Teufel led off the bottom of the seventh with a single, and then Wally Backman ran for him. That gave Teufel time to sit and hope his teammates would save him from the impending media gauntlet. The Mets made just one error in the NLCS, but that miscue by Ray Knight could have cost them Game 3—until Lenny Dykstra's home run saved the day. When Calvin Schiraldi fanned Danny Heep to end the 1–0 World Series opener, Teufel knew what was coming. He'd prepared for it all year with all the *Game of the Week* appearances, *Kiner's Korner* spots, and local news remotes resulting from Cooter's-gate. But this was the World Series. They weren't coming to talk about his having two of New York's four hits against Hurst. When one reporter tried to change the subject during his 25-minute grilling, Teufel dutifully replied, "I'm sorry, I'm only taking error questions now."

"We had five or six months to prepare for that," Teufel, a longtime Mets coach, said of his World Series debut. "But you never get prepared to do something on such a big stage as that. As you can tell, I handled it, I didn't crumble. We were kind of groomed to handle it; you face the media and do what you have to do. Explain what happened . . . but the next day you face it again and talk about it again until the next game's over and then it's pretty much over."

Had the World Series turned out a different way, there would have been a lot more scrutiny on a ball going through a Mets infielder's legs as opposed to someone else's.

Tom Seaver wasn't much heard from during the '86 World Series. He wasn't able to pitch for Boston, but he was there, surrounded by New York writers looking to file features. Seaver could be genuine or nasty—or genuinely nasty—to those he didn't know or didn't want to see. And he didn't want to see the New York press. They had filed a million stories off him, and in October 1986 he neither felt like reminiscing nor predicting his future with a bad knee as he approached age 42.

Ed Sherman just wanted to go home. A little over a year earlier he'd been covering Chicago high school sports for the *Chicago Tribune*, but he'd been appointed the second reporter to cover the Bears, who became *the* sports story of 1985, so when their run ended, he was put on the White Sox beat and he'd worked and traveled almost every day since. He got to know Seaver on the White Sox before the trade to the Red Sox. Though they weren't close, Sherman saw him in the cramped Red Sox clubhouse during the World Series, and asked for an interview. Seaver consented, but after a minute the New York and national media started to crowd around. Seaver left. Sherman figured his exclusive exited at the same time, but a few minutes later, he heard a loud whisper coming from—was that the closet? "Ed, Ed, come here." So he went in the small closet in Shea's visiting locker room and conducted an interview that became the *Sunday Tribune* feature "Seaver Sad on Sideline." It could have been called "Tom Terrific in the Closet."

Seaver was the legend who wasn't pitching, but Game 2 gave the scribes a pitching matchup of the ages to write about. Last year's 24–4 pitcher against this year's 24–4 pitcher: Dwight Gooden vs. Roger Clemens. As with Gooden in 1985, there was no reason to bother counting the votes for the Cy Young Award in November because it had been obvious by July who'd win it.* The most impressive pitcher of the night turned out to be Elie Wiesel, famed author, Holocaust survivor, and winner of the 1986 Nobel

* Clemens would get the bonus of the AL MVP in 1986, while in '85, for reasons still unclear, Gooden got just one first-place vote for NL MVP.

Peace Prize, who threw out the first pitch. As often happens with much-hyped pitchers' duels, this one was a dud.

Under the rotation system in place for a decade, 1986 would have been the year for a designated hitter in the World Series—and in odd-numbered years pitchers batted in all games in the Series. Before the 1986 post-season began, Commissioner Peter Ueberroth and the rules committee opted for a change: Rule of the park. So in the National League park the pitcher batted, keeping designated hitter Don Baylor's 31 homers and 94 RBI on the bench at Shea. Roger Clemens, batting for the first time in his career, bunted right to Keith Hernandez, the ultimate defender of the bunt. Hernandez hurried and bounced the throw to second. Everyone was safe. Three straight run-scoring hits followed, including what would be Bill Buckner's sole RBI of the World Series.

After the Mets cut the lead to 3–2, Davey Johnson let Gooden bat with two on and the Mets down by two in the fourth. He grounded out. After long home runs to Dave Henderson and Dwight Evans, Gooden walked off the mound in the fifth with the Mets down by four. Not pinch-hitting for Gooden was one of several controversial decisions. Davey Johnson also sat slumping Ray Knight and Mookie Wilson (hitting a combined .140 in the postseason) in favor of Howard Johnson and Danny Heep, who both went hitless in Game 2.

Gooden actually outlasted Clemens, who was pulled in the bottom of the fifth. Steve Crawford, who didn't have a win in 1986 until the playoffs, was credited with the 9–3 victory. As the NBC camera focused on the full moon, known in October as the harvest moon, Vin Scully commented, "It's been the Red Sox doing the harvesting." The press would do the harvesting of the Mets.

"Where did the magic go?" Ed Sherman asked in the *Chicago Tribune*. "The Super Team of 1986 is being '86ed' by a team that was left for dead after eight innings last Sunday in Anaheim," wrote Tim Rosaforte in the *Fort Lauderdale Sun-Sentinel*. Jim Murray of the *Los Angeles Times* said that sudden slugger Dave

Henderson "turned Dr. K into Dr. Gopher." *New York Times* columnist Dave Anderson said the 108-win Mets "were in shambles." Peter Pascarelli of the *Philadelphia Inquirer* wrote that the Mets were in "dire straits," and he didn't mean the British rock group. Though to quote lead guitarist Mark Knopfler from Dire Straits' 1986 Grammy-winning album *Brothers in Arms*, victory seemed "so far away."

Nine runs and 18 hits were the most allowed by the Mets in their 28-game postseason history—that was as many runs as the Mets allowed in their entire five-game victory over the Orioles in the '69 World Series. The '86 Mets had a lot of work to do to get their own world championship rings.

The Shea Stadium parking lot hawkers were desperate to dump their official World Series merchandise—and knockoffs—as midnight approached, their prices reducing with every step taken by patrons who just wanted to leave the windy, trash-strewn lot, the weekend a disaster. Both customer and seller were of the same mind, though different motivation: After this incredible season, was this the last time the Mets would play at Shea in 1986?

"The ballpark is the star," wrote Martin F. Nolan, author of the dystopian series *Logan's Run*—not named for former Boston Brave Johnny Logan. The *Boston Globe* published a special section with Red Sox essays from New England's literary set in October, an All-Star lineup of, among others, Stephen King, John Updike, David Halberstam, Doris Kearns Goodwin, George Will, and outgoing Yale president/incoming National League president A. Bartlett Giamatti. Nolan hit the sweet spot: "Fenway has been the talisman for the poetically inclined. It is old, it is idiosyncratic and a frequent citadel of dashed hopes—all enduring themes of literature. Fenway is the ultimate protagonist of lit'ry life, a survivor."

Albeit a little cramped and worn in the 1980s, Fenway was—and remains—New England's ecumenical shrine, and it was just a set of Sox shy of being the game's oldest park in 1986. Comiskey Park, christened on Chicago's South Side in 1910, plus Tiger Stadium, opened under a different name the same day as Fenway in 1912, also had survived the ballpark purge of the 1960s and 1970s. A lot about baseball is just surviving. If the '86 Mets wanted to survive the week and not go down as one of the best teams to ever flop in October, changes were in order.

Davey Johnson decided to go with a three-man rotation, dropping Sid Fernandez as starter in Game 4. He reinserted Ray Knight and Mookie Wilson into the lineup—Danny Heep would serve as designated hitter. And he told the players to skip the Monday workout at Fenway Park and relax at the Sheraton.

"We flew to Boston and I cancelled the workout," Davey Johnson stated, as if it weren't ingrained in Mets history as one of the franchise's greatest off-field decisions. "I couldn't get away with that today. If I did that today I'd probably be fined $250,000, I don't know. But I just felt like we needed a break, you know?"

Having barely survived the Astros, the Mets were flat at Shea to open the World Series. Did they need more reporters asking them why they weren't playing well, or the hassle of answering more questions about Gooden? And the Mets had just been to Fenway a month earlier for the charity game against the Red Sox, so they'd seen the big wall and taken a few swings at it. No one needed the extra rest more than Gary Carter. Calling every pitch of the Astros series, catching 28 innings in less than 28 hours, and feeling sore in every part of his body, Gary and his wife, Sandy, slept until noon, had room service, then slept again. "You think about it, of course, you're in the middle of the World Series, but mentally and physically, that's the best thing [Johnson] could have done," Sandy Carter said. "Maybe it was taking a chance."

No team had ever lost the first two games at home and won the World Series—at least not until the year before, when the Royals rallied to stun the Cardinals in seven games in the '85 Series. The history of the Red Sox could be wonderful—Ted Williams,

Bobby Doerr, Luis Tiant, Carlton Fisk, Fenway Park—and it could be haunting: seven-game World Series losses in 1946, 1967, and 1975, a track record of falling apart at crucial moments, and a fan base convinced that anything bad that could happen, would happen. Now they were up two games to none. All they had to do was win twice over the next week and a 68-year championship drought/plague would end at last. And you know who would have been a great pitcher to push them to that goal? Bob Ojeda.

No pitcher had ever faced his former team in the World Series the year after a trade. Bobby O. became the patron saint for pitchers wanting to stick it to their old teams. It didn't hurt that the Mets hung a crooked number on the Red Sox before he even took the mound.

If Lenny Dykstra's climactic home run to win Game 3 of the NLCS was one of the best endings in Mets history, Game 3 of the World Series had to be just about the best beginning. Everyone associated with the Mets was well aware that no major league team to that point had ever rallied from three games to none in the postseason . . . but three pitches into the game, everything felt different. Dykstra's home run down the right field line shocked the Fenway crowd and enlivened the Mets bench. "It hyped everyone up," Ojeda said after the game. "It was a shot in the arm for me"—though not literally. The lefty reported that his arm, for a change, felt fine.

Things were not fine for Boston's starting pitcher. The Mets hooted, hollered, and hammered thin-skinned—and, at 150 pounds, thin-framed—Dennis "Oil Can" Boyd. The son of a Negro Leaguer in Mississippi, Boyd took it as a sign of disrespect that the Mets had blown off the Monday workout with their team down two games to none. But that was just everyday Oil Can anger. When he didn't make the All-Star team in July he went into an All-Star fit. He wound up AWOL, suspended, hospitalized, and under observation for an ongoing drug problem, later admitting to ESPN that he was high on something every time he pitched. Oil Can still managed to win 16 games for the year.

Leadoff home runs can be one-pitch anomalies. It was the rest of the inning that confirmed the momentum shift. Backman and Hernandez both singled, and Carter doubled into the gap for a second run. "The Can is leaking in the first inning," Vin Scully remarked as action started in the Boston bullpen. Still, Boyd had a chance to get out of it with just the two runs. Darryl Strawberry fanned on a 3–2 pitch, his 17th K in 29 postseason at bats. Then Boyd got Ray Knight to hit a grounder to third with the runner breaking for home. Hernandez would have been out from here to Hartford, so he stopped and headed back to third. Gedman threw back to Wade Boggs in the baseline instead of shortstop Spike Owen at the bag. Safe! There was one problem: Carter was standing next to third base. Now *he* was in a rundown, dead to rights. Hernandez faked a dash home and Marty Barrett stopped and looked back to third, allowing Carter to dive back into second. "Score the Play Moe to Larry to Curly" was the *New York Times* headline the next day for a play that looked like a postscript to "The Curly Shuffle." N'*yuk*! N'*yuk*! N'*yuk*!

Danny Heep, the first designated hitter in Mets history, then singled up the middle to score both Hernandez and Carter. Boyd's comment that he would master the Mets had rubbed the opposition the wrong way—and his manager. "I remember the lines across the paper: 'Oil Can Boyd said *I can beat the Mets*,'" McNamara recalled years later for ESPN. "Well, we were down 4–0 after the first inning and I could have choked him for, you know, let a sleeping dog lie."

Ojeda lulled the Sox into a slumber, payback for his Boston tenure that grew sour with time. Undrafted in 1978 out of his hometown College of the Sequoias, the California lefty signed with Boston for $500 and a ticket to Elmira, New York. Just once in parts of six seasons did he throw 200 innings for the Red Sox, and his career ERA at Fenway coming into that night was 4.39. Longtime Frank Cashen lieutenant Lou Gorman, hired as Red Sox general manager in January 1984, made several good trades:

acquiring Don Baylor, Tom Seaver, Dave Henderson, and Spike Owen during the '86 season. He viewed the trade of Bob Ojeda the previous December as shoring up Boston's system with players he was familiar with from the Mets, and bringing back a promising young arm in Calvin Schiraldi. The ever candid Ojeda, on the other hand, told NBC, "Part of me is still here, beyond a doubt because I left some blood here and some tears here, as dramatic as that sounds, and I grew up here. But I belong somewhere else now."

Ojeda never let Boston in the game and won his 20th game of the year—regular and postseason combined—on that bloody, teary field. Boyd settled down, retiring 18 of 19 Mets after Heep's hit, but in the seventh a two-run single by Carter made it 6–1. Carter ended the inning by being caught in a rundown—this time the Red Sox got him, though it did take four throws. Roger McDowell finished the five-hitter, the first World Series game won by the Mets in 13 years. Dating back to 1973, the Mets had lost four straight Series games. They were ready to start a new streak.

Ron Darling was coming home. Born in Hawaii, where his father served as an Air Force mechanic, he grew up in Massachusetts, watching the backs of Jim Rice and Dwight Evans from the Fenway bleachers. Now he would face them at Fenway in the World Series. Though he'd pitched well against the Red Sox three days earlier, that was in the familiar surroundings of Shea Stadium, where it was easier to convince himself that it was business as usual, even though it was the first game of the World Series. Pitching in Boston was different.

Fenway was known yet unknown, a park he'd never pitched in but knew intimately. For all the people the Worcester-raised, Yale-educated, *GQ* cover boy might have had in the stands pulling for him—or, pulling for him to pitch well but for the Sox to win—plenty of others called to him in that unmistakable accent, "Dahling, you suck!" Then he saw his father on the field. Ron Darling

Sr. was part of the color guard for that night's national anthem. They stood near each other on the field while Natalie Cole sang the anthem, father and son exchanging only a quick greeting and a handshake, but as Ron Jr. recalled in *The Complete Game*, a meeting on the field in the biggest game of his life with the man who taught him to play was "enough to erase the thought of what my arm might have been telling me out in the bullpen."

He labored through the first two innings. Rice came up with a man on third and two outs in the first inning and walked. Don Baylor, making his first World Series appearance after 2,072 regular season games—and four losing ALCS—also walked. With the bases full, Darling stayed ahead of Evans and got him to ground out to end the inning. Though old high school nemesis Rich Gedman doubled to start the second inning, he was stranded at third when Wade Boggs lined out. Darling allowed baserunners in all but one inning—none scored.

Mets wives watched from left field. At Shea Stadium they were almost always behind home plate, protected by an attendant from gawkers and drunks. At Fenway they were on their own. "We were so far out," recalled Sandy Carter, whose husband always waved his glove or made a discreet acknowledgment that he'd spied her in the stands. Not so at Fenway. "He wasn't stretching his neck, but he could not find us in the stands. [The Mets] put the Boston wives right behind home plate; they put us in left field. It was a wild crowd out there. They weren't really nice to us when they found out we were Mets wives."

Boston's battery couldn't figure out how to pitch to Gary Carter with a man on in the fourth inning. Al Nipper was making his first outing in 17 days—and was Boston's second choice for the start. The Red Sox had acquired Tom Seaver with the idea that if they reached the World Series, he would start Game 4. Injured Tom Terrific could not pitch, so Ordinary Al did.

Nipper cruised the first time through the lineup, but his luck ended with Carter's second at bat. He crushed a Nipper fastball over the Green Monster to put the Mets on the board. Later in the game against Steve Crawford, Carter hit a curveball over the net and under a yellow van across Lansdowne Street. It was his second consecutive three RBI game. When Gary Carter dreamed of playing in the World Series, this was what he imagined. And Sandy Carter had a great view of both home runs in left field, and a great comeback to the rude fans around her. "I could say, 'Ha, ha, that's my husband hitting that ball right there over that fence.'" Lenny Dykstra's wife, Terri, did not have as good a view of her husband's second home run in as many nights, but the result was the same. This one even had some pinball action, bouncing into the right field stands after it hit Dwight Evans's glove.

Roger McDowell, who had not allowed a run in 11 postseason innings, surrendered two runs in the eighth to make it 6–2, but Jesse Orosco finished up as Mets fans chanted "Let's go Mets" at Fenway, the hometown crowd too worn out and too bummed out to retaliate. The World Series that had looked like a Mets romp before it started, and a Red Sox runaway two games in, was now even. And the home team had yet to win a game.

That ended Thursday night, as did Bruce Hurst's World Series scoreless streak at 15⅓ innings. He allowed a Tim Teufel homer in the eighth and a two-out RBI single to Mookie Wilson in the ninth, but Hurst completed the 4–2 win by fanning Lenny Dykstra. With the Red Sox beating up Dwight Gooden once more and regaining the World Series advantage, Boston fans were back in their full-throated glory, taunting Darryl Strawberry with chants of "Dar-ryl! Dar-ryl! Dar-ryl!" Strawberry turned and tipped his cap. The crowd roared.

Could the Red Sox win the world championship that had eluded them since 1918? That team had been anchored by 23-year-old Babe Ruth, who won two World Series games on the mound and was in left field when the final out was made in Game 6—as a late-inning defensive replacement.

13

"Can You Believe This Ballgame at Shea?"

October 25, 1986

METS–RED SOX WAS A BITTER FEUD THAT EXISTED FOR ALL OF 10 days and then melted away like an October blizzard. One side has learned to get past it. The other sees it as its greatest achievement. Gary Thorne knows both sides.

The Mets gave Thorne a shot in New York after just one year of minor league broadcasting experience, plopping him in the radio booth to work with the venerable Bob Murphy in 1985. Thorne was an assistant district attorney in his native Bangor, Maine, but he still called hockey games at his alma mater, University of Maine, and helped bring minor league baseball back to the state as part owner of the Class AAA Maine Guides. Peter Gammons spent summers in the area and raved in the *Boston Globe* about Thorne's calls. The Mets listened and hired Thorne.

To ask a born-and-bred Mainer if he grew up a Red Sox fan is like asking if he likes melted butter with his lobster. Ed Coleman, a future Mets radio host raised on the Red Sox in Massachusetts in the same era, put it this way: "The agony is passed down from generation to generation."

"It was my whole life during the Ted Williams era as a kid," said Thorne, now an Orioles broadcaster, his booming voice turning the telephone into a transistor radio dialed back to the mid-1980s. "People lived and breathed by the ballgames. It was talked about as much as the weather is talked about, which is saying a hell of a lot. So it mattered. It mattered a lot."

It mattered all across the country. Boston, the town that adored baseball yet was treated so rough by the baseball gods, was on the cusp of breaking a 68-year drought. That they might beat New York—hated whether the Yankees or the Mets were running roughshod—made it all the more appealing nationwide. Yet for all the plotlines and twists and turns, the 1986 World Series had been unmemorable. Not a single lead had changed hands, three of the games weren't close, and Bruce Hurst made small leads seem huge in the other two games. Tim Teufel's error in the opener and two first-inning plays in Game 3—Lenny Dykstra's leadoff home run and Boston's botched rundown—were the signature plays of the World Series through five games. Yet Game 6 would make the Series worthy of all the eyes on it. No one would be sitting at a spring training game in March of 1987 asking, "Who won the World Series last year?" This game you could not forget. Even if you tried.

Bob Ojeda, pitching on three days' rest for the first time in his career, faced Bill Buckner with one on and one out in the first. Though he had a .282 career average against the Mets in what amounted to a season's worth of games (156) as a Dodger and Cub, New York's pitching had improved a bit since Buckner moved to the other league in 1984. He stepped to the plate in Game 6 batting .174, one run scored, one knocked in, and nary a walk in 23 World Series at bats. Ojeda started him off with a ball and then the heavens opened up and disgorged . . . an actor.

Michael Sergio had been on the ABC soap opera *Loving*, but he had also appeared in an *ABC Afterschool Special* in the spring of 1986 called "Getting Even: A Wimp's Revenge." And on the night of Game 6 he did just that—if you can call jumping out of an airplane and landing on the field at a packed stadium wimpy. Foolish? Yeah. He was incensed by a Red Sox banner tied to a mass of balloons during Game 4 in Boston, and came up with a plan. He told David Letterman two nights after the jump that it was "the easiest jump I've ever done."

Today such a stunt would be cause to clear the stadium and deploy SWAT teams—a threat to homeland security. In 1986—15 years before 9/11 changed unauthorized aerial ascents on crowded public areas from prank to peril—Sergio was met by two stadium security guards who escorted him to the Mets dugout, pausing long enough to get a high-five from Ron Darling. Lucky for Sergio, a judge with Mets season tickets denied the $10,000 bail the district attorney's office asked for, but Sergio's later refusal to name the pilot would get him sentenced for contempt. While he was serving time at the Metropolitan Correction Center in Manhattan during June of 1987, Banner Day's most insistent and repeated bed-sheeted plea was "Free Sergio!" Senator Alfonse D'Amato intervened with Transportation Secretary Elizabeth Dole, asking to release his constituent on "humanitarian grounds." There is no known tie to the influence of Banner Day, but the record does show that six days after the banner displays, Sergio was free three weeks into a six-month sentence. Everyone loves a winner.

But on the night of October 25, 1986, it looked like the winner would be Boston. Sergio's disturbance caused barely a ripple on the field. Mets second baseman Wally Backman saw the parachutist appear "right over my head" and land on the infield grass between the mound and first base. "It was different," he conceded. "I thought it was kind of cool what he did, but that wasn't my focus. My focus was trying to win that game." Less than one minute after Sergio touched down a dozen feet from the mound, Ojeda threw the next pitch.

Buckner flew out and Jim Rice walked, bringing up Dwight Evans. Mets fans tried a derisive "Dew-ey" chant like the one

Darryl Strawberry had endured at Fenway. (They had much more luck with the "Ro-ger" chants for Clemens.) Evans, a Boston hero in Game 6 of the 1975 World Series against Cincinnati, rifled a double to score Wade Boggs with the first run of this Game 6. Because the ball hit the base of the wall near the 371-foot mark and caromed to Lenny Dykstra, Rice held at third. Playing in the only World Series of his Hall of Fame career—he'd been injured during the 1975 World Series—Rice was still standing at third when Rich Gedman flied out to end the first inning.

The bottom of the first was much less eventful, thanks to Roger Clemens. Pitching with five or more days' rest he was an unbeatable 9–0 in '86, and he had a track record for closing down titles: winning the clincher in the College World Series and the Class AA title for New Britain, both during the summer of 1983, plus the deciding contest for the '86 pennant 10 days earlier. Clemens was the man you wanted on the mound. The Mets had wanted him, too, and might have had him if the current Red Sox GM had been more diligent.

Back in 1981 Frank Cashen's new regime chose Clemens from a junior college outside Houston in the 12th round of that draft. The lone memorable Met picked ahead of Clemens that year was a fifth-round infielder who never got above Double-A but later became the team's GM: Steve Phillips. With Clemens, the Mets had the bad luck that none of their top scouts had seen him pitch (two of Clemens's starts were rained out). The Mets hesitated in negotiations and the University of Texas swooped in and carried him away to Austin, with legendary coach Cliff Gustafson telling Clemens he'd be a key member of a College World Series–winning staff for his home state. And he was. But the number one pitcher for Texas—and the 1983 College World Series Most Outstanding Player—was not Clemens, but another UT pitcher from Houston: Calvin Schiraldi.

With three first-round picks that year the Mets could have had both Clemens and Schiraldi. The Mets spent the fourth overall pick in '83 on Eddie Williams, an infielder who never played 100 games in a season in the majors, and never played one inning as a Met. One selection after the Red Sox chose Clemens with the 19th pick, the Mets took outfielder Stanley Jefferson. And then with the 27th pick they chose Schiraldi. Within three years the Mets traded Williams, Jefferson, and Schiraldi, bringing back veterans who helped them win. Of course it is always tempting to imagine a what-if rotation of Nolan Ryan, Dwight Gooden, and Clemens—especially during the first four innings of Game 6, when the Rocket had a no-hitter going.

Though it seemed the Mets went down easily, they made Clemens work. He threw 73 pitches through those four innings (49 strikes), with a third of those pitches reaching 95 miles per hour or higher. The pitch count was a few years away from becoming an adhered-to number for starting pitchers, but pitching coaches and managers kept an eye on it in '86. And then they ignored it. Clemens had thrown 143 pitches in the opener of the ALCS, which he lost. His next start was three days later. Now he was well rested and held a 2–0 lead in the bottom of the fifth. Roger McDowell was throwing in the Mets bullpen as the bottom of the order had a chance to bat, though that was a slight concern given that Clemens had pitched to one batter over the minimum.

Darryl Strawberry, the only Met to reach base so far against Clemens, got aboard with his second walk. He stole second and on the next pitch Ray Knight singled up the middle to break up the no-hitter, the shutout, and the mood. Mookie Wilson's single to right hopped off Dwight Evans's chest for an error—no doubt hitting a spot where the turf had been replaced due to marauding fans more than a month earlier. Knight took third and the Mets had men on the corners with nobody out. As Danny Heep batted for Rafael Santana, the crowd mock-chanted Clemens. A double play should have shut them up, but this DP tied the game—the first time in the Series the score was knotted at any point beyond 0–0. With the bases cleared, Davey Johnson had no reason to bat for his starter. On the 99th pitch by *Ro-ger, Ro-ger*, Ojeda grounded out to second.

After Ojeda retired the Red Sox in what turned out to be his last inning, the Mets put runners on the corners against Clemens in the bottom of the sixth, but he caught Carter looking and got Strawberry to swing at the high fastball he'd been laying off earlier in the game. His groundout ended the threat.

The Red Sox took the lead in the seventh against McDowell by playing small ball: no hits, a walk, an error, and a groundout on a hit-and-run. The lone hit by the Red Sox ended the inning. Rich Gedman singled to left and Rene Lachemann waved Jim Rice home. Wilson, long maligned for his arm and coming off shoulder surgery, gunned the ball on the fly to Carter, who applied the tag for the third out. Mookie's two assists were as many as any outfielder in the World Series. Both his throws stunned Boston, snuffed rallies, and ended innings.

Still, the Red Sox had the lead. Clemens retired the Mets in order in the seventh and reporters in the press box started toying with potential leads for the Sunday paper. When they looked up from their keyboards, they saw that Clemens was out of the game. With Dave Henderson on first, Spike Owen laid down a bunt—a strange move if the pitcher was up next. Clemens was summoned back to the bench, removing his batting glove and helmet. A blister had opened up on his right hand in the fifth inning, keeping him from throwing breaking pitches. He threw 135 pitches in seven innings against the Mets, 3 fewer pitches than he'd thrown in his record-setting, 20-strikeout, complete game against the Mariners in April.

Thus began an argument that still continues in dark corners of New England. Did the pitcher ask out or did the manager yank him? On one side you have John McNamara, whom Dave Stapleton, among others, called "probably the worst manager

I ever played for, from the minor leagues on up." On the other side you have Roger Clemens, his reputation forever damaged by legal wrangling after his trainer accused him of using steroids and human growth hormone during a late-career revival after he left the Red Sox in the late 1990s. In the middle stands pitching coach Bill Fischer, who offered this insight in the ESPN series *Battle Lines*: "From that point in time, Roger could have [gone] back out there, I think, but John decided against it." As with other questionable maneuvers, it doesn't matter why it was done so much as that it was done. That's what remains all these years later.

And while the idea of removing the Cy Young winner and MVP two innings shy of a world championship in favor of the much-maligned Boston bullpen seems insane in retrospect, the truth is that the bullpen hadn't cost Boston anything. So far. Schiraldi had pitched just once before that night, getting the save in Game 1; Bob Stanley had logged six innings in relief. Neither man had allowed a run to that point and the bullpen's 3.40 ERA was just a smidge worse than the Mets pen (3.21).

That McNamara chose to use rookie Mike Greenwell to bat for Clemens is yet more grist for the mill. Don Baylor, the 1979 MVP who would win a Silver Slugger and finish in the top 15 in the MVP voting in 1986, had two opportunities to pinch-hit in the eighth inning, yet he remained on the bench. Mike Greenwell, not the All-Star he would become, but a green outfielder without enough service time to even qualify as a rookie, struck out as pinch hitter for Clemens. Then when McDowell walked the next two batters and southpaw Jesse Orosco came in to face lefty-swinging Bill Buckner . . . well, let's just say Game 6 was, is, and will always be a second-guesser's paradise.

Future Manager of the Year Don Baylor*questioned John McNamara's decision, too. Baylor, who had started 13 times at

* Don Baylor, the first manager in Colorado Rockies history, was voted the 1995 National League Manager of the Year. Of course, the award is of dubious worth because John McNamara was the AL Manager of the Year for 1986.

first base with just one error in 1986, said after the game that he was "a fucking cheerleader." He watched Buckner line out to center against the lefty, snuffing the eighth-inning rally. Baylor never was used in Game 6.

Not that it was Davey Johnson's finest managing, either. He brought in his best reliever, Orosco, to throw one pitch. After stranding the bases full in the top of the eighth, Orosco was pinch-hit for to begin the bottom of the eighth because the manager had opted not to double switch. He chose the right pinch hitter, though, because Lee Mazzilli singled to start the inning. Dykstra bunted back to the mound and Calvin Schiraldi made the wrong choice, or at least the wrong throw, bouncing the ball to second. Everyone was safe. Loath to bunt under most circumstances, Johnson doubled down on the bunt and Wally Backman's sacrifice moved both runners into scoring position. McNamara countered with an intentional walk to Keith Hernandez to get to Gary Carter. Much is made, fittingly, of his next at bat, but if Carter did not lift a long fly to left to score Mazzilli, that would have been his last plate appearance of the season. And, by swinging at a 3–0 pitch, had Carter made an unproductive out—or hit into a double play—his legacy, as well as that of the '86 team, might be far different today. We'll leave the rest of the mid-'80s conjecture to *Back to the Future*.

Extra innings. A game like this seemed bound for extras, just like yet another Game 6 that is a candidate for that elusive "Greatest Game Ever Played" title. That night in 1975 Red Sox manager Darrell Johnson, working for the '86 Mets as advance scout (and providing the Mets with all kinds of intel about Fenway and his former team), had plenty of tough decisions against the '75 Reds and was bailed out by late home runs by Bernie Carbo and Carlton Fisk. In the top of the 10th in 1986, it looked like John McNamara would get bailed out by Dave Henderson. The game was still going on because the Mets had blown a two-on, none-out situation in the bottom of the ninth when Howard Johnson, batting for Kevin Elster with nobody out, bunted and missed the first pitch. He swung away on the next pitch and struck out on the third pitch from Schiraldi. Lee Mazzilli then launched a deep fly to the warning track, which would score the imaginary runner used in perfect worlds and Wiffle ball. Lenny Dykstra flied out to end the threat.

As Dave Henderson strode to the plate to start the 10th, NBC showed his home run against the Angels and flashed his .409 World Series average. He swung through Rick Aguilera's first pitch, then teed off on his second. The ball shot out to left field and hit just above the *A* in the *Newsday* sign. Home run. The hundreds of writers scattered through the main and auxiliary press boxes started working in earnest on their stories for the late edition. It was approaching midnight. When Marty Barrett singled home Wade Boggs to make it 5–3, many members of the press began moving toward the clubhouse en masse. With hundreds of media descending on the same place, you didn't want to be at the back of the pack. Cover enough games and you know what impending defeat—or victory—looks like. At least you think you do.

"Everybody around me, including me, we all got up—in unison—and started making our way downstairs," recalled Ed Randall, then a reporter for Canada's TSN stationed in the auxiliary press box in right field, and now host of his own radio show on WFAN in New York as well as programs for MLB. "Because how could they possibly blow a two-run lead?"

Bob Costas was in the Red Sox locker room with champagne they'd borrowed from the Mets chilling in ice buckets on wheels. Cellophane was on the lockers to protect the Boston players' belongings from the champagne spray. Jean Yawkey, widow of Tom Yawkey, who'd owned the team from 1933 until his death in 1976 and only knew October anguish, was on her way down to the locker room. The World Series trophy was there already.

With two outs and a chance to add to the lead, up stepped Bill Buckner, already suffering from a painful left ankle he originally injured a decade earlier as one of the fastest Dodgers. Hobbled and all, his six steals were still second on the station-to-station Red Sox in 1986. A former batting champion, All-Star, beloved Cub, and, ironically, the AL leader in assists by a first baseman in '86, he'd achieved his second straight 100 RBI season. But he couldn't buy a hit in the World Series with men on base. In Game 6 alone he'd stranded nine runners. And now in the 10th he was hit by a pitch. Right on the hip. He shambled to first—a perfect time for a pinch runner: Dave Stapleton, whom you'd assume would come on to play first for Buckner in the bottom of the 10th anyway. He'd performed the task for every Boston win in the post-season. Stapleton even loosened up and stretched out, anticipating going in. Like Don Baylor, he never got the call in Game 6.

Wally Backman flew out to left to start the bottom of the 10th, and Vin Scully continued to talk about what might have been for the Mets. "It's tough enough to lose. It's a long enough winter, anyway, but when you have made a decision and it will stick in your craw all winter, it will make the off-season almost interminable." As he spoke, the cameras focused on the morose Mets manager sitting in his accustomed spot between pitching coach Mel Stottlemyre and the water fountain. Davey Johnson got up, took a step as if he were going to pace, and sat back down with a thud, sighing and putting his head back. "And that's the life of a big league manager," Scully narrated.

"You look back and see Davey's head going against the wall," Mookie Wilson later explained. "He's probably trying to figure out, 'How am I going to explain this to the press?' You look down that whole dugout and everybody is sitting there saying, 'Wow. We blew it.' Plain and simple. Some people probably tell you, 'We knew it.' That's a lie."

The ultimate irony was that the man who hated the bunt,* who played for the manager in Baltimore who loathed the bunt, was pictured on his first solo baseball card in 1965 squaring to bunt—with his hands in the wrong position. After all those wins during the 1986 season, the ninth-inning bunt that wasn't was being fitted like an albatross to wear around his neck. Size 108.

Keith Hernandez flied out to center. Two down in the 10th inning. Mookie Wilson was sitting on the bench, his spot not due up for three batters—or five months, when spring training began.

"Here's the catcher, Gary Carter," public address announcer Jack Franchetti said with as much enthusiasm as if there were two outs in the first inning in April. Hernandez did not want to watch it end, could not watch it end. He walked through the dugout, along the catwalk to the clubhouse, banged through the door, and paced at his locker for a moment until he saw Darrell Johnson, the Red Sox manager who'd lost the excruciating 1975 World Series, sitting in the Mets manager's office. Hernandez went in and sat down with Darrell Johnson (no relation to Davey), plus public relations director Jay Horwitz, to watch the end on TV. They didn't say much. Hernandez, who smoked only during the season and gave it up after he retired, lit another cigarette. He said the game was so tense he spent a lot of it standing on the steps behind the dugout so he wouldn't be caught smoking on TV. He went through two and a half packs during Game 6. In the manager's office with the game—and the season—seemingly over, Hernandez cracked a beer. Gary Carter cracked a hit.

The pitcher's spot was due up, the result of an eighth-inning double switch that infuriated Darryl Strawberry. With the season on the line, the Mets sent up a rookie: Kevin Mitchell. Contrary to urban myth, Mitchell was in the dugout the whole time, pants

* It is ironic that the Mets actually sacrificed more times than the Red Sox in the World Series, 6–4. And the Mets were sixth in the majors in 1986 with 75 bunts, 43 by pitchers.

Kevin Mitchell doing it all, 1986 DAN CARUBIA

on, ready to pinch-hit. Where else would he have been? "I'll tell everybody right now: How in the hell was I able to be on deck and get a base hit? I'm a rookie. What the hell am I going to be doing in the clubhouse?" Mitchell said, denying the oft-told story that he had taken off his pants in the clubhouse in the 10th while making plane reservations for home in San Diego. "Everybody has a story to build up the hype. I'm in a World Series game. And I'm learning something, my first World Series. Mookie Wilson told me, 'Be prepared to hit.' . . . Why would I be making a reservation when the Mets pay for your flight to go home? As a rookie? Tell me that."

As an aside, don't ask him about cutting off a cat's head—a myth started by Dwight Gooden and perpetuated even in recent years by Darryl Strawberry. Suffice to say, it's also false. But do ask Mitchell about his at bat against his former minor league roommate, Calvin Schiraldi.

"That was true," Mitchell said. "He would always talk about how he'd pitch me. And I took the first pitch for a strike on an inside fastball.* He always said that he'd start me off with a fastball inside and then he'd throw me a slider. And he did it. And I looked for the slider on the next pitch and got it."

His line drive off the slider landed in center for a hit. The tying run was on. Pitching coach Bill Fischer came out to talk to Schiraldi. "New York, New York" played briefly, and two rolls of toilet paper landed behind home plate at the same instant as strike one. Compared to the coins, batteries, and golf balls the Red Sox outfielders had been dodging all Series, this was like fictional grocery store manager Mr. Whipple throwing Charmin. A foul ball made it 0–2—one strike away.

The toilet paper was cleaned up and the lady behind home plate rolled her arms like a perpetual motion machine. Bo Field, a New Jersey waitress who'd owned the best seats in the house since Shea

* It was a foul ball on a checked swing.

Stadium opened in 1964, rolled and rolled her arms as the Mets rallied and rallied. Author and arbiter of all things Mets, Greg Prince, of the website *Faith and Fear in Flushing*, later mused: "One would like to think the Mets voted her at least a quarter-share for her role in securing our last world championship, but probably not."

Was it Bo Field's mojo? Was it the tripartite of bad karma—naming Marty Barrett Miller Lite Player of the Game and Bruce Hurst as World Series MVP, and a five-second flash of "Congratulations Red Sox" on DiamondVision, all coming up prematurely in the 10th inning? No. It was Ray Knight looping a single to center that scored Carter and sent Mitchell to third. Shea Stadium, which had been epically loud the entire night, rose to ear-crushing levels again after an understandable lull while contemplating the ending of the World (Series). Now the crowd wanted someone else's world to end. Schiraldi's night ended. Bob Stanley jogged in from the bullpen.

Mookie Wilson is a man of God now. He always was spiritual, but now he gives sermons and at the 2015 Queens Baseball Convention he had a large room full of Mets fans rapt as if preaching gospel, the gospel according to Mook.

"I was as focused as I've ever been in my life. . . . Usually it's like one to three pitches and I'm sitting in the dugout . . . I'm thinking, 'Just don't strike out. Put the ball in play.' The greatest thing that could have happened was the wild pitch."

How did he avoid the pitch? "I was taught, 'Don't get hit.' That ball hurts. . . . I was actually cheating. Stanley throws the sinker, so I was actually looking away. . . . So when I saw the ball come inside, I panicked. Yes, I panicked. So I just got out of the way," he said, snapping his fingers as quickly as he jackknifed out of the way of Stanley's pitch. "I think the catcher expected something away also, and when the pitch came inside, it caught him a little off guard."

"It was a sinker that ran inside a little bit and I didn't get it," explained Rich Gedman, a coach in the Red Sox system since 2011. "I think back on it all the time. I think I made a very good effort at it, but I didn't catch it. The thing I always tell people after the fact is that I'm more disappointed that I dropped the ball when I went to pick it up, because I think we had a chance at the plate."

Mitchell scored standing up. The game was tied. It felt like a dream to Mets fans. On the other side it had become a nightmare. "Can you believe this game at Shea?" Vin Scully asked almost 30 million people.

Knight, stranded on second base to end the ninth inning, was on second once more representing the winning run. Wilson, meanwhile, fouled off ball after ball, six in all. "I came up to the plate, we were down. I'm still at the plate, it's tied. I can't lose, man. I'm playing with house money," Mookie said. "That took a lot of pressure off, but I still did not want to strike out." He did not.

The 10th pitch produced the most famous ground ball in Mets history, if not baseball history. It bounced near home plate, took a high hop, and then landed on the dirt just inside the grass cutout near first. On the second roll it went through Bill Buckner's legs. Ray Knight scored the winning run. Many have contended—including Mookie himself—that Wilson would have beaten Bob Stanley to the bag even if Buckner had fielded the ball cleanly. If Wilson had been safe at first on a close play, history could have been entirely different. Knight would not have scored on the play. Howard Johnson, the next batter, may have made an out and the Red Sox could have won in a subsequent inning. But they didn't. Instead, mayhem ensued.

In the visiting clubhouse a few minutes later, the first baseman was surrounded by so many writers that infielder Ed Romero, whose locker was next to Buckner's, took one look, grabbed his clothes, and changed in the trainers' room. Buckner had nowhere to hide. He told the mob of reporters that the ball skipped instead of bounced.

There was no way to explain, though. It does not really matter how a miracle happens, just that it did.

⁓

The first minutes after midnight marked a tolling of the bell for Mets fans old and young, a prayer for the deceased and a promise to those not yet born. Vin Scully would make the national call about the "little roller up along first," which was the way he called every nubber up either baseline throughout the Series. As Mookie Wilson's fateful grounder went "behind the bag," it became the moment that Mets fans could place themselves for decades to come, an unquestionable moment of joy for generations. The future announcers of the Mets were fans of the team—or on the team—living and dying with each swing by Mookie in Game 6.

Gary Cohen, an announcer in the minor leagues in 1986, was in his Virginia apartment jumping up and down, unaware that by the time baseball started again he would be part of the Red Sox family—as an announcer in Triple-A Pawtucket, Rhode Island.* Josh Lewin, who turned 18 the night of Game 6, was a freshman at Northwestern University outside Chicago, and was at that very moment pledging a fraternity based on the raucous atmosphere of the baseball-imbued gathering in front of the very large TV at the Lambda Chi Alpha house. Unlike Ed Randall and others, Howie Rose's job was to stay in the auxiliary press box in right field at Shea Stadium, phoning in the goings-on for WCBS radio. "When Mookie hit the ground ball, I just went utterly berserk. I don't know how I even composed myself to do the 30-second voicer, but that's what we do. We're supposedly professionals. I did

---

* When Gary Cohen went for his interview in Pawtucket in December 1986 and admitted he'd gone mad with joy after the Buckner error, his interviewer was quiet for a time. He then asked, "You're not a Yankees fan, are you?" Cohen said no. And the man responded, "Then don't worry." Cohen spent two years in Pawtucket before being hired by the New York Mets and has been with the team ever since.

that and ran downstairs." Ron Darling ran onto the field to join his teammates celebrating at home plate, realizing it also meant he would start Game 7. Keith Hernandez was hugging everyone in Davey Johnson's office, having not moved because of the mojo created sitting there as the agony turned to ecstasy. Ralph Kiner, who would turn 64 the night of Game 7, was in the house for Game 6—the epic October helping distract him from the sudden passing of his mentor and closest friend from his playing days: Hall of Famer Hank Greenberg.

But none of those past, present, or future Mets announcers was at the microphone at that incredible moment. That was Bob Murphy's job.

> *The worst that could happen is to go to the 11th inning. Mookie Wilson still hoping to win it for New York. Three and two the count. And the pitch by Stanley . . . and a ground ball . . . trickling . . . it is a fair ball . . . gets by Buckner, rounding third Knight. The Mets will win the ballgame! The Mets win! They win!*

After several seconds of nothing but cheers from the crowd, Murphy's radio partner, Gary Thorne, finally spoke.

"Unbelievable. The Red Sox in stunned disbelief." Thorne was in stunned disbelief himself. A son of Maine—where every man, woman, and child is raised a devout Red Sox worshiper—Thorne admitted he always feels a little stunned at the memory: "I watch that play and I still can't believe it happened." Massachusetts-born Ed Coleman, who would spend most of the next three decades in New York covering the Mets for WFAN, grew up in a house with a father who could actually remember the Red Sox winning the 1918 World Series (the senior Coleman was eight at the time). In 1986 Coleman was steeped enough in the lore and loathing of Boston's near misses to handle panicked fans as afternoon drive-time host on WBZ. As he reminisced about that fateful game, which he watched in a Boston bar with future Red Sox announcer Sean McDonough, Coleman, unprompted, quoted Thorne's "stunned disbelief" line to describe his feeling the moment it happened. "I think he hit it on the head pretty much."

On NBC Vin Scully and Joe Garagiola did not utter a word for almost three and a half minutes. The images of the joyous Mets and the heartbroken Red Sox told the story better than even Scully could. Shea Stadium was bedlam, utter bedlam, for all to see. Scully didn't try to sum it up, to shout over the shouting—from the first inning on he spoke about the electricity of the Shea crowd—and he let the images speak for themselves. Scully, rarely boastful in a career worth boasting about, told writer Cee Angi during his 65th season at the microphone in 2014 that being silent after such moments "really is my trademark. Day to day, week in, week out. If something happens and the crowd roars, I shut up." It is hard to call it silence when the stadium was so loud that Ed Randall and the reporters stuck in limbo in the old Jets locker room couldn't hear the sound on the TV cranked full blast while the stadium visibly shook above them, but the absence of words on the NBC broadcast provided this moment an opportunity to breathe, for reflection by those who cherished the game, especially by the people who treasured the team that had just pulled off what minutes earlier seemed utterly impossible.

"It seemed like too long a pause," *New York Times* TV sports pundit Michael Goodwin opined the day after it happened, "but try to come up with a suggestion about what Scully or Garagiola could have said. They made the right choice." All that announcer silence allowed enough time to jump up and high-five everyone around you, make a quick call to someone who had made fun of you in the 1970s for being a Mets fan when Bruce Boisclair was the third-place hitter on the Mets while Thurman Munson batted in the same spot for the Yankees, then mumble a prayer of thanks (even if you hadn't been to church since parochial school) and flick back a tear of joy—all before Scully finally spoke again.

> *If one picture is worth a thousand words, you have seen about a million words, but more than that, you have seen an absolutely bizarre finish to Game 6 of the 1986 World Series. The Mets are not only alive, they are well, and they will play the Red Sox in Game 7 tomorrow.*

But Scully actually got that last part wrong. There was no deciding game the next day.

14

Haven't Had That Spirit Here Since 1969

October 26–27, 1986

It poured Sunday. The end of Daylight Savings Time gave an extra hour of sleep to all who stayed up late celebrating or just basking in the witnessing of a miracle. If 1969 was the miracle the press had called it, and if the transformation from last place to pennant winner in six weeks in 1973 was miraculous, then a three-run rally with two out and none on in extra innings to stave off elimination was miracle number three. Only two are required for sainthood.

No World Series team had ever come up in its last at bat trailing by two runs and wound up winning. When Gary Carter stepped to the plate in the 10th inning of Game 6, the Mets had a 1 percent chance of winning. Michael Mitchell, who wrote about win expectancy in the *SABR Baseball Research Journal* (Spring 2013), checked World Series elimination games since 1903 and verified that the Mets are the lone team to win whose chance of winning could be counted on one hand—or one finger. The next lowest figure is 6 percent, established by the 1960 Pirates (Game 7) and matched by the 2011 Cardinals, who came back from two runs down in the 10th inning of Game 6, though they had runners on base before two were out.

As for meteorology, the rain helped feed the legend of Game 6—and build the hype for Game 7. In Boston's last World Series against the Reds in 1975, Game 6 was rained out for three straight days at Fenway. When the teams finally played, the deferred expectation helped make the game crackle with energy from first pitch to last, ending in a home run and Carlton Fisk's Body English Boogie that forever changed the way we watch home runs on television. It was such an epic game that in memory many thought the Red Sox won the World Series on Fisk's blast. Boston wasn't so lucky. They had an early 3–0 lead in Game 7 in 1975 and lost in the ninth inning on a bloop hit by that year's National League MVP, Joe Morgan, with World Series MVP Pete Rose belly-flopping into third on the play, as if additional emphasis was needed. There was a lesson there for both the Mets and Red Sox: A great Game 6 may be talked about forever, but it guarantees nothing in Game 7.

The rainout allowed a day for everyone to catch up, so those who were out Saturday night, or out to lunch on the first six games of the World Series, could still catch the game for all the marbles. And did they ever watch. For Game 7 the 38.9 rating was the fourth highest ever and 34 million was the largest audience in history for a World Series game. And that was going against ABC's *Monday Night Football.* The Giants-Redskins game had its lowest rating (8.8) to that point since *MNF* started in 1970. Even in a market of divided loyalties, with first place on the line in the contentious Eastern Division of the National Football Conference (a matchup that would prove to be a dress rehearsal for the NFC Championship Game), the local rating in New York was a Nielsen rout in favor of the national pastime: 55.6 to 8.6, with NBC and the Mets pulling a 71 share. The deciding game of the World Series would be a lot closer on the field. Though many who saw the game and even played in it say they never doubted the Mets would win, the outcome was far from assured.

The Mets had avoided a third showdown with Mike Scott in the NLCS by winning that memorable, extra-inning Game 6 in the Astrodome, but this even more memorable extra-inning Game 6 against Boston just got the Mets another date with Bruce Hurst. The same Mets who felt that there was no way they could beat Mike Scott if there was a Game 7 in Houston felt the opposite way about a Game 7 in New York. Even if the opposing pitcher had proved almost as unhittable as Scott.

The extra day allowed the Red Sox to start Bruce Hurst, 2–0 with a 1.06 ERA in the Series, instead of erratic Oil Can Boyd. Ron Darling had an extra day of rest, too, but unlike Hurst, the Mets starter did not continue to dominate his opponent. Both Mookie Wilson and Bill Buckner received cheers in the first inning—even the hardest-core Mets fan could not deny Buckner the tiny validation of a two-out single. He was stranded. The first blows came down in the second inning.

Dwight Evans and then Rich Gedman homered to start the inning, Gedman's drive bouncing off Strawberry's glove and landing over the fence. He looked in his glove and jumped up and down when he saw it wasn't there. To many Mets fans, this drew on bitter memories from the last Game 7 they played. In 1973 Jon Matlack, the lone Met besides Darling to ever start three times in a World Series, had been brilliant in his first two outings and then allowed two home runs in an inning in Game 7. After the second home run in Oakland, Reggie Jackson leapt on home plate. Before Game 7 of the 1986 World Series, Jackson leapt to the phone and called the team that had eliminated his Angels in excruciating fashion less than two weeks earlier. Reggie spoke to Don Baylor, whom he once was traded for; John McNamara, whom he once played for; and Bill Buckner, whom he sympathized with, for obvious reasons. "Reggie told Buck that what happened last night was just part of the game," Baylor relayed in the clubhouse. "He told me just don't let the guys get down. It's easy at this point to just sit back and not take it to them. We're not going to sit back and just be a spectator."

Baylor was a spectator, however, sitting on the bench for the fourth time in the World Series. He would bat a mere 11 times against the Mets and hit .182. Baylor could have replaced Buckner, who hit .188 in 32 at bats. Both of them drove in one run apiece. Jim Rice, who hit .333 in 27 at bats, did not drive in a single run. He never had a chance. The Hall of Fame slugger led off an inning 15 times, each time the result of Buckner having made the third out.

Darling, who had retired all 12 Red Sox he faced with runners in scoring position in his first two starts (excluding Tim Teufel's Game 1 error), allowed a two-out single to Wade Boggs to make it 3–0 in the second. Back in the 1980s Mets fans weren't so fatalistic—that was Red Sox territory—but to some it had to feel a bit like Game 7 in 1973. But the '73 Mets did not have Keith Hernandez. Nor did they have Sid Fernandez. "See if the Mets pitchers can wake up the Mets hitters," Vin Scully said after Fernandez replaced Darling with two on and two out in the third inning.

Despite winning 16 games, fanning 200, and being in the top four in the NL for most strikeouts and fewest hits per nine innings, Fernandez was axed from the rotation when the Mets fell behind two games to none. He pitched twice in relief, tossing four innings to keep the Mets in Game 5 after Gooden was rocked. Now he was pitching to keep the Mets alive. Manager Davey Johnson was concerned but confident. The team had 40 come-from-behind victories, including the mother of all comebacks the previous game.

"Even though we were two runs down, nobody on, one strike away from being eliminated, we came back—that was the mentality of the club that we had built actually over three years," Johnson said in a 2015 interview. As for running a loose clubhouse, with Hernandez in his office in Game 6 as well as Orosco, McDowell, and others in the locker room during the climactic rally, Johnson had an answer for that. "They can say that guys were in there drinking beer or doing whatever. I call bullshit on that. Guys were still in the game and still felt like we had a chance. And we did. And we won.

Keith Hernandez on the field before Game 6 of the 1986 World Series
DAN CARUBIA

"And then the next day when we got down by three runs, nobody was worried. We were going to win that game. And we won it easy." Well, maybe not exactly easy.

Bruce Hurst retired the first four Mets on 11 pitches. After a Ray Knight single in the second, he set down every Met until the sixth. Though they hit some balls hard, Hurst's split-finger fastball seemed to mesmerize the Mets like Scott's—sans scuff. Hurst cruised through the order twice, pitching to one batter over the minimum. No other World Series MVP ever had to go out and prove the voters were right, the chicken-before-hatching counting department releasing the results when the Mets seemed dead in Game 6.* The Mets didn't look so alive as Game 7 flew by. With one out in the sixth, Hurst had retired 11 in a row and Boston had 11 more outs to get to become champions. Within 10 pitches everything changed.

Lee Mazzilli, batting for Fernandez, who fanned four of eight batters (retiring seven), hit a breaking ball into left field for a base hit. Mookie Wilson also pulled a single to left. Tim Teufel came up. The ex-Twin was the lone Met to have faced Hurst prior to the World Series. And in the Series he hit New York's only home run against him and went 4-for-9. To that point in his career, he was a .350 career hitter against Hurst in 20 at bats, and the lefty was careful.

"He was trying to get me to nibble," Teufel explained. "We [later] became teammates in San Diego. As soon as I saw him, he came right over to me and said, 'How did you take this pitch? How did you take that pitch?' He threw me a split-finger and that

* In the euphoria of the Mets comeback, nobody questioned the premature choice of Bruce Hurst as World Series MVP. Yet Dave Henderson hit .435 in the first six games and had the home run that could've—well, should've—ended Boston's long world championship drought. And Marty Barrett hit .480 through Game 6. No Red Sox player would take home 1986 World Series MVP honors.

was his go-to pitch as a left-handed pitcher." It was ball four, loading the bases. Up came the man Mets fans wanted to see more than any player: Keith Hernandez. And it just so happened he had done this before.

In Game 7 of the 1982 World Series, in the sixth inning, southpaw Bob McClure, a pitcher Hernandez faced as a kid in Little League and Babe Ruth ball in Pacifica, California, pitched around Gene Tenace to bring up the lefty-swinging Hernandez with the Cardinals trailing the Brewers. Hernandez cracked a two-run single to tie the game—on his 29th birthday, no less. Now Hernandez had just turned 33, and just as then, he faced a left-hander.

"I was like, 'You've got to be kidding me,'" Hernandez said of the similarities between his sixth inning, Game 7 at bats in '82 and '86. "It was the same situation basically, which I thought was kind of ironic."

Hernandez studied the situation and the pitcher, and then he looked in the stands. "My brother [Gary] was there, and I looked up to where he was sitting in the box seats behind home plate, and he gave me the big power sign," he said. "I got up on my one knee in the on-deck circle and was walking towards home plate, and I just did what I always did in a tight situation, which was take a couple of deep breaths and count to ten, slow everything down and get in the box. I mean you can't run and hide. There I am. I'm either going to do it or I'm not."

The same held for Hurst, who had to protect a three-run lead to end 68 years of waiting in New England. He had limited Hernandez to 1-for-7 so far in the Series. A double play would end the inning and squash the best chance so far to break through against Hurst. After Game 6, however, the mood had changed. This wasn't one pitch away from sure defeat, this was just the sixth inning. But it was time to act.

The crowd was on its feet, Bo Field's arms rolled away in the front row, Hernandez was down a strike in the count, and he swung at a fastball almost shoulder high. The ball landed in left-center, two runs scored, Teufel went to third, and Hernandez clenched his fists in triumph. With so many people at the Giants-Redskins game at the Meadowlands armed with transistor radios and portable TVs, the crowd in New Jersey cheered as one for Hernandez's hit at the same time the Redskins completed a 49-yard play, confounding the players. "It was weird," Washington linebacker Neal Olkewicz said after the Giants' 27–20 win. Despite all the attention for the game at Shea, there were 75,923 at the Meadowlands, with just 941 no-shows. "I'm surprised there were so many people here," Giants quarterback Phil Simms said when the night was over.

There were more cheers across the tristate area when Gary Carter hit the next pitch off the end of the bat and Dwight Evans smothered it with his glove. Hernandez held up—lest he be doubled off and prevent the tying run from crossing the plate—and Evans, with his cannon-like arm, threw to second for the second out. Hernandez stormed off the field yelling at right field ump Dale Ford for not making a call earlier. Carter would bemoan Hernandez not getting a better read on the play, thus costing him a hit and an RBI. But what mattered was the game was tied.

Again it came down to bullpens. Like the Astros before them, the pen did in the Red Sox. Roger McDowell set down Boston in order in the top of the seventh and Calvin Schiraldi came back out for more. Forlorn after Game 6, he told the press, "I don't deserve any more chances." He got another, anyway. As fans chanted "Calvin, Cal-vin" at the former Met, he shook off his catcher and threw a fastball that Ray Knight drilled on a line over the wall in left-center. Knight jumped in the air a little between first and second, and his step on home plate—not the styling stomp of Reggie Jackson against the Mets in 1973—made the cover of *Sports Illustrated*: "Knight Cap." Everyone in the Mets dugout hugged him and then he came out for his last curtain call, pointing toward wife

Nancy Lopez. It was the first home run by the home team in the World Series. Just in time.

The tie broken, the Mets added another run on Rafael Santana's RBI single. Roger McDowell's sacrifice bunt—the first one in the Series handled correctly by Schiraldi—chased the tormented right-hander. Lefty Joe Sambito, a Met in 1985, came in and threw an intentional walk, following an inexplicable base on balls to Backman batting right-handed (his average batting righty in 1986 was 88 points lower than McDowell's). Up came Hernandez with the bases loaded against a left-hander for the second time in as many innings—and he came through again. His sacrifice fly plated what turned out to be a huge run.

After a then Mets record 75 appearances and still-standing marks of 128 innings and 14 wins in relief during the season—plus 14⅓ more innings in the postseason—McDowell was spent. His 1-2-3 seventh inning seemed like ancient history when three straight Red Sox got hits to start the eighth. Evans's double in the gap scored two, with Rice coming home all the way from first—at long last. With the lead down to a run, the tying run on second, and six more outs needed to secure a world championship, Davey Johnson made one last call for Jesse Orosco. Orosco had thrown 11⅔ innings over eight postseason appearances to that point—on top of 81 innings during the season. Like McDowell, Orosco was running on fumes. But in the biggest game of a career that spanned 24 years and a major league record 1,252 appearances—plus 24 more games in October—Jesse was far from messy.

That's not to say there weren't a few hearts extracted from throats at Shea when his first batter, Rich Gedman, hit a line drive. It was snagged by Backman. Dave Henderson, up yet again where a home run would give his team the lead in the late innings, struck out swinging. John McNamara finally inserted Don Baylor as a pinch hitter, but he grounded out and the Mets escaped with a 6–5 lead.

Tired as the Mets bullpen was, it was fresh as a daisy next to the Olde Towne Team's ragged relievers. Having made it a one-run game, here came one more questionable move by McNamara. Bob Stanley had retired the one batter he faced to end the home seventh, and his spot in the order did not come up in the top of the eighth, but McNamara opted to double switch in shortstop Ed Romero—and put Al Nipper on the mound.

Nipper got two strikes on Darryl Strawberry, but the next strike Nipper threw was crushed high over the 371-foot marker in right-center for a blessed insurance run. Treating Davey Johnson's Game 6 double switch as some sort of double cross, Strawberry held a grudge for having been on the bench for all the Game 6 heroics—never mind that the player who pinch-hit in his spot, Kevin Mitchell, singled to keep the epic rally going. Strawberry had a decent season overall, but he had been brutal at Shea, hitting 57 points lower at home, plus he had an 0-for-August in New York, and power numbers that were way down at Shea compared to the road. Shea was always a hard park to hit in, but this was a player with more homers at Shea than anyone in the stadium's history. Maybe it was the pressures of a bad marriage, the drinking, or a dozen other things in '86, but he had been hitless in his last 12 Shea at bats dating to his home run off Nolan Ryan in the NLCS. And he marked the occasion of his first World Series home run by touring the bases in slow motion and coming out for the de rigueur curtain call. Straw brought an extra dose of drama to a team and a city that already had plenty, but everyone pulling for the Mets was thrilled with the extra run. And they wanted more.

Knight singled—his ninth hit of the Series—and took second on a ground ball. Rafael Santana, whose .250 average in the Series was 32 points higher than his regular-season mark, was walked to bring up Orosco. With a two-run lead and three outs to get, there was no way Orosco wasn't batting, or bunting. Joe Garagiola went so far as to say on NBC, "I'd almost bet the house that he's going to bunt." Orosco squared to bunt on the first two pitches, but just as Nipper released the third pitch, Orosco brought the bat back and swung away—the old Butcher Boy play. It was a double-play grounder under most circumstances, but with Romero covering third in anticipation of a bunt, the bouncer went right through the vacated shortstop spot. Knight scored for an 8–5 Mets lead. "Joe, you just lost your house," Scully quipped.

It was Orosco's first hit of the year and the last in a career that continued 17 more seasons. Boston's nightmare in the pitcher's spot was complete—and in the AL park, the Mets produced more runs out of the DH slot. If the oft-beseeched baseball gods did exist, they had thoroughly forsaken Boston.

Fenway Park may have been a jewel to the sporting cognoscenti and the literary set, but Shea Stadium was the place to be right now. The soiled concrete, the nasty bathrooms, the heartburn-inducing food—it did not matter. This was Shea's apex, its first world stage moment beyond the Beatles hitting the big ballpark for the first time in 1964 and the Mets' completion of their upset over the Orioles five years later. Red Sox fans could point to the infernal "Curse of the Bambino." Mets fans could turn to destiny. Who made the last out at Shea that crowned the Mets world champions in 1969? Davey Johnson. The Met on the mound who induced that last out from Baltimore? Jerry Koosman. And who was the player to be named later when the Mets dealt Kooz to the Twins in 1979? Jesse Orosco. As soon as he finished running the bases, Orosco was ready to take the Mets home.

Dave Stapleton, one of the most mentioned unused players in World Series history, played in each of the first two Series games at Shea but not the last two. Ed Romero, a .210 hitter on the year, had his first at bat of the World Series to start the ninth. "I just went up there and tried to do the best I could—I hit a popup to first base, just like everyone else was doing that night," Romero, now a minor league manager, said with a chuckle. Batting champ Wade Boggs hit .352 against lefties in 1986, but he would hit just .160 against Orosco in his career. He grounded out to second base. Two outs, nobody on.

Shea had reached the berserker stage. Roll after roll of toilet paper was being heaved on the field. Fans jumped up and down in the stands, and that's where they'd stay. A squadron of policemen on horseback in the bullpens prepared for deployment. Helmeted troopers lined the dugout. Behind them was Mayor Ed Koch, who'd stayed for less than an inning on Opening Day and now was here in the ninth inning of Game 7. The Shea DiamondVision cued a congratulatory note—for the Mets. But they made sure it did not go up until the third out was secured. This was a different version of waiting, the last minutes of an extended wait for those who stood in the stands or in a bar or in their living room, and whether they'd lived through abandonment by the Dodgers or Giants or M. Donald Grant, or were too young to remember 1969 or 1973, but knew all too well of the big suck that was the late 1970s and early 1980s—for them the last minutes always seemed the longest. And if they got cocky, they could look at the Red Sox players, a few with face in towel, and understand that, as Yogi Berra had said as manager before the Mets made their last-to-first sprint to the 1973 pennant, "It ain't over 'til it's over." If ever a month embodied that sentiment in baseball, it was October of 1986. Even the man who uttered that eternal Yogi-ism had experienced this wisdom in action from too close a vantage point as an '86 Astros coach.

What might go wrong was always somewhere in the back of the mind of most hard-core baseball fans or observers. You can't take a knee or pass the ball or the puck around to kill the final seconds; you have to go get it in baseball. Anything could happen—even with two outs and no one on. But those thoughts grew more remote with each second, drowned out by noise, by anticipation, by the smoke bomb hurled into left field, by strike two to Marty Barrett.

If anyone was going to start a miraculous rally, it would be Barrett. His 13 hits in the 1986 World Series tied Bobby Richardson (1964) and Lou Brock (1968) for the most hits in Series history. Both Richardson's and Brock's teams lost in seven games. With a 2–2 count, Orosco toed the rubber, went into his windup, and threw.

Behind the microphone on WHN, the Mets flagship radio station, sat Bob Murphy. The consummate professional, he never said "we" in the booth. "It was never 'we' with him," his partner, Gary Thorne, said, "although there was never any question about who he wanted to win." Murphy had started his major league broadcasting career with Curt Gowdy at Fenway Park. He'd joined the Mets in 1962, the third man hired after the network veteran Lindsey Nelson and perennial home run champ Ralph Kiner. Murphy had called almost every game in team history. Those who missed—or weren't alive for—his Game 7 call would hear it again and again in the decades to follow as WHN morphed into all-sports WFAN and clunky, expensive personal computers morphed into PCs, and then laptops, and then tablets, and then phones that seemed able to do anything. The Internet allowed the world's documented information to be summoned at a keystroke. And in down moments for Mets fans, Murph's call would be summoned often. It was the call a man waited his entire career for:

> *Now the pitch on the way . . . He struck him out! . . . Struck him out! The Mets have won the World Series! The dream has come true. The Mets have won the World Series, coming from behind to win the seventh game.*

Like Murphy's call, Orosco's reaction was not rehearsed. He threw his mitt into the air, pounded the ground with both fists, sitting alone on the mound for two seconds before Carter and a wave of charging Mets covered him in a sea of white and blue and orange racing stripes. Orosco was buried. To borrow a line from the Sinatra song that—like the city—belonged to the Mets in 1986, they were on top of the heap.

Part III.
Decline

15

Break Up the Mets

A COLD, CLEAR JANUARY AFTERNOON WAS YET ANOTHER DAY IN the long wait between championships in Flushing. This day marked 10,302 days since Game 7 in 1986, or 28 years, 2 months, 14 days. In that time half the teams in the major leagues won world championships, and two-thirds of the current Mets 40-man roster was born—including pitcher Jon Niese (since traded), whose birthday was the very day the Mets were crowned 1986 champions. As Niese grew from boy to adolescent to rookie to veteran, and the Mets grew in irrelevance, the Yankees added five more world championships to the pile, San Francisco made up for lost time with three titles in five Octobers, and the Cardinals won twice, as have the Twins and Blue Jays. Even the Marlins, seven years away from existence in 1986, have won two World Series while being torn apart and built back up numerous times.

With three world championships since 2004, the Red Sox have lost their "woe is us" mantle to become the American League's model of consistency. But New England took the loss to the Mets hard, and there were hard feelings, too. Minutes after the 1986 World Series ended, a riot broke out at the University of Massachusetts at Amherst—almost 100 miles west of Boston. With most of the Red Sox fans profiling white and the outnumbered Mets supporters skewing more black and Hispanic, the confrontation escalated to involve a crowd that the *Harvard Crimson* reported as 12,000. The Massachusetts Commission Against Discrimination reported that the minority students had "reason to fear for their safety," and as a direct result UMass changed its writing curriculum for incoming students to reflect on themes of prejudice.

Hostility occurred on other campuses in Massachusetts as well. Slurs were spray-painted at Smith College while Mount Holyoke responded to racism with a teach-in. The College of the Holy Cross in Worcester was split, if not as dramatically. "We didn't have riots exactly," said current *Newsday* Mets beat reporter David Lennon, who was a Holy Cross freshman in 1986, "but I remember that night in Game 7 . . . being in the dorm and being crushed and commiserating with the rest of the Red Sox fans—the Mets fans running around going crazy and gloating in our faces." Cambridge was quiet, but sad. Bill Nowlin, a founder of Rounder Records as well as author of twenty-odd books on the Red Sox, couldn't sleep after Game 6, so he went for a walk in Cambridge in the middle of the night. "As I was trudging along, I ran into at least four or five other guys—all guys, as it happened—who were quite obviously doing the same thing. I didn't know any of them, and none of us stopped to talk, or even acknowledge each other. We kept our gaze down and avoided eye contact, and kept on silently moping and trudging along."

The Mets causing anger, resentment, and depression to a fan base other than their own? No wonder people still love the 1986 team so much.

That is why 400 people are out on this January afternoon at McFadden's, a restaurant/bar adjacent to Citi Field, located between where Shea once stood and the auto junkyards on Roosevelt Avenue. The hard-core Mets fans, the ones attending the second annual Queens Baseball Convention, don't even notice the junkyards across the street. Wrecks don't bother them. They are survivors.

Shannon Shark, founder of the blog *Mets Police*, serves as QBC 2015 host. It began out of a conversation about the Mets being one of a handful of clubs without a team-run Fan Fest every winter. The Mets did hold one until 2006. In a response not unlike those used by the team to explain the demise of Old-Timers' Day, Banner Day (since reinstated), and reunions for various pennant winners, management said it was too much to ask players to take part in such events in the off-season. *Groan!* It is a common refrain.

"The Mets haven't always embraced their history as much as they should have," says ESPN.com's Adam Rubin, who grew up on Long Island and has covered the Mets since 2003. "They don't do Old-Timers' Day, probably because of the cost involved. When they opened Citi Field, the stadium just wasn't decorated the way you'd think a new stadium for a team would be. They've done a good job since then changing the color scheme, adding the Mets Hall of Fame, the banners outside and stuff. But certainly in general they haven't always done a good job embracing their history."

So the *Mets Police* took the initiative and, with the help of dozens of volunteers—but not the Mets—established the Queens Baseball Convention in 2014. "We're planning to do it again," says Shannon, a media consultant who grew up close enough to Shea to see the stadium lights from his window and later was a vendor at the ballpark—Steve's Ice Cream was his best seller and easy to haul. "The goal now is to do a bigger version of it. Like anything I do, I just like to see things grow year to year." The Mets can be a growth industry, but one limited by the team's lack of understanding or appreciation of the deep connection fans feel with the team. Just like the Mets have never seemed to get Mookie Wilson.

Having spoken, signed, and smiled for three hours at QBC15, Wilson relaxes in a back room. He just wrote a book, with Erik Sherman, in which he broaches the subject of the team's poor attitude toward its history, and toward the 1986 Mets. "Within the Mets organization there was an ongoing trend of not tapping into the knowledge, experience, and winning attitude of our

1986 championship team," Wilson wrote. "Some of it has to do with the hard-partying nature of the team that management has always seemed ashamed of, never mind that these same players put together the best record in team history and the most exciting October the Mets have ever seen. Or may ever see.

"Sure, some of the guys got mixed up in bad situations, but if nothing else, the guys from that championship team are older and more mature now and can warn some of the current Mets about the pitfalls of fame," Mookie went on in *Mookie*—was any other book title even an option? "The Mets have been distancing themselves from the image of our '86 team for some time."

Others disagree. For the past decade the Mets have had 1986 players Keith Hernandez and Ron Darling in the broadcast booth—the team did not, however, retain studio analyst Bob Ojeda, who brought insight and humor to a role where past '86 Mets, Lee Mazzilli and Darryl Strawberry in particular, came up dry. Mets third-base coach Tim Teufel previously managed for the organization in the minors. The man he platooned with at second base in 1986, Wally Backman, served as the team's most controversial '86 alum under contract. A coveted minor league manager who won everywhere he went, his career hit a roadblock when he was fired four days after the Diamondbacks hired him to manage in the majors in November 2004 because of past transgressions that Arizona was lax to investigate and quick to condemn. Domestic disputes with his former wife, as well as a drunk driving conviction and a bankruptcy filing, cost Backman his dream of managing in the major leagues. He was forced to start over in the independent minor leagues, but the Mets brought him back to affiliated baseball. In six years he managed Mets teams at every level of the minors and in four different cities, winning three division titles and earning 2014 Pacific Coast League Manager of the Year. Despite the Mets finishing with losing records from 2011 to 2014 under Terry Collins, Backman remained in the minors as if in Mets purgatory, waiting to one day get the call.

Darryl Strawberry DAN CARUBIA

Backman, mid-50s, his brown hair and mustache long ago turned white, is in midseason form in mid-January at the Queens Baseball Convention. You can see why players relate to his personable style, treating new acquaintances like old friends. Thirteen years in the majors as a 5-foot-9 switch-hitter who could hit from only one side, Backman is a study in determination and perseverance. He advocates for the Mets and their fans retaining these qualities. "When the Mets win another World Series"—and even months before anyone could imagine the Mets making a pennant run, Backman says *when*, not *if*—"I think the '86 team will still be loved like the people love them now. They'll love the next one, too. . . . I'll tell you what, New York is a pretty special place to play. As a former major league player, it's the best place to play."

Backman and his charges are both one step from the majors in Las Vegas, a town synonymous with distractions. When asked what would have happened if the Mets' Triple-A team had been in Las Vegas in the 1980s as opposed to Virginia, he just smiles, shakes his head, and sips his drink.

Unearthing what happened to the Mets after 1986 is like an archeological dig. Most searches start with something missing: Dwight Gooden from the victory parade.

Ideally, a parade would not be held a mere 12 hours after clinching a World Series, but thanks to the rainout it went off at noon the day after Game 7. It was a sprint for everybody to get there.

"Somehow Bobby Ojeda wound up at my house, my condo in New York, and slept on the couch—my brother slept in the other bedroom," Keith Hernandez said of the night of revelry that followed the 1986 clinching against the Red Sox. "The morning came and we were late, so Bobby and I got in a cab and raced downtown and we got to the staging area and we couldn't get anywhere close to the cars. The people recognized us. And there were these wrought-iron, 7-foot fences to get over—or 6-foot fences—and the fans literally lifted us up sideways, like a mosh pit, and pushed us over the side so we could get over the fence. And I got into my car. Barely."

There was one car for each participant with a driver and security agent. Even for the announcers. "People had climbed up the light poles and were 18 deep and coming out the windows," Gary Thorne recalled. "It was an unbelievable day." And then they went in and had lunch.

"It was the worst TV show in the world because nobody told us that when the parade ended at City Hall, they were going to go inside for lunch," Len Berman said of the NBC-TV broadcast. "We're on the air live. We just had to talk. I remember [news anchor] Chuck Scarborough and I were on the air for an hour. I don't know what we talked about." The conversation concerned the best team in baseball—after all, they owned the town. They were given the keys to prove it.

The lasting image of the City Hall ceremony was Keith Hernandez and Gary Carter, who would soon be named the first captains in Mets history (Mex came first). They held up the World Series trophy together at City Hall: Carter's end was carried a bit higher in his sharp gray suit with blue tie and broad grin, while Hernandez grimaced through a hangover in jeans, a Mets T-shirt, and a blue corduroy team hat. Oscar and Felix in an *Odd Couple* revival.

"I should have dressed a little more appropriately," Hernandez apologized three decades later. "I didn't even get a chance to shower. I just went." It didn't matter what you wore. All that mattered was that you were there. And that's not something every Met could say.

Dwight Gooden was home watching on TV. He'd been up all night snorting cocaine with people he barely knew. Gooden was in such bad shape he pretended not to be home when Darryl Strawberry knocked on the door, offering a ride to Shea for the parade. Mets PR head Jay Horwitz called repeatedly, asking if he could send a car. Doc's mother called, too. And his fiancée. Gooden just ignored everything. "What happened to Dwight Gooden?" questions shifted into off-season mode. On April 1, 1987, the answer came.

WHN was a few months away from becoming the country's first true all-sports radio station, WFAN. It was a country music station, of all things, but due to owning radio rights to the hottest team in town, the station featured plenty of sports. Gary Thorne was making his daily WHN report from St. Petersburg, one of the last days there before the team relocated to Port St. Lucie the following spring. Thorne's morning broadcast was anything but perfunctory. Howie Rose, who also worked for WHN, was in New York preparing for his first season as host of the new *Mets Extra* before and after every game on radio. Rose remembered the announcement clearly. "The first thing he said was a bombshell hit the Mets camp this morning at about 11," Rose said. "The Mets were so hated, I thought the bombshell—oh my God, did some crazy people blow up St. Pete or whatever? Then he went on to talk about Doc. It was just like a knock to the gut."

Gooden had let his growing addiction and paranoid delusions obscure common sense. He insisted during an off-season interview that he would include a proviso for voluntary drug tests in his new contract, even though the union prevented such clauses from being mandatory. In a four-month span he had missed the victory parade, had a son with a woman who was not his fiancée, called off the wedding, and been arrested for fighting with Tampa police. The Mets called Gooden's bluff, and the drug test provision was in his new $1.5 million contract. He failed the first test he took. It was April 1, two years to the day after a *Sports Illustrated* story about a Mets rookie named Sidd Finch who could throw 168 miles per hour. Gooden was no April Fool's joke.

He chose rehab over a yearlong suspension without pay, but the '87 Mets were a different ball club even before that. Free agent Ray Knight took the team's one-year offer in the collusion era personally. So the World Series MVP moved on to Baltimore and

Howard Johnson could now play every day in New York—HoJo responded with the first of three 30-homer, 30-steal seasons in 1987. Kevin Mitchell was gone, too, traded home to San Diego in an eight-player deal for Kevin McReynolds. Both moves made the Mets stronger, on paper. That paper would not be ticker tape streaming down on the Mets down Broadway in an October 1987 parade. Or any other time soon.

Preaching to the converted, Mookie Wilson, a deacon at his church in South Carolina, spoke to the crowd at the Queens Baseball Convention about what the Mets lost during the 1986 off-season.

"You need something other than talent to win," he said. "We were missing important parts of the psyche of that team. I don't think we ever recovered from losing Kevin Mitchell. . . . 'You push me, I'll push you, and your sister.' That was Ray Knight. Half the fights we had, Ray Knight started them. But he was that good. He was that presence. I hate to use the word *enforcers*, but that's what they were. You mess with me. I've got Mitch and I've got Ray Knight. Whatcha gonna do?"

Kevin McReynolds wasn't messing with anybody. Almost everyone agrees that McReynolds was a very good player, but opinions differ as to whether he was an ideal fit for that Mets team. Mookie said McReynolds was "the guy that you would invite to dinner every Sunday afternoon, but he's not the guy I'm bringing to New York to win a championship." Writer Jeff Pearlman, who grew up watching the 1980s Mets, thought the McReynolds trade was the right move, but he admitted that the laconic left fielder was "kind of a paycheck player." Mets announcer Gary Cohen said McReynolds "just didn't care." Retired *Newsday* columnist Steve Jacobson said, "Kevin McReynolds gives you only what's on the scoreboard." Jacobson's colleague and Mets beat writer Marty Noble, on the other hand, came to McReynolds's defense, calling him "perhaps the best left fielder the Mets have ever had. By far. . . . All he did was play well," Noble chuckled. "There's nothing wrong with that."

But getting rid of a player who would be NL MVP and play in a World Series again in the 1980s—two feats the Mets came close to but missed—was the bigger issue. Kevin Mitchell never saw it coming. "I was very surprised," Mitchell said, noting that the thrill of playing in his hometown was offset by playing under high-strung Larry Bowa, and he was traded by the Padres to the Giants in July of '87. "I thought I was going to be around a long time with the Mets. I guess they felt that I was a bad influence on Darryl Strawberry and Dwight Gooden. And I tell people to this day: How can I be a bad influence on guys that were already in the big leagues before me? My mindset is strong, stronger than theirs. They [were] in the big leagues before me. I have no control over those two guys. I went on and did my thing. I don't drink. I don't smoke. I never did drugs."

Mitchell underwent back surgery in late 2014 that left him unable to move, and he regained strength and mobility over time. Because of his father and brother's tragic history with drugs, however, he endured extreme pain rather than take medication. "I refuse to take it," Mitchell said. "My addiction is life." If only some of the players the Mets *didn't* trade had had a similar resolve.

The 1986 Mets are now known almost as much for their late-night partying as they are for their late-inning magic, thanks to *The Bad Guys Won*, the 2004 bestseller by Jeff Pearlman. For any other writer to try to duplicate Pearlman's level of detail of off-the-field exploits is a fool's errand. It's been done and done well. Before that the *Sports Illustrated* writer was best known for spending a day with John Rocker in 1999 and bearing witness to the inner, über bigot that would earn the former Braves reliever a suspension and a place in the Redneck Hall of Fame.

As a 14-year-old in Mahopac, New York, Pearlman was a hard-core Mets fan in 1986. When he started working on the book in the early 2000s, he was unaware of the extent of the team's partying, the destruction of the plane coming back from Houston, the liberties taken by the players while filming the "Let Go Mets" video, the straying on the road, or the way the Mets held court after hours at watering holes like Port Washington's Finn McCool's. No one before had delved into the team's extracurricular activities. "To them it was like telling an old frat story," Pearlman said. Older and wiser, many of the '86 veterans are more guarded now.

"There's no way with Twitter and cell phones, iPhones, that the '86 Mets could have lived that way—there's no way," Pearlman said. "At Finn McCool's getting wasted and someone would videotape it. Or some woman would have taken pictures [of] her hooking up with . . . No. Impossible."

The Mets had survived on talent, attitude, and grit in the late innings in October 1986. It is difficult to explain analytically how a team can win a championship when half its postseason wins occur when trailing or tied entering the ninth inning. And that does not even include being down three runs in the sixth inning of Game 7 against Boston.

"Yeah, I think the front office didn't like the drug rumors they heard," Pearlman said. "The thought that Mitchell was just like Gooden and Strawberry, there's definitely a racist element there. They decided to change it up. . . . If they beat the Dodgers in '88, we're not even having this discussion." But they didn't beat the Dodgers in the 1988 NLCS. After averaging 98 wins over five years, the Mets had their one trophy, plenty of impressive statistics, and a lot of laughs, but that's it.

On a sun-splashed afternoon at spring training, the 25th anniversary of his first spring with the Mets, Bob Ojeda sat in the far end of the sleepy press box in Port St. Lucie. Still an analyst for SportsNet New York at the time, he spoke of what he thought happened to the Mets after 1986. It was Bobby O. at his best—blunt and brutally honest.

"I don't know if it's just my opinion or a lot of my teammates would agree, but we really cheated the Mets fans, Frank Cashen,

Joe McIlvaine, all the people who put together that team," Ojeda said. "They put together a team that should have won five World Series. We were a magnificent team. The problem was we were out of control. And no one could control us. We were a wild, crazy, talented bunch, that for the life of me I can't see how we became this out of control.

"The core team, that main team, hell, that whole '86 team, shouldn't have been broken up. But I think Frank Cashen, one of my favorite people of all time, felt for our own safety, he needed to break that team up. We were that out of control. And I think as he built that team up and wanted to keep it together, Frank always cared for us as people and then as players. And I think realistically, for our own well-being, I think he tried to protect guys against themselves."

You never doubted that Bobby O. cared. After the Mets started both postseason series with losses in '86, he got the Mets on the board with wins each time—and when it comes to Game 6, he started two of the most memorable such contests—and his team won both. Somehow. A hedge clipper accident the week the Mets clinched the NL East in 1988 kept him from pitching against Los Angeles in that year's NLCS. The Mets did not make a second World Series appearance during the most successful period in franchise history. Something different went awry each of the years that followed.

In 1987 there were numerous injuries, a patched-together pitching staff, Dwight Gooden missing two months due to rehab, and a Terry Pendleton home run that the Mets never got over. In 1988 the Mets ran away from the pack late to win the NL East, but they did not have the good fortune that visited them in October 1986. The Mets did not pull out three wins in their last at bat in the NLCS against the Dodgers like they had against the Astros. They were not able to duck Orel Hershiser in Game 7 like they had Mike Scott in 1986—in a case of what might have been if the Mets hadn't beaten the Astros in 16 innings in '86, the

Mets played a Game 7 in '88 and were shut out by the league's most dominant pitcher for the pennant. In 1989 the Mets tried to reinforce their pitching by forking over a king's ransom in young arms—including Rick Aguilera—to Minnesota for Frank Viola, and traded center fielders Mookie Wilson and Lenny Dykstra in separate, disastrous deals, while also giving away Roger McDowell as part of the Juan Samuel trade. The '89 team finished a distant second to the Cubs, the lone season Davey Johnson's Mets did not win 90 games. A year later the Mets won 91 times, but they were no longer Johnson's club. Johnson was let go despite what is still the most wins (595) and highest winning percentage (.588) in team history.*

Bud Harrelson took over as manager in May 1990 and by then just a handful of '86 regulars were still in Mets uniforms: Dwight Gooden, Darryl Strawberry, Howard Johnson, Tim Teufel, Sid Fernandez, Ron Darling, and Bob Ojeda. Within a year only Doc, HoJo, and El Sid remained. Strawberry, who in a decade in the Mets system saw just one losing season—his rookie year in New York—went home to Los Angeles in a drug-induced, career-wrecking disaster. Ojeda was sent to the Dodgers that same off-season in a deal that brought Hubie Brooks back to New York. Drained of their best players and relying on prospects who did not pan out, the Mets were done as a power. The Yankees took over New York once more. They have yet to relinquish control, even in the wake of a Mets pennant in 2015.

"Years later I still feel we owe people," Ojeda said. "We owned New York City. It was a tremendous feeling. We loved it. We all cherished it. But it should not have been a one-time thing."

---

* In 17 years managing the Mets, Reds, Orioles, Dodgers, and Nationals, Davey Johnson had a .562 winning percentage and finished first six times, though 1986 was his lone World Series as a manager.

16

Tilting at Windmills

For a franchise that has yet to win another World Championship, the 1986 Mets certainly are memorable. Rob Neyer and Eddie Epstein wrote *Baseball Dynasties* in 2000 about the greatest teams in history. Neyer's top 10 dynasties slot the '86 Mets at number eight, with just one team since then on the list: the 1998 Yankees at number three (the 1939 Yankees are number one and the 1970 Orioles are second). In the years since Neyer cowrote the book, no team has jarred the Mets from his list. "I don't believe any team since 2000 has enjoyed a three-season run that would rank higher than those Mets," he said in 2015. It is also worth noting that using the *Dynasties* methodology of standard deviation and winning percentage, among other factors, the Mets were the only one-time champion in the top 10, fitting since the nine different World Series champions crowned between 1982 and 1990 represent the longest period in baseball history without a repeat.

Back when the 1986 Mets were fresh in everyone's mind, Bill James lauded them in his 1987 *Abstract*. Every number spoke of how much the '86 Mets dominated.

> *In what areas of play were they outstanding? They led the league in both ERA and runs scored. If you focus on the offense, they led*

> *the league in two of the three most important basic categories (batting average and walks drawn) and missed by only a few of leading in the third (home runs). They led the league in both on-base percentage and slugging percentage. They outhit their opponents .263–.236. They outhomered their opponents 148–103. They bested their opponents in doubles (261–215), walks drawn (631–509), and positive strikeouts (1,083–968). . . . There may never have been a pennant winner which had such an extraordinary balance of pitching and hitting.*

In 2009 ESPN.com writer David Schoenfield rated the top sports moments of the 1980s and picked Game 6 of the 1986 World Series as number two. Number one? "Miracle on Ice," the 1980 U.S. Olympic hockey team—back when the United States used amateurs—beating the Soviets in Lake Placid. Can't argue with the order of miracles there.

Even before the Mets beat them for the 2015 pennant, Cubs fans didn't have much good to say about New York, but the Mets did win over one Cubs fan—for a day at least. He even referenced Shea daredevil Michael Sergio: "I considered parachuting here into the Rose Garden," President Ronald Reagan joked when he met the Mets at the White House in November of 1986, "but the Secret Service had a little something to say about it." The president was funny and irreverent, though he called the Mets "the other team in New York." He ignored that half the Mets weren't there, though Dwight Gooden made it this time. After handing over a pile of personalized Mets swag, Fred Wilpon told the president, "We intend to be back here next year." Five presidents and counting . . .

Yet '86 can still work its magic. Heather Quinlan was 12 years old that year, young enough to have slept through Buckner (her mother's screaming woke her up), but of an age where she fell in love with the team forever. She's spent the last couple of years making

Presidential get together 1986: back row, from left are Gary Carter, John Gibbons, Bob Ojeda, Rick Aguilera, Lee Mazzilli, and Dwight Gooden. At the podium Mets president Fred Wilpon gives a gift to 40th US President Ronald Reagan. GETTY

a documentary on the '86 club—and she's seen the replay of the climactic play of Game 6 of the World Series a few times now. "I still get choked up," said Quinlan, who previously produced and directed *If These Knishes Could Talk: The Story of the NY Accent*. "As lousy as the '80s were in New York, too. It was dirty and graffiti, but I still kind of feel like everything before 9/11 was a more innocent time. . . . I was at the ticker tape parade and besides that being a great day—the greatest day of my life, right?—I'll talk about it to people who were there and they say, 'I got off from school,' or 'I got off from work.' That was the icing on the cake. Like it was almost a national holiday or something. That's what it felt like."

The victory parade was a once-in-a-lifetime occurrence for many Mets fans. Though some were fortunate to have been paying attention in 1969 as well as for the 1973 pennant, the 2000 Subway Series, an event anticipated for four decades, wasn't much fun to lose. Mets fans of any age could say the same thing about the 2015 loss to the Royals. For the Mets, who average one World Series appearance per decade, losing the last baseball game played in a given year is more discomforting than watching David Lynch's 1986 mystery *Blue Velvet*. "You've got about one second to live, buddy!"

The Yankees have always been the bane of the Mets fans' existence. The Yankees were the established team when the Mets were born, and the New Breed stole away some fans who were bored of the Yanks' U.S. Steel–like efficiency and wanted something new. There were periods when a Mets-leaning youth could get through grade school without hearing the words "the Mets suck" and know the truth in these torments. The Mets held their own in the late 1960s and early 1970s, and you heard it here that the Mets were *the* team in New York from 1984 to 1993. The day Bret Saberhagen sprayed bleach at reporters in the Mets locker room during the 103-loss summer of '93—just after Vince Coleman threw a firecracker at a toddler for kicks—the press ran from the Mets. Others followed.

"They went downhill and the Yankees took over, and now of course the Yankees own the town because every young person growing up was a Yankees fan," said Len Berman, who grew up on the Yankees and Mickey Mantle, started at NBC-TV in the year of the Mets in '86, and saw the change of the guard. "Now you're 20 years away from Derek Jeter's rookie year." Or 20 A.D.—After Derek.

"Quinnipiac University does a study every year, and at this point it's probably like a 2-to-1 advantage for the Yankees over the Mets in terms of the New York area for teams people root for," explained ESPN.com Mets reporter Adam Rubin in a back field at Mets spring training in 2015. "It's been six straight losing seasons, so a generation of kids probably is more likely to gravitate toward the Yankees."

How can that change? As Berman said repeatedly when talking about the '86 Mets, "We wouldn't be talking if they didn't win." And how will they win? Pitching.

When you have a staff of hot, young studs, it can make every day an event. "You wanna watch the game?" invokes the immediate follow-up: "Who's pitching?" The Mets hope that their 2015 and forward rotation of Harvey, deGrom, Syndergaard, and Matz—don't forget Wheeler, another young stud who sat out 2015 with Tommy John surgery*—has the health, the resiliency, the hubris to match Gooden, Darling, and Fernandez of 30 years ago (and how could you forget Ojeda?). Or that they can be what Seaver, Koosman, and Matlack were to the generation before them. Baseball can change in an instant—an injury, a trade, an inexplicable loss of effectiveness. Success is fragile, especially for the Mets.

"The Mets, with the young talent they have, should sustain the success they're going to have now for a while," Rubin said. "Undoubtedly they'll start swaying people back in their direction. But obviously that takes a number of years to affect the size of a fan base. I have no doubt that if they can keep this nucleus together and the pitching becomes what you think it's going to be, that they'll rule the city in the not too distant future. They'll have a winning record this year," Rubin boldly predicted in March of 2015, when more people were bullshit than bullish on the Mets' chances. He was right.

Contacted after the Mets' appearance in the 2015 World Series, Rubin expounded on the Mets' jump from possible contender to improbable league champion. "Certainly they transformed the team via trades, emboldened by the Nats' struggles," he said, referring to favored Washington staggering down the stretch. "So I'm not surprised they went from an 84-or-so win team to a playoff team. I don't think anyone envisioned at the start of the season that they'd be a playoff team, but it should be sustainable because of the starting pitching." The assertion is admirable, but the words "should" and "sustainable" have been said of the Mets before: 1969, 1986, 2000, and many other years. Yet the 1973 "Ya Gotta Believe" team—a more surprising pennant winner than even the '15 Mets—stand as the only Mets club to reach a World Series less than a decade after

---

* Zack Wheeler's particular surgery included repairing his ulnar collateral ligament (UCL) as well as his pronator teres tendon, often called the flexor pronator tendon.

the franchise's previous trip. Yes, it's never been easy to be a Mets fan; even that white knuckle October of 1986 is better to relive than it was to endure the first time, when all seemed lost.

The Mets are the team of the underdog—in New York. Outside the metropolitan area, it will take some effort to be hated anywhere close to the '86 team, which was loathed for its dominance-cum-arrogance—the Pirates had a late 1980s ad campaign that went, "The Mets: another good reason to hate New York." Mayor Ed Koch, that big baseball fan, responded by asking, "Where is Pittsburgh?"

"America hates New York because they see New York as an army of occupation—teams with 'New York' on their jersey have to get used to it," explained retired *Newsday* columnist Steve Jacobson, who has experienced every boom and bust cycle in New York baseball since the 1950s. "The Mets made all those fans thirty years ago. They still have a fan base. They still have fans that don't want to give up on them."

Winning today isn't a matter of just putting together the talent. It's about the money. Though let's be honest: Money has always made the difference. In the early 1980s the Mets had to wait for the farm system to churn out players; then Frank Cashen cashed in the excess prospects, who'd been played up in the press, and brought back established players with big contracts the Mets could afford to pay. When the Mets signed Keith Hernandez to a five-year, $8.4 million extension—crazy money in 1984—Fred Wilpon smiled and told reporters, "Keith, it's a pleasure to pay the money." Two years later the Mets roster was chock full of young players not making a lot, but that championship team had three of the six highest-paid players in the game (Carter, Foster, and Hernandez) and a $15.3 million payroll that was fourth in baseball behind the Yankees, Cubs, and Braves. By 1992 the Mets were still near the top with a $44 million payroll under new general manager Al Harazin, a longtime Cashen lieutenant who'd taken over because Joe McIlvaine, tired of waiting for Cashen to retire in New York, went to San Diego. Harazin veered away from the Cashen model—homegrown foundation, augment through trades, no high-priced free agents. McIlvaine wound up as Mets GM soon enough, but only after the team hit rock bottom in 1993, its assets squandered. The Mets had a losing record for six straight years—at the same time the Yankees were ascending.

In May 1998 the Yankees had won 31 of their first 40 and the Mets, though above .500 under Bobby Valentine, were 9 games out of first and drawing poorly. That's when co-owner Nelson Doubleday emerged from the shadows to insist the Mets make a play for future Hall of Famer Mike Piazza after general manager Steve Phillips—who'd replaced McIlvaine—initially said the team wasn't interested in the best catcher in baseball. The Mets made the trade and eventually signed Piazza to the largest contract in history at the time: seven years, $91 million. The Mets also signed another of their own free agents, Al Leiter (four years, $32 million). Doubleday said, "We needed Mr. Piazza. And we need Mr. Leiter. And we're lucky enough to be in a market where we're able to afford it." That statement may now sound as out of place as the Mets owning the town, but the side of New York where the Mets play was considered a big market. Once upon a time.

Coming to New York as vice president and GM, Frank Cashen regarded Doubleday as his boss and Fred Wilpon as a nuisance, telling the team president that if he set up a permanent office at Shea Stadium, "I was going back to my old job." Though they had a relatively smooth relationship after that, the way Wilpon wound up with that permanent office vexed Cashen. "To be honest, I never fully understood how the legal paper ever survived the due diligence inspection by the purchasing partners," wrote Cashen, who died at 88 in 2014. "It authorized an individual who had only a reported 5 percent of the team to have sole option to purchase the team if it was ever sold."

Doubleday had funded the $21.1 purchase of the club from the Payson family in 1980, with Wilpon emerging as president despite the fact that his investment, matched by brother-in-law Saul Katz, was just $650,000. Six years later Doubleday sold his publishing empire, which had been more of a family obligation than a passion for the fun-loving yet publicity-shy Doubleday. The Mets were separate from the deal with German publisher Bertelsmann, but the team technically had to change hands. The agreement to purchase the Mets in 1980 stated that Wilpon had the right of first refusal if the team were sold. So Wilpon and Doubleday became equal partners in the fall of 1986.

In 2002 Wilpon bought out Doubleday, whose relationship with Wilpon had become contentious. One of the biggest sticking points was that Wilpon, a real estate developer, wanted to build a new Ebbets Field and Doubleday preferred to renovate Shea Stadium. After a divisive valuation of the team at close to $400 million—about $100 million less than Doubleday sought—Doubleday cashed out at $135 million, when debt was cancelled out.* The takeover was complete.

Where did they get the money? Fred Wilpon had worked his way up in the real estate market, getting lucky a few times, and always had his calls returned as a member of a miniscule group of people who owned a major league team in the country's biggest market. That helped business. So did Bernie Madoff.

Fortune had it that Madoff befriended the Wilpons. Madoff's decades-long Ponzi scheme bilked some $65 billion from his victims, including Fred and Jeff Wilpon, plus brother-in-law Saul Katz, who had $550 million tied up in almost 500 accounts. On December 11, 2008, it all disappeared quicker than a Mets lead in September.

* Nelson Doubleday died in 2015 at age 81.

Another favorable valuation—this time by the trustees representing those swindled by Madoff—determined that the Wilpons, though a net winner, were not on the hook for hundreds of millions as initially believed. Still, the Mets lost a reported $70 million in 2011 and the payroll has yet to approach its pre-Madoff levels—but Bobby Bonilla still gets paid. The ire and irony of taking the $5.9 million owed for Bonilla to leave quietly in 2000 and paying the contract out over 25 years, starting in 2011, at $1.16 million per, was a Madoff special that is further ammunition for detractors. Though in reality the Mets actually come out ahead financially in the arrangement.* Even a win is seen as a loss.

Amidst the mess general manager Sandy Alderson came aboard, the ship taking on water faster than debt. Considered by some the grandfather of "Moneyball"—the application of analytical statistics and evaluations to help build rosters—Alderson promised a top-to-bottom rebuild that the previous regime had never fully committed to. Rebuilding also bought time, since the Mets did not have the kind of money to spend as when the Madoff money spigot seemed to make all things possible. Even when they were floundering on the field in the early 2000s, the Mets were often second—a distant second, mind you—to the Yankees in payroll in MLB. They just were terrible spenders. "Look at the contracts he's signed," said Marty Noble, who now covers the Mets for MLB.com. "My God! I mean they spent millions and millions and millions of dollars and got no return and then you have people say he's cheap? He might be out of money now. No one knows how much money they do or don't have at this point."

They surely would have had more money if not for crushing autumn losses in the final years at Shea Stadium, though the old ballpark nonetheless drew more than 11 million over its last three seasons. (Smaller Citi Field, by contrast, took five years to draw

* *Business Insider* evaluated the deal in 2013 and found that the Mets will come out $9 million ahead, while Bonilla actually gave up $10 million he could have earned if he'd invested the $5.9 million at 8 percent interest in 2000.

that many fans, albeit with higher overall ticket prices and a losing team.) "We all know now that they were one swing away from getting to the World Series [in 2006], and they probably would have won that World Series—you would think, the way the Cardinals beat the Tigers," said *Newsday*'s David Lennon.* "But that was a huge missed opportunity. Then you go to collapses in '07 and '08, which for me as a reporter, the collapse in '07 was nothing I had ever—for as much experience as I had—I had never been around anything like that."

As excruciating as it was, at least the Mets were in a race then. It took until the seventh season at Citi Field to finally have what Fred Wilpon once called on WFAN a "meaningful game in September"—or any month, for that matter. "It's a great park—I think it's a tremendous park, one of the better ones in baseball," explained WFAN Mets beat reporter Ed Coleman early in the 2015 season. "But it has to be full, or somewhat full, for it to have some life and have some character. I think that will happen when the team wins." Like colleague Adam Rubin, Coleman was prescient.

Howard Megdal, a featured writer for *Capital New York*, *Sports Weekly*, and other publications, endured a short-term ban from the Mets press box following the release of his 2011 book *Wilpon's Folly*, which chronicled the black hole that swallowed the team's finances and much of the hope attached to the club.

The Mets quickly rescinded Megdal's ban after a media outcry, but 2011 was not a good year for Mets and PR. That spring a *New Yorker* article by Jeffrey Toobin not only documented the rise and fall of the house of Wilpon, but featured the owner's churlish reactions to his three biggest stars at the time. David Wright "wasn't a superstar." Jose Reyes, who that year became the first Met to win a batting title and then left as a free agent to a divisional

* The Tigers committed crucial errors in all five games of the 2006 World Series and were outscored by the Cardinals, 22–11.

foe, "had everything wrong with him." Carlos Beltran, who pronounced 2005 the beginning of "the new Mets" when he arrived in a swirl of cache and cash, was deemed damaged goods from the owner's box and shipped to San Francisco in July of '11 in exchange for highly touted pitching prospect Zack Wheeler. This is not to say that Fred Wilpon was wrong in his valuations. Five years have shown he was not far off the mark, but he did hand superstar money to Wright, who hasn't been much healthier than Reyes or Beltran. Still, caustic barbs aren't what a fan base wants to hear from an owner who hemorrhages money and adamantly refuses to sell. Nor does any Mets fan want to hear the owner say, "We're snakebitten, baby."

Megdal has remained one of Wilpon's severest critics, even as he raises his children as Mets fans. "The only reason [Wilpon] managed to hang on this long," he says, "is an unprecedented boom in the value of regional sports networks, which meant that suddenly the Wilpons had $2 billion in equity, 65 percent of $2 billion because that's what SNY is estimated to be worth, to borrow against instead of 65 percent of $1 billion." This doubling of value occurred after the sale of the Dodgers by Frank McCourt for $2 billion in 2011. He turned a $1.2 billion profit on the mess he created in Los Angeles, but the reason he sold was that commissioner Bud Selig seized the team. McCourt even dragged down the Mets on his way out, saying that unlike the Wilpons, he had never asked for an emergency—and secret—bridge loan to keep his team running, as the Mets did when they needed $25 million to survive a cash crunch in late 2010.

"The question is why is the league perfectly comfortable with the Mets owners taking and diverting and siphoning off the equivalent of a major league payroll toward company debt before they spend a penny on the Mets?" Megdal said. "And that's what they've done for years because they are financing—that's not even paying down the debt. That's not even a long-term solution. That is financing $250 million against the team. More than $600 million in debt against SNY. And $43 million plus in annual debt balloon payments. Against Citi Field."

The Wilpons continue to be supported by new commissioner Robert Manfred, who took over for old Wilpon crony Bud Selig, whose Machiavellian ascension to the baseball throne created a permanent schism between Wilpon and Doubleday in 1992. The latter was an ally to deposed commissioner Faye Vincent, the closest thing to an independent commissioner that baseball may see.

"You want to figure out in the New York market, why one team has a $200 million payroll and the other one is maybe $100 million, maybe 100, that's a questionable number. And the answer is that money all goes to Sterling debt," Megdal said in June 2015. By November 2015 the Mets had a pennant flying in Queens, and sold scads of T-shirts, hats, and sweatshirts to both the bandwagon fans and hardcores willing to dish out almost $1,000 on the secondary market for standing room only tickets for the World Series in Flushing.

You figured Mets detractors would change their tune after the pennant, even as the team's free agents prepared to sign elsewhere, but in his regular column in *USA Today Sports Weekly*, Megdal did not let the Mets off the hook. Not at all.

"The Mets checked in 20th of the 30 teams in baseball last season, in the vicinity of the Colorado Rockies, Milwaukee Brewers, and Minnesota Twins. This is not an ephemeral exercise in which New York fans demand more money spent—it is that when one owns a New York team, the revenue that comes in is greater, absolutely enormous, and far outstrips the money coming into, for instance, the Rockies, Twins, and Brewers," Megdal wrote in the paper hitting newstands less than three weeks after the Series ended, all the while noting that attendance increased almost 20 percent and the team made as much as $60 million in additional revenue.

Others are also on point. As David Lennon of *Newsday* put the Mets financial priorities, "That's just not the way a big-market team behaves." It is not lost on the generation too young to remember 1986—Megdal, for the record, was six—that a pennant, however glorious, is still a step short of a world championship. Too many people are still waiting for their '86.

Thirty years ago a buildup of homegrown talent culminated in one of the greatest Octobers in baseball history. Two books written on those few weeks in 1986 were titled *One Strike Away* (by Dan Shaughnessy in 1987) and *One Pitch Away* (by Mike Sowell in 1995), the closeness of those titles reflecting the closeness of those series. The teams that did not win wallowed in their lost opportunity for a long time. Greg Prince, cofounder of the *Faith and Fear in Flushing* website and author of a book of the same name, put it in perspective.* "How achingly close the Angels and the Astros and the Red Sox came to winning and what that must have felt like for their fans," Prince said. "Not that I cared in October of 1986, but decades later, it underscored just how fortunate we were. The Angels fan waited another 16 years, the Red Sox fan 18 years, and the Astros fan had to change leagues and keep waiting. So glad that wasn't us. So glad I was wrong when I was sure that was going to be us."

Red Sox catcher Rich Gedman called the pitches that resulted in the miraculous Game 6 comeback in the 1986 World Series. Pitches that can never be called back, no matter how much time passes or how many championships Boston goes on to win. With the Red Sox indeed one strike away from winning their first title since 1918, Gedman missed corralling Bob Stanley's sinker to Mookie Wilson, losing a lead, a game, and a friend in the process. "Those are the types of things that break up friendships. Me and Bob Stanley were very close during those times and it seemed like we became a little distant after."

---

* The *Faith and Fear* masthead is shared by Greg Prince and Jason Fry, a former *Wall Street Journal* online reporter and now author of a *Star Wars* fiction series.

Gedman doesn't have much sympathy for the Mets. Still employed by the Red Sox, as hitting coach for the Class AA Portland Sea Dogs, he stands in an empty dugout on a perfect summer afternoon in Maine. A son of New England who saw the shared dream of six states stomped in a New York minute, he doesn't pause when told how long it's been since the last Mets world championship, a figure extended since the 2014 interview. "It wasn't 86 years," he says, looking toward the replica Green Monster in use at Hadlock Field. "That's a long time."

17

Kid's Curtain Call

MANY OF THE 1986 METS STAYED CLOSE TO THE GAME, BECOMING announcers or branches on the Davey Johnson managing tree. Gary Carter did both. He always wanted more, which did not make him the most popular '86 Met with his teammates. He squeezed every bit of talent he had out of his body, not something every member of that team—or any team—can say. He was a role model in a time when most athletes weren't concerned about that. As for being self-centered, it's hard for people living in a time of Twitter, Facebook, Instagram, and the selfie stick to retroactively consider anyone egotistical.

"The one thing that they forgot was when the gong rang, partner, he was some kind of player," Mel Didier, Expos scouting director in the 1970s, told Buck Martinez during a 2014 Mets–Blue Jays exhibition broadcast at Olympic Stadium. "I tell you what, he got after it as good as anybody. And of course that made him end up in the Hall of Fame." In an Expos hat. The All-American Kid is in Cooperstown wearing the hat of a defunct Canadian team. He wanted his plaque to represent him as a Met.

"You know they gave him no choice," Sandy Carter said of Gary's 2003 induction. "In fact, when they told him this is what you're going

Marv Albert interviews Gary Carter after Game 4 of the 1986 World Series. NATIONAL BASEBALL HALL OF FAME LIBRARY, COOPERSTOWN, NY

to go in as, Gary was like, 'Really? But the Expos aren't going to be around.' Everybody knew they were not going to be a team anymore—and the truth was we had great memories, 11 [years] with the Expos. And the Mets, there was nothing better than that [world championship]. So I said, 'Maybe it's a blessing, honey, that they didn't give you a choice.' He would have liked half and half."

Great athlete, excellent student, and first to help an old lady across the street, Gary Carter was a fresh-faced, blond paperboy out of central casting. He even married his high school sweetheart from Fullerton, California. You'd swear his Sunny Hills High was a rival school on *The Brady Bunch*. If that was somehow true, Carter's team would have won with him at quarterback.

As a paperboy he had a strong enough arm that his throws of the *Culver City News* landed true on the porch, yet he was conscientious enough to get off his bike and place the paper on the porch if he missed, which was rare. His natural smile and ebullient personality ensured that he made far more in tips than the paltry dime he was paid for every $1.50 monthly subscription he collected. His mother made him put all the money in the bank, except for $3 per month, which he spent on baseball cards. At age 10 he also helped take care of a neighborhood boy about his age who was disabled and, to use the parlance of the day, "mentally retarded." Carter helped him walk and eat and even changed him. Carter thought about what his pastor said about being a good Christian. "One of the first things we had to be was grateful," he recalled in a book by Bill Staples and Rich Herschlag, *Before the Glory*. "I was paid to watch that young man, but what I really got out of it was the kind of gratitude I thought the pastor was talking about."

If, as his detractors thought, Carter was always looking for the national spotlight, he sure found it early. At the age of seven he won the first Punt, Pass, and Kick national contest for his age group. He received a paid trip to Washington D.C. and was taken to the Oval Office. President John F. Kennedy had been called to his ill father's bedside, but a signed letter of congratulations from JFK meant far more than the PP&K bust of each of the first winners displayed at the Pro Football Hall of Fame in Canton, Ohio. Carter went to the finals again at age 11, but he lost when he slipped on the frozen grass at Wrigley Field during his punt. Nonetheless, the powers at PP&K knew charisma when they saw it and awarded him a trip to New York to film a commercial about the program with famed announcer Chris Schenkel. Carter was paid $1,000 to demonstrate how the competition worked, but he gave away most of the money to "protect my amateur status." Kid really felt that way.

It seemed a childhood out of a Disney movie, and it ended while he was just 12 with a few words called by a neighborhood kid while Carter was playing baseball: "Gary, you'd better go home. Your mom died." Leukemia claimed Inge Carter at age 37. A first-generation daughter of German parents, she instilled in Gary his drive, energy, and even his fetish for neatness. His father remarried, but his mother always remained next to Gary's heart. When he was dying of brain cancer he told his wife Sandy, "Well, honey, I lived twenty years longer than my mom. It's too soon, but I'm going to see my mom and dad in heaven." Kid really felt that way.

A two-time high school All-America quarterback, Carter was recruited to play football all over the country, even after missing his senior football season with a knee injury. He committed to play both baseball and football at UCLA in 1972. He changed his mind a few days later when the Montreal Expos made a generous offer at the time for a third-round pick: $35,000, plus an extra $7,500 when he reached the majors. The Expos, a club created just three years earlier, were still among the worst organizations in baseball, but their decision to draft Carter was an organizational turning point—a 2015 ranking of the best pick in each year of the draft by ESPN.com chose Carter as the best pick for '72.* Carter, an infielder in high school, would have the opportunity to move fast up the ladder, but he would have to switch to catcher. Mel Didier never had any doubts.

"We're going to work your butt off," Didier told the 18-year-old Carter after signing. "And we're going to drive you. And you're going to block a million ground balls in the dirt. But one day you're going to be an All-Star catcher for 10 years." Didier was wrong—Carter was an All-Star 11 times. And All-Star MVP twice.

Expos players had doubts. Veterans derisively hung the nickname "Kid" on Carter in 1973 spring training, and it stuck. "Hey, Kid, why don't you get us some ice cream," pitcher Mike Torrez asked/demanded as Carter watched the veterans play cards. He took the name as a badge of honor, much the way Cincinnati's Pete Rose took Mickey Mantle's 1963 spring training taunt of

* Gary Carter's 1986 Mets teammates Darryl Strawberry and Dwight Gooden were ESPN.com writer Christina Kahrl's best draft picks in 1980 and 1982, respectively.

"Charlie Hustle" and turned it into a credo. "It was always just 'Kid,'" reporter Marty Noble points out. "No one ever said *the*." Montreal pitchers initially didn't want Kid catching them, preferring buddy Barry Foote. Managers Gene Mauch and Harvey Kuehl played Carter in the outfield, where he'd rarely played until he debuted in the major leagues in 1974. An All-Star as a rookie in 1975—he played an inning as defensive replacement for Rose in right field—Carter injured himself in Jarry Park's outfield the following year. He missed half the season and the Expos won just 55 times. New manager Dick Williams, who'd been to the playoffs four times in eight seasons—with two world championships in Oakland—was hired in 1977 to oversee the club's transfer to Olympic Stadium and its transformation from laughingstock to contender. One of his first orders of business in Montreal was settling the catching situation.

"I saw right through their sugar and spice and realized that they wanted Foote because he was their friend. Foote wouldn't push them, wouldn't challenge them to be better. He'd buy them beers," the late Hall of Fame manager wrote in *No More Mr. Nice Guy*. "Carter reminded me of a young Dick Williams, only nicer. He spent his time in the dugout cheering like hell and his time on the field cocky as hell, living by the verbal challenges and the pumped fist. The pitchers hated him. But then, maybe it was good they hated somebody. The last time they were happy, they lost 107 games."

The Expos, bursting with talented young players, had more victories than any team between 1979 and 1983, yet they won just one division title—and that came during the truncated 1981 strike season. After Rick Monday's crushing home run gave the Dodgers the lead in the top of the ninth inning in the decisive game of the NLCS at the Big O, Carter came up with the season down to its final out—that situation rings a bell. He drew a walk. Though the Expos lost the game, Carter hit .429 in 35 at bats in his first taste of the postseason (an extra playoff round was added for the first time, due to the strike). As Jonah Kerri points out in his history of the Expos, *Up, Up, & Away*, Carter was second only to Philadelphia's Mike Schmidt in Wins Above Replacement in the major leagues between 1977 and 1984. Schmidt won two pennants and two MVPs in that span, but Kid's seven-year, $14 million contract with the Expos in 1982 surpassed the Phillies third baseman's deal and was the highest in the National League.* The Expos, who had drug issues that made the mid-1980s Mets look like Boy Scouts, faded to fifth place in 1984. And management decided to move clean Carter. It was, in Kerri's words, "The first time an Expos owner ever cited finances as the overriding reason to let a star player go . . . with Carter the first big domino to fall." New York was moving in the other direction. Unlike the June 1977 Tom Seaver deal—a four-for-one trade that signified surrender—this four-for-one deal in December 1984 signaled that the Mets were all in.

Two months of conversations between Frank Cashen and Expos president John McHale settled the deal. That was from the perspective of the ball clubs; the Carters were in the process of building their dream house in Montreal and welcoming newborn son D. J. "He was a month old when we found out the Expos wanted to trade Gary," Sandy Carter said. "The Mets picked up the last five years [of his contract]. And it was so nice to be wanted so badly."

The Mets didn't just pick up the contract; they found the family a rental house near where owner Nelson Doubleday lived and handled the Montreal home. "The Mets paid, I think, 75 percent of the loss when we sold the house because we built it and sold it so quick," Sandy Carter said. "They picked out basically the home in Oyster Bay Cove. They were great."

Gary Carter could concentrate on baseball in a new city, and the family did what it did best: watch Dad play. The Carters lived the major league life, a team effort. From the baby to the All-Star

* Yankees outfielder Dave Winfield was the lone major league player paid more than Gary Carter upon signing his 1982 deal.

catcher, there were few days off. Birthday parties at a friend's house? Sorry. Going to Great Adventure during a homestand? Um, no. Going to a sleepover when Dad was getting ready to go on a road trip? You wouldn't even ask. Though the kids went back to the same Florida school every September, they were home-schooled once the season started in April. The family ate together at home before games and traveled to Shea in shifts. They didn't miss many games, and Gary Carter—despite playing the most important position, batting in the middle of the order, and being one of the highest-paid players in the game—didn't miss any of their births, even in an age when few players dared ask.

"It became part of our lives," eldest daughter Christy (Carter) Kearce said. "We were up there for most of the season, and then school would start and Mom would get us situated, and then we would go back and forth to see Dad, which was cool." The best day came in September 1986, when Sandy picked up daughters Christy and Kimmy early from school.

"Guess where we're going?"

"Seven-Eleven! Slurpees!"

"No. We're catching a flight and we're going to New York!"

The family headed to New York for the 1986 NL East clincher. "I'll never forget because there were people jumping on the screen and rolling down it [onto the field]," Kearce recalled. "When we went home with Dad in the car, people were banging on the window of the car, carrying big things of sod. We were like, 'Why would anybody take sod?' People were completely out of control. They did a lot of damage."

The Mets did plenty of damage in 1986, to the National League—not to mention New England—and also to bars, women, planes, and a plate glass window in a Houston club. But the glitz fades, stories of late-night exploits turn from cool to embarrassing, and insight comes with age. In the 1980s it was easy to be jaded, or maybe even a jerk, but Carter signed every autograph and was home every second he could be—even though an intervention was needed to get him to hang up his uniform. When his contract with the Mets expired—Keith Hernandez left at the same time, the same way—the National League's top catcher of the 1980s toured San Francisco and Los Angeles as a backup, setting the NL record for most career games caught, a record he still holds (2,056). His final stop was with the Expos, who were fighting for a playoff spot—they finished second, again. Carter smacked a game-winning double off the wall at the Big O in the final at bat of his career. One last curtain call.

The Carters settled in the Palm Beach area, where the Expos had spring training, and Kid served as an announcer with the fledgling Marlins and later in Montreal, which broadcast few games by the late 1990s. But he longed to teach the game. Carter rejoined the Mets as a minor league manager—among his players to reach Flushing were Jon Niese and Bobby Parnell. After he managed Class A, the Mets wanted him to move up to Double-A Binghamton, but he said no. And he was out of the Mets organization. When Willie Randolph was on the hot seat in New York in 2008, Carter said in an interview he'd like the job. Another mistake. Some of the same criticisms surfaced as when he was a player.

"He really wanted to be a major league manager," Sandy Carter said. "He really, really desired that . . . because he did the independent league, he did the Long Island Ducks, and out in California, the [Orange County] Flyers, or whatever it was—but he was asked by Palm Beach Atlantic [University], and Kimmy was already there for five years, so she liked to tease him that she got the job for him. . . . He loved working with these young kids. They were like sponges. They were just like, 'Show me this, tell me that.'"

It was not the big leagues, but it was home. A Christian university just 15 minutes away, Palm Beach Atlantic allowed him to see more of his middle child, the one Carter born in Montreal.

Kimmy did not fall far from the tree. When she started playing fast-pitch softball in high school, her father recommended she play catcher and taught her on his old major league equipment. She was recruited in college for both soccer and softball. She chose the latter—and always wore number 8. A four-year starter at Florida State, she played both behind the plate and in right field, was All-ACC three times, set the FSU single-season and career marks for RBI as a senior captain (among a slew of records), and helped the Seminoles place third in the 2003 College World Series. Just like the big leagues, the family did not miss many games.

"I could always hear my family's voices in the stands. I always heard encouraging, motivating words . . . or even tips from my dad that would help me during the game," Kimmy (Carter) Bloemers said. "He always kept score with his own scorebook and wore his FSU attire head to toe. I am tearing up just remembering how special those times were for me."

Daughter and Kid had three years coaching at the same school until brain cancer claimed his life at age 57 in 2012. He was inducted into the Palm Beach Atlantic Hall of Fame in 2015 and had his number retired as well. Quite a few people thought the number might also hang on the wall at Citi Field.

Sandy Carter has nothing but good things to say about the Mets, but when asked whether she thought his number would be retired by the team, she stopped. "Yeah. Truthfully, I did. Do I think they should? Yes. I'm his wife. It's not like there's so many retired."

"Like the Yankees," Kearce added, finishing the thought. As if eavesdropping on the October 2014 conversation, the Yankees soon announced that three more numbers would be retired the following year to bring the total of players so honored to 21 and counting.

Until the Mets announced the retiring of Mike Piazza's number 31 after his election to the Hall of Fame in January 2016, Tom Seaver's 41 had been the only player number retired in the franchise's first 54 seasons. Unlike Carter, "NY" adorns the caps on the Cooperstown plaques of Piazza and Seaver. Number 8 was worn by six Mets after Carter left in 1989, though it has been out of circulation in Flushing since his 2003 induction into the National Baseball Hall of Fame. It is not the same as hanging the number on the wall—as the Expos did for number 8.*

D. J. Carter, in film production in California, is as surprised as anyone why the Mets have not followed suit. "Absolutely," he said. "I still think they should retire his number. It honestly doesn't make sense to me why his number has not been retired with them. My dad cherished his years as a Met and the Mets have done everything but retire his number."

"I truly am surprised the Mets have not retired my dad's number," Bloemers said. "Even though he only played five years [in New York], he was loved by the fans, he was considered the missing puzzle piece for the team, he is a Hall of Famer, he represented the Mets in a very positive way the way he lived his life and was a good influence, and he was an awesome ballplayer who helped them win a World Series. Sounds good enough to me."

It is sad that Gary Carter, the man who would not let the 1986 season die, was the first of the 1986 Mets to pass on. Keith Hernandez wept on TV when commenting on his cocaptain's death at age 57 on February 16, 2012.

"Gary played with so much pain and had to go through so much preparation for his knees before every game," Hernandez reflected in 2014. "And he was tenacious and overcame everything. . . . The fact that he died so young gives you a sense of mortality, and I think it affected a lot of guys. I know it did me. I've lost

* When the Expos became the Washington Nationals, they ignored Montreal's retired numbers and put them back in circulation. So much for Rusty Staub and Andre Dawson (both 10), Tim Raines (30), and Carter (8). No other franchise has done that to former players, with the exception of the Reds, in 1942.

several teammates over my 17 years in the big leagues; this one really hit me hard. We were the same age."

"He came to the park and prepared himself, through the injuries, through the hurts of it," said Tim Teufel, who played with Carter and managed at the same time he did in the Mets system. "Catching so much, he kind of grinded through. He's sorely missed."

Jeff Pearlman wrote *The Bad Guys Won* several years before Carter became ill. "I don't think a lot of them had a great love for Gary Carter," Pearlman said. He compared it to not being best friends with everyone in your Boy Scout troop or French class. "You go back to your 10th reunion—for your high school class—and you still have the shared bond over something you did. Together."

"Gary was such a rock," Len Berman said. Carter was his go-to guy for interviews on NBC-TV. "It's just sad. It always bothered me a little bit. I can't tell you what happened in that locker room, but supposedly some of the other players weren't wild about Gary because he was always genuinely nice to everybody. . . . And what's wrong with being cooperative with the media? It doesn't mean you're a suck-up. It doesn't mean anything."

Mets teammate Randy Niemann recalled an extra-inning game in San Diego, which Carter caught all of—of course. The Mets missed curfew for flying out of that airport and had to bus two hours north to Los Angeles, fly from LAX, stop to refuel in Kansas City, and arrive in New York the next day around 10 a.m. Niemann sat across the aisle from Carter, who spent most of the flight answering fan mail, of which there was no shortage. "That was just who he was," Niemann said. "He was the kind of person that loved doing what he was doing and really loved giving back to people. People took the time to write to him. He took the time to not only sign an autograph, but write a personal note and send it back to them. That's just who he was. That's what I'll always remember about him."

Carter's 1986 backup Ed Hearn named his son Cody Carter Hearn after the man he sat behind as a rookie, a gesture that still touches the Carter family. "Other people saw other things that I don't think I saw or really just cared that much about," Hearn said. "That was the Camera Kid syndrome, so to speak. But today, looking back and thinking about all those years, I see that more, that part of him that other guys saw back then. Part of how I was raised, I was influenced by my parents using guys like Gary Carter [as role models]. Back in the day, say, Tom Landry type, Roger Staubach—you know, guys that were good athletes, but they were men of good character, even godliness."

"It's such a shame that we lost him," his Mets manager, Davey Johnson, said in 2015. "Let me tell you about Carter, what people don't understand. Gary Carter, and I learned this early on when he first came over, Gary had a book on every hitter in the league. . . . He demanded a lot out of our young pitchers. I sometimes had to get on him: I said, 'Gary, you're asking these guys to throw curveballs when they're behind in the count.' He said to me, 'They've got to learn how to do it.' I said, 'Geez, these guys are hard throwers; some of them don't have that much command.' But he had a book on every hitter in the league. I saw it. And how to pitch them in different counts. And I said, 'I'm not going to get in your way. Try not to ask too much out of them.' He was the best."

Carter was more concerned with running the team on the field than fitting in off it. It is kind of funny how the two most crucial Game 6 heroes, Gary Carter and Mookie Wilson—though not the closest of friends—were teetotalers and very religious on a team known for late-night revelry.

"There's nothing cool about him," Pearlman said of Carter. "And that was a cool team. You know, they were a bunch of guys who thought they were cool. Gary Carter was the anti-cool. He was kind of a geek. . . . There's nothing wrong with being a geek.

It's probably the more admirable way to be. But you're not going to fit in with the cool kids in the smoking section."

To reinterpret Davey's Johnson line from the 1986 championship celebration—and Jeff Pearlman's book title: The bad guys won, but the good guy did quite well for himself. The good guy is very much missed. So is his team.

Acknowledgments

Every writer needs help. I was fortunate to find it from several sources. When it came to getting in touch with the people for this book, I was aided by a roster full of people. From professional baseball organizations I need to thank Andrew Buchbinder of the Springfield Cardinals; Chris Cameron of the Portland Sea Dogs; Chris Chenes of the Tri-City Valley Cats; Chris Glass at Mid-Atlantic Sports Network; Shannon Forde, Ethan Wilson, and Jay Horwitz of the New York Mets; plus Kevin Sornatale at SportsNet New York. The Queens Baseball Convention truly is baseball like it oughta be, and Shannon Shark of *Mets Police* should be lauded on his gradual ascent from Shea vendor to QBC czar. Also thanks to Keith "Media Goon" Blacknick for keeping the QBC running smoothly and to Stephen Keane of the Kranepool Society, who conducted the Mookie Wilson QBC interview onstage and kept going backstage with Mook and Wally Backman. Also thanks to Alan Cohen, James Jayo, Heather Quinlan, and Mark Simon, who helped track down elusive subjects. A conversation with Mark at the first QBC in 2014 helped me decide to write this book when I was toying with pursuing another subject. Heather—look for her film on the 1986 Mets—along with Bill Nowlin and Erik Sherman were on the trail of the same '86 animal and were helpful, friendly, and supportive.

To keep this to a one-volume set, I had to leave a lot out, but one of the better stories that didn't get in was how Dan Carubia walked in with a camera bag and no credential (or ticket) hours before Game 6 of the World Series and got pictures on the field of the Mets taking batting practice. A fine photographer with a salesman's persuasiveness, he let me use his best work from that night—and other on-field shoots—in this book. A more conventional source, the National Baseball Hall of Fame, came through again with wonderful images of the team and the era. Thanks to John Horne and everyone at the Hall.

Larry Arnold sent a homemade collection of DVD highlights meticulously culled from Mets games—and local newscasts—taped throughout 1986. I cannot begin to explain how thorough these DVDs were and how much they helped this process, and even changed the way I approached the book. Because I spent most of the '86 baseball season in Boulder, Colorado, taking a summer class at the University of Colorado, sloughing off, and not owning a functioning TV, I saw many of these games "live" for the first time via Larry's DVDs. Jeff Marcus came in late out of the bullpen and helped to transcribe interviews. Alan Silverman provided computer punch off the bench. There would be no book without my agent, Anne Marie O'Farrell, or Lyons Press with Keith Wallman serving as editor, Stephanie Scott working with photos, and Ellen Urban helping with late edits caused by a pennant nobody saw coming but many appreciated.

I also must note the contribution of the late Greg Spira, an avid Mets fan and baseball researcher, who left behind some boxes in my attic that turned out to be a treasure trove of clippings from numerous sources pertaining to 1986. I wish I could tell my old colleague how helpful this unexpected find was for this project. I will say, however, that like the '86 Mets he dearly loved, Greg is very much missed.

As always, I am indebted to my family for their patience and support through the long process. Thank you, Debbie, Tyler, and Jan. Words fail to describe how much you mean to me. My father, not a huge baseball fan, took me to ballgames and later helped provide tickets for what was the greatest period of Mets prosperity in franchise history. My mother cared even less for baseball, but she lit candles at Our Lady of Sorrows in October of '86 for me as much as the Mets. Every little bit helped. My brother Mark and his wife, Pam, took me to frigid Game 1 of the World Series. My brother Michael and sister Marie were dutifully happy for me, and the Mets.

Linc Wonham took me in when I wandered west in the spring of 1986, and we two diehard Mets fans pieced together what was happening in Queens through box scores, one-sentence *Denver Post* reports, and Wiffle ball séances. And a great summer turned spectacular when John Salerno joined us. Back east come fall, John Booth, Alec Dawson, Mike Kaplan, Paul Lin, Paul Lovetere, and Jim Singer were among those I sat with at Shea for the first five postseason home games. Broke but beaming, I watched the last two games from Shea in Lovetere and Doug Kline's dorm room in Virginia. It was there I also watched Game 6 of the NLCS with the late Chris O'Brien—Otis and I were friends but we became brothers for those 282 minutes as day turned to night and the Mets turned into pennant winners. And to Dave Bird, Al Gildersleeve, Todd Radom, and my many Red Sox friends—I am sorry yet not repentant.

I ended the book with Gary Carter because he refused to let the World Series end on his watch. Without that effort there would be no book. Character endures, and so do deeds. Gary Carter was the missing piece that changed a good team into a great one, and he is the piece that is missed now as '86 is revisited. His family's cooperation and devotion to his legacy is inspiring. Sandy, Kimmy, Christy, and D. J. each told me that Gary's one stated goal for enduring all the pain that went with catching—much of it on artificial turf—was to win a World Series. He never quit. Everyone could use a little more of that '86 attitude.

Notes

Part I. Dominance

Chapter 1: The Waiting

4. "The first airline where attitude is as important as altitude": *Airways News*, http://airwaysnews.com/html/timetable-and-route-maps/people-express-airlines-timetables-route-maps-and-history/1983-june-1-people-express-airlines-timetables-route-maps-history-and-advertising-/23537.
4. "By the night of the third game there was a little more edginess to it.": Interview with Gary Cohen, December 21, 2014.
4. "It wasn't the first press box I was kicked out of.": Interview with Peter Golenbock, February 11, 2015.
5. (all among the top dozen shows in the Nielsen ratings): "TV Ratings: 1985–1986," ClassicTVHits.com, www.classictvhits.com/tvratings/1985.htm.
5. a scuffle with Mariano Duncan of the Dodgers a few weeks earlier: Davey Johnson and Peter Golenbock, *Bats* (New York: G. P. Putnam's Sons, 1986), 299.
6. So Johnson had no real choice but to go with Aguilera,: Ibid., 314.
9. and chomping on a Belgian waffle,:"Readers Remember," *New York Times*, April 20, 2014.
10. he opened Gil Hodges Lanes on Ralph Avenue in 1961: "Gil Hodges, Ex-Dodger Star, Sure of a Hit with 48 Modern Bowling Lanes," uncredited newspaper clipping, February 9, 1961.
10. to Payson to indulge in her whim to become part owner.: Joan M. Thomas, "Joan Payson," SABR Baseball Biography Project, http://sabr.org/bioproj/person/88dc3fa9.
11. a deal—pitcher Bill Denehy and $100,000: John Saccoman, "Gil Hodges," SABR Baseball Biography Project, http://sabr.org/bioproj/person/c8022025.
11. home to the world champion St. Louis Cardinals the following month.: Bing Devine, *The Memoirs of Bing Devine: Stealing Lou Brock and Other Winning Moves by a Master GM* (New York: Skyhorse, 2011).
11. during the bloody Battle of Okinawa during World War II. Saccoman, "Gil Hodges."
12. We're looking far beyond .500.": Leonard Koppett, *The New York Mets* (New York: Collier Books, 1974), 189.

12. Gil Hodges said before the season that the Mets could win 85 games: Ibid., 184.
13. quickly rubbed the ball on *his* shoe at the behest of Hodges.: Interview with Jerry Koosman, July 10, 2011.
14. increases in teams' contributions to pension and medical benefits funds.: Jack Lang and Peter Simon, *The New York Mets: Twenty-Five Years of Baseball Magic* (New York: Henry Holt, 1986), 117.
14. when Mass is over I go over to chat with them," Staub recalled.: Interview with Rusty Staub, June 22, 2010.
14. two days shy of his 48th birthday.: Lang and Simon, *New York Mets*, 118.
14. "It's probably the most disappointing thing in my career that I didn't get a chance to play for him.": Staub interview.
18. The *New York Daily News* was their forum.: Lang and Simon, *New York Mets*, 156.
18. Once the money started, things changed." Interview with John Stearns, March 8, 2011.
19. 43-year-old real estate developer named Fred Wilpon.: Lang and Simon, *New York Mets*, 175.
20. "It was all pure junk," he wrote in his autobiography.: Mookie Wilson with Erik Sherman, *Mookie: Life, Baseball, and the '86 Mets* (New York: Berkley, 2014), 84.
21. what good baseball looks like. That's fun.": Interview with Shannon Shark, May 14, 2015.
23. "It's not a matter of trying harder. We just have to win more games.": Keith Hernandez and Mike Bryan, *If at First: A Season with the New York Mets* (New York: McGraw-Hill, 1986), 327.

Chapter 2: Life of Collusion

27. players with one-year contracts. John Helyar, *Lords of the Realm: The Real History of Baseball*: (New York: Villard, 1994), 329–30.
27. depend on your response to these problems.: Ibid., 331.
28. a businesslike way before we, as a sport, are bankrupt.": Ibid., 333.
29. cost $4 million four years later.: Ibid., 311.
29. But there's a lot of people making more.": Associated Press, "Royals Sign Brett to 'Lifetime' Contract,": *Sarasota Herald-Tribune*, May 8, 1984.
29. Murray for $13 million over five years in Baltimore.: Helyar, *Lords*, 325.
30. Go solve it.": Ibid., 334.
30. you would push the red one.": Ibid., 322.
30. more annually than the Yankees. Murray Chass,: "Yankees Offered Richest TV Pact," *New York Times*, May 1, 1982, www.nytimes.com/1982/05/01/sports/yankees-offered-richest-tv-pact.html. Helyar, *Lords*, 380.

32. Angels that August in a cost-cutting move. "Blockbusters in Winter Meetings History,": CBSSports.com, November 30, 2010, www.cbssports.com/mcc/blogs/entry/22297882/26161798.
33. a pitcher in a big ballpark like ours.": Whitey Herzog and Kevin Horrigan, *White Rat: A Life in Baseball* (New York: Harper & Row, 1987), 171.
33. and now we're back to 40.": "Mets Obtain Ojeda in 8-Player Trade." *New York Times*, November 14, 1985.
33. that's going to help you get back to the big leagues.": Interview with Davey Johnson, March 31, 2015.
35. big leagues as a backup catcher, like a utility guy.": Davey Johnson interview.

Chapter 3: Exquisitely Bored

36. wind down after a game, a road trip, or a season.: Dwight Gooden and Ellis Henican, *Doc: A Memoir* (Boston: Houghton Mifflin Harcourt, 2013), 72.
38. and issuing a siren's call to Dr. K.: Ibid., 71–73.
38. This is how I wanted to feel.": Ibid., 75.
39. was produced by the MLB Players Association Chris Otto, "Important Message from Papergreat and Some 1980s Baseball Players,": Papergreat.com, March 25, 2014, www.papergreat.com/2014/03/important-message-from-papergreat-and.html.
39. (the average salary in 1985). Average Wage Index, :Social Security Administration, www.ssa.gov/oact/cola/awidevelop.html.
39. 12 percent increase per year for a decade. Vin Getz, "Major League Baseball's Average Salaries 1964–2010,":Sports List of the Day, December 5, 2011, http://sportslistoftheday.com/2011/12/05/major-league-baseballs-average-salaries-1964-2010. "Minimum Salary," Baseball-Reference.com, www.baseball-reference.com/bullpen/minimum_salary.
40. hung around with some wrong people." Michael Goodwin, "Baseball and Cocaine: A Deepening Problem,": *New York Times*, August 19, 1985, www.nytimes.com/1985/08/19/sports/baseball-and-cocaine-a-deepening-problem.html.
40. "drug problems because of an identity crisis.": Murray Chass and Michael Goodwin, "Cocaine: Baseball's Black Eye," *Chicago Tribune* via *New York Times* News Service, August 19, 1985, http://articles.chicagotribune.com/1985-08-19/sports/8502240237_1_dale-shiffman-prosecution-cocaine.
40. to keep the gram bottles in his back pocket from breaking.: Murray Chass, "Cocaine Disrupts Baseball from Field to Front Office," *New York Times*, August 20, 1985, www.nytimes.com//1985/08/20/sports/cocaine-disrupts-baseball-from-field-to-front-office.html.
41. "I did it almost every day during the winter.": Ibid.
41. hampered them and diluted their talent,: Ibid.

41. "Stool Parrot," but he flew off with no jail time.: Aaron Skirboll, *The Pittsburgh Cocaine Seven: How a Ragtag Group of Fans Took the Fall for Major League Baseball* (Chicago: Chicago Review Press, 2010), 155.
42. 20 of 111 counts and served two years in a federal penitentiary.: John McCollister, *The Good, the Bad, and the Ugly: Heart-Pounding, Jaw-Dropping, and Gut-Wrenching Moments from Pittsburgh Pirates History* (Chicago: Triumph Books, 2008), 43.
42. similar offenders were usually charged with a misdemeanor.: Skirboll, *Pittsburgh Cocaine Seven*, 138–39.
42. take responsibility for what adults do.": Ibid., 177.
42. players used cocaine in 1980.": Ibid., 173.
42. "How could I know what the percentage was?":Keith Hernandez and Mike Bryan, *If at First: A Season with the Mets* (New York: McGraw-Hill, 1986), 282–83.
43. drug users on the 1980 Cardinals.): Chass, "Cocaine Disrupts Baseball."
43. he later identified as "never massive.": Hernandez and Bryan, *If at First*, 282–83.
43. was with Bowie Kuhn as commissioner.: Thomas Rogers, "Blue Suspended for the Year," *New York Times*, July 27, 1984, www.nytimes.com/1984/07/27/sports/blue-suspended-for-the-year.html.
44. Martin had been suspended 33 games in 1984: Jane Gross, "The Toughest Year for Jerry Martin," Players, *New York Times*, May 15, 1984, www.nytimes.com/1984/05/15/sports/players-the-toughest-year-for-jerry-martin.html.
44. "But I have no idea what the commissioner will do.": Joseph Durso, "Hernandez Is Facing Future with Optimism and Doubts," *New York Times*, February 5, 1986, www.nytimes.com/1986/02/05/sports/hernandez-is-facing-future-with-optimism-and-doubts.html.
45. instead of at home in Newport Beach, California?: John Helyar, *Lords of the Realm: The Real History of Baseball* (New York: Villard, 1994), 340–41.
45. third drug test in three seasons.: Sam McManis, "The Troubling Career of Michael Ray Richardson," *Los Angeles Times*, February 28, 1986, http://articles.latimes.com/1986-02-28/sports/sp-12889_1_drug-policy.
45. and subpoenaed but not called to testify in the drug trials Glen Macnow,: "Baseball Drug Case Now Goes to the Jury," *Orlando Sentinel*, September 19, 1985, http://articles.orlandosentinel.com/1985-09-19/sports/0330110021_1_john-milner-renfroe-willie-mays.
46. long before and long after the Pittsburgh trials. Inquirer Wire Services,: "Ueberroth Punishes Baseball Players Linked to Drugs," *Philadelphia Inquirer*, March 1, 1986, http://articles.philly.com/1986-03-01/news/26081366_1_conditional-suspensions-drug-trials-drug-testing.
46. United Press International named drugs the number one sports story of 1985.: Skirboll, *Pittsburgh Cocaine Seven*, 210.
46. transgressions demands the actions I have taken.": Michael Goodwin, "Baseball Orders Suspension of 11 Drug Users," *New York Times*, March 1,

1986, www.nytimes.com/1986/03/01/sports/baseball-orders-suspension-of-11-drug-users.html.
46. drug testing infringed upon players' rights.: Skirboll, *Pittsburgh Cocaine Seven*, 212–14.
47. or for whatever reason, we will include it.": George Vecsey, "The Test-Tube League," Sports of the Times, *New York Times*, January 19, 1986, www.nytimes.com/1986/01/19/sports/sports-of-the-times-the-test-tube-league.html.

Chapter 4: The Perfectly Strange Couple

48. tickets than any R-rated film since *The Exorcist* in 1973. "Domestic Grosses Adjusted for Ticket Price Inflation,": Box Office Mojo, www.boxofficemojo.com/alltime/adjusted.htm.
49. was a creator of *Perfect Strangers*.: "Dale McRaven," IMDb.com, www.imdb.com/name/nm0574471.
49. you can drink during the season,": Robert Lipsyte, "Spring of '62: Revisiting the Dawn of the Mets," *New York Times*, February 19, 2012, www.nytimes.com/2012/02/20/sports/baseball/remembering-the-mets-first-spring-in-1962.html.
49. empty bus leaving at five o'clock.": Anthony McCarron, "If You Think Today's NY Mets Are Bad, Then You Must Not Remember the 1962 Squad of Casey Stengel, Richie Ashburn and Marv Throneberry," *New York Daily News*, January 14, 2012, www.nydailynews.com/sports/baseball/mets/today-mets-bad-not-remember-1962-mets-casey-stengal-richie-ashburn-marv-throneberry-article-1.1006140.
50. resurrection of Bob Gibson, only younger, wilder, and dressed in blue.: Interview with Kevin Horrigan, February 12, 2015.
51. "New York Mets—1986 NL East Champions.": Richard Justice, "Mets Reached Their Lofty Expectations Quite Easily," *The Washington Post*, October 4, 1986.
51. begin their reign as NL East champs" proclaimed the *Liberty Champion* Steve Davis,: Sportscene, *Liberty Champion*, March 26, 1986.
51. the defending NL champion Cardinals. UPI, "Yanks and Mets Favored,": *New York Times*, January 8, 1986, www.nytimes.com/1986/01/08/sports/yanks-and-mets-favored.html.
51. "The Baseball Bible" was based in St. Louis!: "TSN's 1986 Predictions," *The Sporting News 1986 Baseball Yearbook* (St. Louis: Sporting News, 1986).
51. they won the last two years anyway.": Joseph Durso, "Cards Shed Scars and Brace for Challenge," *New York Times*, March 16, 1986, www.nytimes.com/1986/03/16/sports/cards-shed-scars-and-brace-for-challenge.html.
51. front page of *USA Today* instead of the Cardinals.": Interview with Steve Jacobson, January 22, 2015.
54. seven of them were on big league rosters.": Interview with Whitey Herzog, March 6, 2014.

54. ninth-place rings,": Herzog recalled, laughing. Ibid.
55. had just won the World Series as a manager.": Ibid.
55. to appeal to above the manager.": Leonard Koppett, *The New York Mets* (New York: Collier Books, 1974), 160.
56. talent than his more experienced personnel.": Jack Lang and Peter Simon, *The New York Mets: Twenty-Five Years of Baseball Magic* (New York: Henry Holt, 1986), 105.
56. a great friend of mine.": Herzog interview.
57. frustrated and bored with the job.": Whitey Herzog and Kevin Horrigan, *White Rat: A Life in Baseball* (New York: Harper & Row, 1987), 86.
57. worst decision I ever made in my life," he said.: Herzog interview.
57. beat him out for the job with the abysmal Rangers.: Herzog and Horrigan, *White Rat*, 87.
57. situation in Kansas City with a good, young team.": Herzog interview.
59. "We got cheated," he said later. :Herzog and Horrigan, *White Rat*, 134.
59. even that was in the short term.: Ibid., 132.
59. giving away more than you know.": Ibid., 128.
59. 'Who was Keith Hernandez traded for?' I'm honored.": Kevin DuPont, "Keith Hernandez Sent to Mets for Allen, Ownbey," *New York Times*, June 16, 1983, www.nytimes.com/1983/06/16/sports/keith-hernandez-sent-to-mets-for-allen-ownbey.html.
60. in an interview the night of the trade.: "Why Cardinals Dealt Keith Hernandez in 1983," RetroSimba.com, http://retrosimba.com/2013/06/12/why-cardinals-dealt-keith-hernandez-30-years-ago.
60. Whitey's hands were sort of tied there.": Horrigan interview.
60. They don't visit your locker room, you know.": Interview with Keith Hernandez, January 15, 2015.
61. to get their attention.": Herzog and Horrigan, *White Rat*, 151–52.
61. "an irresistible contract" Steven Crist,: "New Mets Training Complex to Put St. Lucie West on Map," *New York Times*, February 3, 1988, www.nytimes.com/1988/02/03/sports/new-mets-training-complex-to-put-st-lucie-west-on-map.html.
62. on the other side of the state.: Richard Firstman, "No Joy in St. Pete," *Newsday*, March 19, 1987.
62. He went down.: Mookie Wilson with Erik Sherman, *Mookie: Life, Baseball, and the '86 Mets* (New York: Berkley, 2014), 123.
62. thus sparing him more damage.: Joseph Durso, "Mets' Wilson Hurt; Right Eye Injured," *New York Times*, March 6, 1986, www.nytimes.com/1986/03/06/sports/mets-wilson-hurt-right-eye-injured.html.
63. repaired right shoulder to fully recuperate.: Wilson with Sherman, *Mookie*, 124.
63. and Lenny Dykstra at the time.: Bob Sherwin, "Kevin Mitchell—At Home in the Hood—New Mariner Escaped Ghetto, Not Questions about Him and His Friends," *Seattle Times*, February 16, 1992, http://community.seattletimes

.nwsource.com/archive/?date=19920216&slug=1475979. "Roger Jongewaard Dies at 75; Longtime Baseball Scout," *Los Angeles Times*, June 20, 2012, http://articles.latimes.com/2012/jun/20/local/la-me-roger-jongewaard-20120619-1.
63. including another team's manager Jeff Pearlman,: *The Bad Guys Won* (New York: HarperCollins, 2004), 69–70.
63. I didn't think baseball was like that.": Interview with Kevin Mitchell, March 31, 2015.
63. and not for the last time.: Art Spander, "Giants' Kevin Mitchell Has Come a Long Way," *Chicago Tribune*, July 26, 1987, http://articles.chicagotribune.com/1987-07-26/sports/8702240691_1_josie-whitfield-kevin-mitchell-darryl-strawberry.
64. derailed what many thought would be a fine career.: Joseph Durso, "Gibbons, Promising Met Catcher, Is Hurt." *New York Times*, March 26, 1984.
64. He just never recovered.": Interview with Mookie Wilson, January 10, 2015.
65. after not being on the roster when camp began: "Mets Invite 10 More," Sports People, *New York Times*, February 4, 1986, www.nytimes.com/1986/02/04/sports/sports-people-mets-invite-10-more.html.
65. does it?" Sisk asked after getting the news.: Joseph Durso, "Sisk, Gardenhire Sent Down by Mets," *New York Times*, April 4, 1986, www.nytimes.com/1986/04/04/sports/sisk-gardenhire-sent-down-by-mets.html.

Chapter 5: Comet, Computation, and Chemistry

66. even though Halley was dead.: Elizabeth Howell, "Halley's Comet: Facts About the Most Famous Comet," Space.com, February 20, 2013, www.space.com/19878-halleys-comet.html.
67. no weaknesses. And we didn't.": Interview with Davey Johnson, March 31, 2015.
68. mad after that," Johnson said that night.: Jim Naughton, "Gooden Able to Rise to the Occasion," *New York Daily News*, April 9, 1986.
70. Have it framed.": Interview with Kevin Horrigan, February 12, 2015.
70. each person that we played against.": Interview with Whitey Herzog, March 6, 2014.
70. "Optimize the Oriole lineup.": Davey Johnson interview.
71. I use it as another tool.": "Davey Johnson, the Mets, and Sabermetrics," *Misc. Baseball* (blog), December 4, 2009, https://miscbaseball.wordpress.com/2009/12/04/davey-johnson-the-mets-and-sabermetrics.
72. but this was out-of-the-box thinking in 1986.: Rich Lederer, "Abstracts from the Abstracts. Part Ten: 1986 Baseball Abstract," BaseballAnalysts.com, November 29, 2004, http://baseballanalysts.com/archives/2004/11/abstracts_from_21.php.
73. may have been invisible to the naked eye.": Interview with John Thorn, October 2, 2014.

73 fn. In the days before sabermetrics, he sort of understood all that stuff instinctively.": Horrigan interview.
73. score more runs," Cook told Johnson.: Davey Johnson interview.
74. against the reigning Cy Young winner.: Whitey Herzog and Kevin Horrigan, *White Rat: A Life in Baseball* (New York: Harper & Row, 1987), 6.
75. "The mid-'80s changed that for me.": Interview with Ricky Horton, February 27, 2015.
76. "We had some help there."): Herzog interview.
76. players don't get the job done," Herzog said.: Herzog and Horrigan, *White Rat*, 20–21.
77. the home opener spoiled.: Jim Naughton, "Error in 13th Foils Mets," *New York Daily News*, April 15, 1986.
77. ball to go through Johnson's legs.": Herzog and Horrigan, *White Rat*, 22.
79. a public strip search. Every time.": Mike Lupica, "Driving Home a Lesson," *New York Daily News*, April 17, 1986.
79. the attendant a "stupid bitch.": Dwight Gooden and Ellis Henican, *Doc: A Memoir* (Boston: Houghton Mifflin Harcourt, 2013), 79.
79. didn't do anything wrong.": Jim Naughton, "'I'm Not a Violent Person.'" *New York Daily News*, April 17, 1986.
79. no way you are getting the win.": Lupica, "Driving Home a Lesson."
81. and do it the other way.": Interview with Wally Backman, January 10, 2015.
81. "The thing Teufel does best is hit.": Murray Chass, "Mets Trade to Help Hitting," *New York Times*, January 17, 1986, www.nytimes.com/1986/01/17/sports/mets-trade-to-help-hitting.html.
82. Strawberry in his first Mets draft in 1980.: J. Frank Cashen, *Winning in Both Leagues: Reflections from Baseball's Front Office* (Lincoln: University of Nebraska Press, 2014), 99.
82. the reason he became a GM: Ibid., vii.
82. "Go on, go on, hit.": Interview with Marty Noble, February 25, 2015.
84. I wanted to hit a home run and did.": "1986 Mets: A Year to Remember," www.dailymotion.com/video/x129dhn_1986-mets-a-year-to-remember_sport.
84. Then you have great chemistry.": Davey Johnson interview.
84. and that put Ray on fire.": Noble interview.
84. even if they hated New York.: "Al Capone's Vault," https://www.youtube.com/watch?v=P84OKTUx6LY.
85. to figure it out pretty quick.": Interview with Tim Teufel, March 12, 2015.
86. vaunted running game was grounded.: Tim Rosaforte, "Tarp Accident Throws Coleman Out of Lineup," *Fort Lauderdale Sun-Sentinel*, October 14, 1985, http://articles.sun-sentinel.com/1985-10-14/sports/8502140738_1_tarp-vince-coleman-cardinals-teammates.
87. fight sequence on the campy 1960s show *Batman*.: "Bat-Fight Words," Bat-Mania.com, www.bat-mania.co.uk./trivia/batfight_words.php.
87. "Every game with these guys seems like this.": Phil Pepe, "Mets-Cards 'Crucial' Series," *New York Daily News*, April 25, 1986.

87. you'd see his glove sticking up.": Phil Pepe, "Mets on the Verge of Sweeping Cards," *New York Daily News*, April 27, 1986.
88. the way they beat us last year.": Jim Naughton, "How Sweep It Is for Mets," *New York Daily News*, April 28, 1986.
88. especially the Cardinals.": Noble interview.
88. We're out of the race.": Herzog and Horrigan, *White Rat*, 197.

Chapter 6: Top Gun

90. words of the *Washington Post*, "made America love war.": David Sirota, "25 Years Later, How 'Top Gun' Made America Love War," *Washington Post*, August 26, 2011, www.washingtonpost.com/opinions/25-years-later-remembering-how-top-gun-changed-americas-feelings-about-war/2011/08/15/gIQAU6qJgJ_story.html.
91. the average movie ticket was $2.75.: Sirota, "25 Years Later." *1986 Remember When . . . A Nostalgic Look Back in Time.* Birmingham, AL: Seek Publishing.
91. stated that they had seen the movie.: Mark Evje, "'Top Gun' Boosting Service Sign-ups," *Los Angeles Times*, July 5, 1986, http://articles.latimes.com/1986-07-05/entertainment/ca-20403_1_top-gun.
91. Ford Escort cost 89 cents per gallon.: *1986 Remember When.*
91. Navy got script approval.: Robert Lindsey, "'Top Gun': Ingenious Dogfights," *New York Times*, May 27, 1986, www.nytimes.com/1986/05/27/movies/top-gun-ingenious-dogfights.html.
91. ejector seat failure.: Jacob V. Lamar Jr., "The Pentagon Goes Hollywood," *Time*, November 24, 1986, http://content.time.com/time/magazine/article/0,9171,962933,00.html.
92. triumph over the forces of Communism.": Lindsey, "'Top Gun': Ingenious Dogfights."
92. the template for a new Military-Entertainment Complex.": Sirota, "25 Years Later."
92. for second place. Dismissed.": Chip Proser, *Top Gun* script, revised April 4, 1985, www.dailyscript.com/scripts/TopGun.html.
94. "Walkman" entered the *Oxford English Dictionary* in 1986.: Meaghan Haire, "A Brief History of the Walkman," *Time*, July 1, 2009, http://content.time.com/time/nation/article/0,8599,1907884,00.html.
94. Bronx wasn't safe for families to venture to.: "This Day in All Teams History, May 1st," NationalPastime.com, www.nationalpastime.com/site/index.php?action=baseball_team_search&baseball_team=All+Teams&fact_Month=05&fact_Day=1.
94. Dwight Gooden *losing* than any Yankee pitcher winning.'": Frank Brown, "The Grapple for the Apple,": *New York Daily News*, August 3, 1986.
95. for the award-winning television show *Mad Men*. :Michael Bierut, "Jerry Della Femina, Mad Men, and the Cult of Advertising Personality," The Design

Observer Group, July 25, 2010, http://designobserver.com/feature/jerry-della-femina-mad-men-and-the-cult-of-advertising-personality/14668.
95. 'Baseball like it used to be.'": Frank Brown, "The Grapple for the Apple."
95. a study the previous year from the city comptroller.: Ibid.
96. the Mets get the big screen.": Ibid.
97. were four axes under Billy Martin's. Moss Klein, "Managerial Merry-Go-Round," *The Sporting News 1986 Baseball Yearbook* (St. Louis: Sporting News, 1986).
97. To New Yorkers, it's all Mets.": Frank Brown, "The Grapple for the Apple."
99. 300 million riders during the 1980s.: "When the New York City Subway Was the Most Dangerous Place on Earth," All That Is Interesting, http://all-that-is-interesting.com/new-york-subways-1980s#1.
99. $3.50 in 1986 (including deposit).: William R. Greer, "Beer Prices Up Since Bottle Law," Consumer Saturday, *New York Times*, March 15, 1986, www.nytimes.com/1986/03/15/style/consumer-saturday-beer-prices-up-since-bottle-law.html.
100. you might as well lose in California.": Interview with Mookie Wilson, January 10, 2015.
100. turned the trip into a California trifecta.: Ed Leyro, "A Brief History on West Coast Road Trips for the Mets," StudiousMetsimus.com, August 8, 2013, http://studiousmetsimus.blogspot.com/2013/08/a-brief-history-on-west-coast-road.html.
100. owed him something,": Davey Johnson said of Heep after the game. Jim Naughton, "Heep Helps His Cause," *New York Daily News*, May 17, 1986.
101. you're a regular every day.": Mets-Dodgers, *ABC Sunday Afternoon Baseball*, May 18, 1986.
101. fans definitely have an effect on our play.": Steve Zabriskie pregame interview with Keith Hernandez, WOR-TV, May 27, 1986.
102. into "Boooom" for Foster's resurgent power.: Bill Gallo, "From Boo to Boom" (cartoon), *New York Daily News*, June 7, 1986.
103. did not move for a full minute.": Mets-Dodgers, WOR-TV, May 27, 1986.
103. and buried the hatchet. Jeff Pearlman,: *The Bad Guys Won* (New York: HarperCollins, 2004), 94.
104. Knight admitted on *Kiner's Korner* after the game: *Kiner's Korner*, WOR-TV, May 31, 1986.
104. "It's a tainted win, but they'll take it.": Ibid.

Chapter 7: Not Your Father's Mets

107. who is going to have a good year for me." :Marty Goldensohn, "Having a Field Day at Spring Training," *Newsday*, March 3, 1987.
107. no more key injuries.": Howard Johnson interview, *New York Mets Pregame Show*, SportsChannel, June 2, 1986.

108 "probably cost the Mets the pennant.": Jack Lang, "Mets Left Short Without HoJo, Straw," *New York Daily News*, June 3, 1986.
108. tired from playing, traveling, or partying. Graham Roberts,: "Why Amphetamines Found a Home in Baseball," *New York Times*, March 31, 2006, www.nytimes.com/imagepages/2006/03/31/sports/01greenies_graphic.ready.html.
108. fn. first tested for steroids.: Jack Curry, "With Greenies Banned, Up for a Cup of Coffee?" *New York Times*, April 1, 2006, www.nytimes.com/2006/04/01/sports/baseball/01greenies.html.
108. cope with it by partying.: Darryl Strawberry with John Strausbaugh, *Straw: Finding My Way* (New York: Ecco, 2009), 64–65.
109. he wouldn't say otherwise.": Ibid., 82–83.
109. and we got pretty harsh sometimes.": Ibid., 82.
109. before the 1985 Pittsburgh drug trials.: Ibid., 98.
110. their second brawl of the season.: Jim Naughton, "Brawling in Pittsburgh," *New York Daily News*, June 7, 1986.
110. chokehold and wouldn't let him go.":Interview with Kevin Mitchell, March 27, 2015.
110. some 2,500 handwritten, handheld signs: Joseph Durso, "Mets Top Pirates Twice, Run Winning Streak to 6," *New York Times*, June 16, 1986, www.nytimes.com/1986/06/16/sports/mets-top-pirates-twice-run-winning-streak-to-6.html.
111. two-run single against former Met Jeff Reardon in the 10th.: Michael Martinez, "Mets Win in 10th on Strawberry Hit," *New York Times*, June 17, 1986, www.nytimes.com/1986/06/17/sports/mets-win-in-10th-on-strawberry-hit.html.
112. more of a smarter pitcher this year.": Jack Lang, "Doc OK with Fewer K's," *New York Daily News*, June 3, 1986.
113. more highly of me than I did of myself.": Mookie Wilson with Erik Sherman, *Mookie: Life, Baseball, and the '86 Mets* (New York: Berkley, 2014), 42–54.
113. Mookie made the All-Tournament team and Hubie did not).: "All Tournament Teams," *2009 Guide: NCAA Men's College World Series Records, 1947–2008* (Indianapolis: NCAA, 2008), 46, http://fs.ncaa.org/Docs/stats/baseball_cws_RB/2009CWSfull.pdf.
115. and received their blessing.: Wilson with Sherman, *Mookie*, 55–57.
115. Preston, a future All-Star center fielder.: Ibid., 64–66.
116. and mental aspect of the team change.": Mookie Wilson discussion at Queens Baseball Convention, January 10, 2015.
117. has established himself.": Jim Naughton, "For Mets, 2-Headed Leadoff Man," *New York Daily News*, June 13, 1986.

Chapter 8: Sledgehammer

119. the eventual foundation of Turner Network Television (TNT).: "Milestones," TBS Superstation, http://cgi.superstation.com/about_us/milestone.htm.
119. more than double the Yankees' take at that point—: John Helyar, *Lords of the Realm: The Real History of Baseball* (New York: Villard, 1994), 380.
119. was still not wired for cable.: Jesus Rangel, "At Long Last, Cable Comes to Brooklyn," *New York Times*, May 13, 1986, www.nytimes.com/1986/05/13/nyregion/at-long-last-cable-comes-to-brooklyn.html.
120. places like Grand Island, Nebraska, had been enjoying for years.: Josh Barbanel, "Cable TV Comes to Queens in a Test Two Decades After Manhattan Got It," *New York Times*, December 10, 1985, www.nytimes.com/1985/12/10/nyregion/cable-tv-comes-to-queens-in-a-test-two-decades-after-manhattan-got-it.html.
121. "Boy, the Mets really blew it tonight, huh?": *The Seinfeld Chronicles* pilot episode, https://vimeo.com/82691805.
122. averaging almost two innings per relief outing. :Bill Gallo, "*Daily News* Met Player of the Month: June" (cartoon), *New York Daily News*, July 2, 1986.
123. emigrated from southern Italy to Long Island in the 1850s.: "About Fireworks by Grucci," Grucci.com, http://www.grucci.com/main.html?pgid=10.
124. In either league.": New York Mets vs. Houston Astros, WOR-TV, July 3, 1986.
124. like the NBA All-Star Game.": Interview with Keith Hernandez, July 14, 2008.
126. including one to Davey Johnson.: Steve Wilder, "Met Report Card," *New York Post*, July 11, 1986.
127. but don't show me up.'": Joseph Durso, "Mets Win on Fernandez's 2-Hitter," *New York Times*, July 12, 1986, www.nytimes.com/1986/07/12/sports/mets-win-on-fernandez-s-2-hitter.html.
127. breaking his wife Lisa's nose during a postseason altercation Darryl Strawberry with John Strausbaugh,: *Straw: Finding My Way* (New York: Ecco, 2009), 87–91.
127. hit a home run and celebrated.": *NBC Game of the Week Pregame Show*, July 12, 1986.
128. posted bond of $8,000 each, Ojeda and Aguilera $800 apiece.: Michael Martinez, "4 Mets Arrested in Fight," *New York Times*, July 20, 1986, www.nytimes.com/1986/07/20/sports/4-mets-arrested-in-fight.html.
128. still thankful he left early that night.: Interview with Ed Hearn, March 27, 2015.
128. whose birthday they had been celebrating.: Dave Anderson, "Cooter's Joins Copa," *New York Times*, July 21, 1986, www.nytimes.com/1986/07/21/sports/cooter-s-joins-copa.html.
128. That's something that's way beyond me.": Interview with Tim Teufel, March 12, 2015.

131. routine fly ball to right field.": "1986-07-22 Mets at Reds," https://www.youtube.com/watch?v=dljM3PyIiXI.
133. just once per inning.: Dick Young, "Orosco, McDowell do Curly Shuffle," *New York Post*, July 24, 1986.
133. "Helped us win a game.": Interview with Davey Johnson, March 31, 2015.
133. but I'd rather have the win.": Len Berman interview with Roger McDowell, *Live at Five*, network, July 23, 1986.
134. You can't push us around.": Jim Naughton, "HoJo's 3-run HR Wins Brawlgame," *New York Daily News*, July 23, 1986.

Chapter 9: Just Routine, Ma'am

136. very Kiss-Me-I'm-Italian.": E. M. Swift, "Hometown Kid Makes Good; Lee Mazzilli, Brooklyn's Very Own, Has Become a Met Star and Budding Idol," *Sports Illustrated*, July 23, 1979, www.si.com/vault/1979/07/23/823810/hometown-kid-makes-good-lee-mazzilli-brooklyns-very-own-has-become-a-met-star-and-budding-idol.
136. a conflict with his first love, baseball.: Jon Springer, "Lee Mazzilli," SABR Baseball Biography Project, http://sabr.org/bioproj/person/e0629b8b.
138. ever trade Lee Mazzilli?": J. Frank Cashen, *Winning in Both Leagues: Reflections from Baseball's Front Office* (Lincoln: University of Nebraska Press, 2014), 109.
139. rest of '86 and the $650,000 owed him in '87.: "Mazzilli Joins Tidewater," *New York Times*, August 2, 1986, www.nytimes.com/1986/08/02/sports/mazzilli-joins-tidewater.html.
139. three homers over the past two months should get.: Interview with Marty Noble, February 25, 2015.
139. a Mookie Wilson with a more popular player.": Jim Naughton, "Foster: Is It Racial?" *New York Daily News*, August 6, 1986.
139. manager responded, "Performance dictates,": Ibid.
139. I got it all straight.": Noble interview.
140. reaching 500 home runs, was also unrealized.: Len Berman interview with George Foster, WNBC-TV, August 7, 1986.
140. can't condone and I can't have.": Carl Cherkin interview with Davey Johnson, WOR-TV, August 6, 1986.
141. before the last game on the schedule.: Jim Naughton, "Mets Make Hit Parade," *New York Daily News*, August 8, 1986.
141. and play in New York.": Pregame show, WOR-TV, August 8, 1986.
141. that he couldn't throw in the outfield.": Interview with Mookie Wilson, January 10, 2015.
142. be considered restraint of trade.": *SportsCenter*, ESPN, August 10, 1986.
143. got to be Ed Hearn.'": Interview with Ed Hearn, March 27, 2015.
144. guys would be fresh tomorrow.": Interview with Randy Niemann, May 29, 2014.

147. until the collision an instant later.: Jim Naughton, "Dykstra Gets Davey Off Hook," *New York Daily News*, August 28, 1986.
147. "Just your routine double play.": Mets vs. Padres, WOR-TV, August 25, 1986.

Chapter 10: Everybody Wang Chung Tonight

149. which "Get Metsmerized" was purported to rip off, er, emulate.: Evan Wiley, "The 12 Worst Songs Ever Recorded by Athletes," Bleacher Report, July 29, 2008, http://bleacherreport.com/articles/42124-the-12-worst-songs-ever-recorded-by-athletes.
151. combined tenures in the big leagues.: Debbi del Condo, "Pint-Sized Martha Quinn Is a Growing Presence on MTV," *Orlando Sentinel*, April 21, 1985, http://articles.orlandosentinel.com/1985-04-21/entertainment/0290200192_1_martha-quinn-mtv-veejay-thing-on-mtv. Melissa Leon, "Martha Quinn, Nina Blackwood & More Original MTV VJs Tell All," The Daily Beast, May 7, 2013, www.thedailybeast.com/articles/2013/05/07/martha-quinn-nina-blackwood-more-original-mtv-vjs-tell-all.html.
152. profile that month in *New York* magazine.: Joe Klein, "Let's Go Mets!" *New York*, September 29, 1986.
153. anyway, in 13 interminable innings.): Mike Sielski, "The Mystery of the 1978 Mayor's Trophy," *Wall Street Journal*, May 21, 2011, www.wsj.com/articles/SB10001424052748704816604576335411148026014.
153. costing him money on the road teams' share.: Bill Madden, *Steinbrenner: The Last Lion of Baseball* (New York: Harper, 2010), 278.
153. in the middle of it.": Interview with Steve Jacobson, January 22, 2015.
153. bigger than the Giants winning the Super Bowl.": Interview with Len Berman, March 30, 2015.
154. ended the Mayor's Trophy game in New York.": Peter Gammons, "Coming Attraction in Fenway?" *Sports Illustrated*, September 15, 1986, www.si.com/vault/1986/09/15/113943/coming-attraction-in-fenway.
154. throwing his baseball wealth in your face.": J. Frank Cashen, *Winning in Both Leagues: Reflections from Baseball's Front Office* (Lincoln: University of Nebraska Press, 2014), 116.
154. you're not looking around in wonderment.": Jim Naughton, "A World Series Pre-Phew!" *New York Daily News*, September 6, 1986.
155. major league mark with 50 homers allowed.): Jayson Stark, ". . . But That Doesn't Mean the Drama's Over," *Philadelphia Inquirer*, September 16, 1986, http://articles.philly.com/1986-09-16/sports/26075936_1_astros-staff-indians-edwin-correa.
156. during an upper-deck fracas at the Vet.: A. J. Mass, *Yes, It's Hot in Here: Adventures in the Weird, Wooly World of Sports Mascots* (New York: Rodale, 2014), 36–37.
156. it will be champagne.": Jim Naughton, "Mets Shave Magic Number to 1," *New York Daily News*, September 17, 1986.

159. just kept running and killed me.": Interview with Wally Backman, January 10, 2015.
160. he wasn't able to," Hernandez recalled.: Interview with Keith Hernandez, August 13, 2008.
161. but it feels so much better.": *Kiner's Korner*, WOR-TV, September 17, 1986.
161. 'Yeah, at the present time.'": Frank Brown, "Cashen Rues Fans' Eve of Destruction," *New York Daily News*, September 16, 1986.
161. dubbing Flynn "MVG": Most Valuable Groundskeeper.: Bill Gallo, "Pete Saves the Day" (cartoon), *New York Daily News*, September 19, 1986.
162. day game the next day.": Interview with Pete Flynn, August 22, 2009.
162. can tear up the field anytime.": Brown, "Cashen Rues."
164. 108 is a pretty good number.": Interview with Davey Johnson, March 31, 2015.
166. band The Bangles and "Walk Like an Egyptian.": "Billboard Hot 100, Sales and Airplay," *Billboard*, December 20, 1986.

Part II. Destiny

Chapter 11: Scuff Enough

169. was awaiting trial in the fall of 1986.: Jon Beeman and Evan Lange, "The Bernhard Goetz Trial: A Chronology," http://law2.umkc.edu/faculty/projects/ftrials/goetz/goetzchrono.html.
172. overcome the Astros in their backyard.": Interview with Keith Hernandez, December 22, 2014.
172. was deemed to be the worst.: Thomas Boswell, "Astros Bear Eerie Likeness to 1985 Royals," *Washington Post*, October 2, 1986.
173. "I don't believe I ever made a wrong call.": Doug Harvey and Peter Golenbock, *They Called Me God: The Best Umpire Who Ever Lived* (New York: Gallery Books, 2014), 1.
174. Bill Doran's relay throw and avoid a double play.: Vic Ziegel, "Ojeda Also 'Pops' Up With Speed on the Basepaths," *New York Daily News*, October 10, 1986.
175. and come back to win a game.: "1986 NLCS, Game 3: Astros @ Mets," https://www.youtube.com/watch?v=OnWikVkgSJM.
176. That's what he's here for.": Phil Pepe, "Dykstra! Dykstra!" *New York Daily News*, October 12, 1986.
176. good bench and a good bullpen.": Interview with Davey Johnson, March 31, 2015.
177. game that it was the right call.: Jack Lang, "Umps Made the Right Call," *New York Daily News*, October 12, 1986.
177. "You go with your best.": Pepe, "Dykstra! Dykstra!"
178. at Shea closing with "I'm Down.": "The Beatles Setlist at Shea Stadium, New York, NY, USA: August 15, 1965," Setlist.fm, www.setlist.fm/setlist/the-beatles/1965/shea-stadium-new-york-ny-2bd7b08e.html.

178. LCS shutout record set in 1974 by noted scuffer Don Sutton.: Tim Rosaforte, "Scott Deceives Mets Once Again with Three-Hitter," *Orlando Sentinel*, October 13, 1986.
178. adopting the designated hitter to be his greatest achievement: Robert McG. Thomas Jr., "Charles (Chub) Feeney, 72, Dies; Ex-President of National League," *New York Times*, January 11, 1994, www.nytimes.com/1994/01/11/obituaries/charles-chub-feeney-72-dies-ex-president-of-national-league.html.
180. His talent beat my talent.": Interview with Marty Noble, February 25, 2015.
180. It was crazy given the importance of it.": Interview with Ed Randall, May 6, 2015.
181. a spot like right now.": Jerry Izenberg, *The Greatest Game Ever Played* (New York: Henry Holt, 1987), 65.
181. "Don't let them do it.": Gary Carter with Phil Pepe, *Still a Kid at Heart: My Life in Baseball and Beyond* (Chicago: Triumph, 2008), 50.
181. one behind his back," a jubilant Carter said after the game. :"Two-for-22 but All Smiles," *New York Daily News*, October 15, 1986.
181. get back to where some real people are.": Jack Lang, "Astros Get Death Threats," *New York Daily News*, October 15, 1986.
183. *Houston Post* featured the headline "We Wuz Robbed.": Game 6, 1986 NLCS, A&E Home Video.
183. replay could not change his view.: Robbie Andreu, "Bang-Bang Play Shot Down Astros' Early Scoring Threat," *Orlando Sentinel*, October 15, 1986, http://articles.sun-sentinel.com/1986-10-15/sports/8603030073_1_astros-replays-craig-reynolds.
183. "grain by grain, to run out.": Bob Ojeda, "The Glory and the Pain of Pitching," *New York Times*, May 26, 2012, www.nytimes.com/2012/05/27/sports/baseball/the-former-met-bob-ojeda-relives-both-glory-and-pain.html.
184. Everybody knew we needed to win this damned game.": Davey Johnson interview.
184. fn. but I haven't scuffed every ball that I've thrown": Craig Calcaterra, "Knock Me Over with a Feather: Mike Scott Admits to Scuffing Baseballs," NBCsports.com, November 4, 2011, http://mlb.nbcsports.com/2011/11/04/knock-me-over-with-a-feather-mike-scott-admits-to-scuffing-baseballs.
185. position over the last eight seasons.": 1986 World Series Collector's Edition DVD, Game 6, NLCS.
185. because I can't stand them.": Izenberg, *Greatest Game*, 34.
185. "I'm emotional, too.": Ibid., 113.
186. Smith throws up there a strike now.": 1986 World Series Collector's Edition DVD, Game 6, NLCS.
187. getting pretty excited." The Mets were pretty excited in Texas, too.: Interview with Mark Simon, April 15, 2015.
187. didn't factor in a 16-inning game.": Interview with Keith Hernandez, December 22, 2014.

188. from the indoor stadium after his home run.: Mike Sowell, *One Pitch Away: The Players' Stories of the 1986 League Championships and World Series* (New York: Macmillan, 1995), 174–75.
190. only words were those of encouragement.: Carter with Pepe, *Still a Kid*, 54–55.
190. whatever pitches Gary called.": Interview with Jesse Orosco, April 16, 2015.
190. nothing but those sliders and struck him out.": Interview with Keith Hernandez, December 22, 2014.
191. are mobbing Jesse Orosco!" "Bob Murphy (announcer),": StateMaster.com Encyclopedia, www.statemaster.com/encyclopedia/Bob-Murphy-(announcer).
191. On one side or the other.": 1986 World Series Collector's Edition DVD, Game 6, NLCS.
191. columnist Mike Lupica, "0-for-Scott": Mike Lupica, "Mets-Astros War a Piece of History," *New York Daily News*, October 16, 1986.
192. more than $7,000,: J. Frank Cashen, *Winning in Both Leagues: Reflections from Baseball's Front Office* (Lincoln, University of Nebraska Press, 2014), 137.
192. glad we don't have to try.": Phil Pepe, "Greatest Game Ever," *New York Daily News*, October 17, 1986.

Chapter 12: So Far Away, So Good

193. New Jersey, New York, and Pennsylvania.: "Census Regions and Divisions of the United States," U.S. Census Bureau, www2.census.gov/geo/pdfs/maps-data/maps/reference/us_regdiv.pdf.
194. four World Series broadcasts since 2010 to surpass it.: "World Series Television Ratings," Baseball Almanac, www.baseball-almanac.com/ws/wstv.shtml.
194. Even if we had to fight.": Interview with Kevin Mitchell, March 27, 2015.
195. the most boring 1–0 game ever.": Interview with John Thorn, October 2, 2014.
197. taking error questions now.": Dan Shaughnessy, *One Strike Away: The Story of the 1986 Red Sox* (New York: Beaufort Books, 1987), 235.
197. and then it's pretty much over.": Interview with Tim Teufel, March 12, 2015.
198. "Tom Terrific in the Closet.": Interview with Ed Sherman, May 20, 2015.
199. Rule of the park.: Inquirer Wire Services, "Rules Committee Votes to Allow DH in World Series Games in AL Parks," *Philadelphia Inquirer*, March 28, 1986, http://articles.philly.com/1986-03-28/sports/26083467_1_dh-rule-designated-hitter-rule-american-league.
199. Red Sox doing the harvesting.": 1986 World Series Collector's Edition DVD, Game 2.
199. Ed Sherman asked in the *Chicago Tribune*.: Ed Sherman, "'Way We've Played' Amazing to Mets," *Chicago Tribune*, October 20, 1986.
199. Tim Rosaforte in the *Fort Lauderdale Sun-Sentinel*.: Tim Rosaforte, "Duel a Boston Massacre," *Fort Lauderdale Sun-Sentinel*, October 20, 1986, http://

articles.sun-sentinel.com/1986-10-20/sports/8603030989_1_world-series-fifth-game-roger-clemens-wasn-t.
200. "turned Dr. K into Dr. Gopher.": Jim Murray, "What's He Doing in the Series? Just Hitting .555!" *Los Angeles Times*, October 20, 1986, http://articles.latimes.com/1986-10-20/sports/sp-6417_1_world-series.
200. "were in shambles.": Dave Anderson, "The Boston Tee Party," *New York Times*, October 20, 1986.
200. Mets were in "dire straits,": Peter Pascarelli, "Red Sox Shell Gooden to Go 2 Up, Mets' Bats Are Silent in 9–3 Loss," *Philadelphia Inquirer*, October 20, 1986, http://articles.philly.com/1986-10-20/sports/26058971_1_boston-bullpen-mets-fenway-park.
200. Yale president/incoming National League president A. Bartlett Giamatti.: Dan Shaughnessy, *At Fenway: Dispatches from Red Sox Nation* (New York: Three Rivers Press, 1996), 64–65.
200. protagonist of lit'ry life, a survivor." :Martin F. Nolan, "From Frazee to Fisk: Park Is Unique, So Is Its History," in *The Red Sox Reader*, revised edition, ed. Dan Riley (Boston: Houghton Mifflin, 1991), 3–4. Originally published in the *Boston Globe*, October 6, 1986.
201. we needed a break, you know?": Interview with Davey Johnson, March 31, 2015.
201. "Maybe it was taking a chance.": Interview with Sandy Carter, October 21, 2014.
202. for a change, felt fine. Murray Chass,: "The World Series '86: Mets' Fast Start Runs Down Red Sox," *New York Times*, October 22, 1986, www.nytimes.com/1986/10/22/sports/the-world-series-86-mets-fast-start-runs-down-red-sox.html.
202. every time he pitched. "Oil Can Boyd,": ESPN *E:60*, http://espn.go.com/video/clip?id=7882764.
203. as action started in the Boston bullpen.: 1986 World Series Collector's Edition DVD, Game 3.
203. looked like a postscript to the "The Curly Shuffle.": Joseph Durso, "Score the Play Moe to Larry to Curly," *New York Times*, October 22, 1986, www.nytimes.com/1986/10/22/sports/score-the-play-moe-to-larry-to-curly.html.
203. let a sleeping dog lie.": "Battle Lines - 1986 World Series - Red Sox/Mets," https://www.youtube.com/watch?v=8fEPmxQgZnw.
203. and a ticket to Elmira, New York.: Bob Ojeda, "The Glory and the Pain of Pitching," *New York Times*, May 26, 2012, www.nytimes.com/2012/05/27/sports/baseball/the-former-met-bob-ojeda-relives-both-glory-and-pain.html.
204. But I belong somewhere else now.": 1986 World Series Collector's Edition DVD, Game 3.
205. telling me out in the bullpen.": Ron Darling with Daniel Paisner, *The Complete Game: Reflections on Baseball, Pitching, and Life on the Mound* (New York: Alfred A. Knopf, 2009), 70–76.
205. they found out we were Mets wives.": Sandy Carter interview.

206. hitting that ball right there over that fence.'": Sandy Carter interview.

Chapter 13: "Can You Believe This Ballgame at Shea?"

207. passed down from generation to generation.": Interview with Ed Coleman, May 13, 2015.
208. It mattered a lot.": Interview with Gary Thorne, November 10, 2014.
208. three days' rest for the first time in his career,: Dan Shaughnessy, *One Strike Away: The Story of the 1986 Red Sox* (New York: Beaufort Books,1978), 248.
209. "the easiest jump I've ever done.": "10-27-1986 Letterman: Rich Hall, Michael Sergio," https://www.youtube.com/watch?v=4jiw4rzszy4.
209. into a six-month sentence.: "Parachutist Gains Release from Jail," *Gainesville Sun*, June 13, 1987.
209. trying to win that game.": Interview with Wally Backman, January 10, 2015.
212. complete game against the Mariners in April.: Shaughnessy, *One Strike Away*, 65.
213. from the minor leagues on up.": Mike Sowell, *One Pitch Away: The Players' Stories of the 1986 League Championships and World Series* (New York: Macmillan, 1995), 262.
213. but John decided against it.": "Battle Lines - 1986 World Series - Red Sox/Mets," https://www.youtube.com/watch?v=8fEPmxQgZnw.
214. "a fucking cheerleader.": Shaughnessy, *One Strike Away*, 252.
215. possibly blow a two-run lead?": Interview with Ed Randall, May 6, 2015.
215. The World Series trophy was there already.: "Bob Costas on 1986 World Series," Archive of American Television, https://www.youtube.com/watch?v=BxHL-mIW8vY.
216. he never got the call in Game 6.: Sowell, *One Pitch Away*, 260.
216. make the off-season almost interminable.": 1986 World Series Collector's Edition DVD, Game 6.
216. life of a big league manager,": Scully narrated. Ibid.
216. 'We knew it.' That's a lie.": Mookie Wilson at Queens Baseball Convention, January 10, 2015.
217. Jay Horwitz, to watch the end on TV.: Interview with Keith Hernandez, October 5, 2008.
217. two and a half packs during Game 6.: 1986 World Series Collector's Edition DVD, bonus disc interview with Keith Hernandez.
219. As a rookie? Tell me that." Interview with Kevin Mitchell, March 27, 2015.
219. looked for the slider on the next pitch and got it." Ibid.
220. our last world championship, but probably not.": Greg Prince, "The Lady Behind Home Plate," *Faith and Fear in Flushing,* October 15, 2012, www.faithandfearinflushing.com/2012/10/15/the-lady-behind-home-plate/#sthash.7IunyBeT.dpuf.
220. it caught him a little off guard.": Mookie Wilson at Queens Baseball Convention, January 10, 2015.

221. I think we had a chance at the plate.": Interview with Rich Gedman, August 12, 2014.
221. "Can you believe this game at Shea?": Vin Scully asked almost 30 million people. 1986 World Series Collector's Editing DVD, Game 6.
221. but I still did not want to strike out.": Mookie Wilson at Queens Baseball Convention, January 10, 2015.
221. and changed in the trainers' room.: Interview with Ed Romero, July 31, 2014.
221. ball skipped instead of bounced.: Art Spander, "The Same Old Story," October 26, 1986, in *The Art Spander Collection* (Dallas: Taylor Publishing, 1989).
222. the very large TV at the Lambda Chi Alpha house.: Interview with Josh Lewin, January 10, 2015.
222fn. "Then don't worry.": Cohen spent two years in Pawtucket before being hired by the New York Mets and has been with the team ever since. Interview with Gary Cohen, December 22, 2014.
223. and ran downstairs.": Interview with Howie Rose, March 30, 2015.
223. sitting there as the agony turned to ecstasy.: Interview with Keith Hernandez, October 5, 2008.
223. Hall of Famer Hank Greenberg.: Ralph Kiner with Joe Gergen, *Kiner's Korner* (New York: Arbor House, 1987), 1. Ralph Kiner with Danny Peary, *Baseball Forever* (Chicago: Triumph Books, 2004), 203.
223. Mets win! They win!: "The Call," *Never Forget '69* (blog), October 25, 2011, http://neverforget69.com/?p=1306.
223. I still can't believe it happened.": Thorne interview.
224. hit it on the head pretty much.": Coleman interview.
224. and the crowd roars, I shut up.": Cee Angi, "'We've Been Friends Long Enough You'll Understand,'" SB Nation Longform, June 2, 2014, www.sbnation.com/longform/2014/6/2/5764256/vin-scully-career-retrospective-dodgers-broadcaster-profile.
224. stadium visibly shook above them: Interview with Ed Randall, May 6, 2015.
224. made the right choice.": Michael Goodwin, "NBC Scored in Game 7, Too," TV Sports, *New York Times*, October 29, 1986, www.nytimes.com/1986/10/29/sports/tv-sports-nbc-scored-in-game-7-too.html.
225. in Game 7 tomorrow.: 1986 World Series Collector's Edition DVD, Game 6.

Chapter 14: Haven't Had That Spirit Here Since 1969

226. and wound up winning.: 1986 World Series Collector's Edition DVD, Game 7.
226. runners on base before two were out.: Interview with Michael Mitchell, May 18, 2015.
227. the Mets pulling a 71 share.: Michael Goodwin, "NBC Scored in Game 7, Too," TV Sports, *New York Times*, October 29, 1986, www.nytimes.com/1986/10/29/sports/tv-sports-nbc-scored-in-game-7-too.html.

228. and just be a spectator.": Ed Sherman, "Reggie Tries to Cheer Up the Red Sox," *Chicago Tribune*, October 27, 1986.
229. and two out in the third inning.: 1986 World Series Collector's Edition DVD, Game 7.
231. And we won it easy.": Interview with Davey Johnson, March 31, 2015.
232. pitch as a left-handed pitcher.": Interview with Tim Teufel, March 12, 2015.
232. I thought was kind of ironic.": Interview with Keith Hernandez, December 22, 2014.
232. either going to do it or I'm not.": Ibid.
233. Phil Simms said when the night was over.: Chris Cobbs, "Giants Provide More Cheer for N.Y.: They Beat Redskins, 27–20, to Gain 3-Way Tie for Lead," *Los Angeles Times*, October 28, 1986, http://articles.latimes.com/1986-10-28/sports/sp-8093_1_giant-lead.
233. thus costing him a hit and an RBI.: Jeff Pearlman, *The Bad Guys Won* (New York: HarperCollins, 2004), 258.
233. "I don't deserve any more chances.": Dan Shaughnessy, *One Strike Away*, 253.
236. "Joe, you just lost your house," Scully quipped.: 1986 World Series Collector's Edition DVD, Game 7.
236. Romero, now a minor league manager, said with a chuckle.: Interview with Ed Romero, July 31, 2014.
238. never any question about who he wanted to win.": Interview with Gary Thorne, November 10, 2014.
238. from behind to win the seventh game.": "Bob Murphy (announcer)," StateMaster.com Encyclopedia, www.statemaster.com/encyclopedia/Bob-Murphy-(announcer).

Part III. Decline

Chapter 15: Break Up the Mets

241. that the *Harvard Crimson* reported as 12,000.: "World Series Touches Off Racial Clashes," *Harvard Crimson*, November 15, 1986, www.thecrimson.com/article/1986/11/15/world-series-touches-off-racial-clashes.
241. incoming students to reflect on themes of prejudice.: Marcia S. Curtis, "Crisis and Response: A Writing Program's Self Exam," www.umass.edu/writingprogram/teaching/database/CrisisAndResponseAWritingProgramsSelfExam.html.
241. Mount Holyoke responded to racism with a teach-in.: "World Series Touches Off Racial Clashes," *Harvard Crimson*.
241. going crazy and gloating in our faces.": Interview with David Lennon, March 12, 2015.
241. silently moping and trudging along.": Interview with Bill Nowlin, May 6, 2015.

242. take part in such events in the offseason.: Wendy Thurm, "It's Fan Fest Season; Well, for Most Teams," FanGraphs, January 24, 2014, www.fangraphs.com/blogs/its-fan-fest-season-well-for-most-teams.
242. done a good job embracing their history.": Interview with Adam Rubin, March 12, 2015.
242. to see things grow year to year.": Interview with Shannon Shark, May 14, 2015.
243. image of our '86 team for some time.": Mookie Wilson with Erik Sherman, *Mookie: Life, Baseball, and the '86 Mets* (New York: Berkley, 2014), 244–45.
243. it cost Backman his dream of managing in the major leagues.: Jack Curry, "The Past Costs Backman His Job, Only Four Days After Receiving It," *New York Times*, November 6, 2004, www.nytimes.com/2004/11/06/sports/baseball/06backman.html.
245. it's the best place to play.": Interview with Wally Backman, January 10, 2015.
246. And I got into my car. Barely.": Interview with Keith Hernandez, December 22, 2014.
246. "It was an unbelievable day.": Interview with Gary Thorne, November 10, 2014.
246. I don't know what we talked about.": Interview with Len Berman, March 30, 2015.
246. a chance to shower. I just went.": Interview with Keith Hernandez, December 22, 2014.
246. cocaine with people he barely knew.: Dwight Gooden and Ellis Henican, *Doc: A Memoir* (Boston, Houghton Mifflin Harcourt, 2013), xi.
247. Gooden just ignored everything.: Ibid., xvi–xvii.
247. It was just like a knock to the gut.": Interview with Howie Rose, March 30, 2015.
247. voluntary drug tests in his new contract: Gooden and Henican, *Doc*, 93.
247. was not his fiancée, called off the wedding: Ibid., 92.
247. arrested for fighting with Tampa police.: Ibid., 96–99.
247. He failed the first test he took.: Ibid., 102–3.
247. '87 Mets were a different ball club even before that.: Ibid., 103–4.
248. and I've got Ray Knight. Whatcha gonna do?": Mookie Wilson at Queens Baseball Convention, January 10, 2015.
248. bringing to New York to win a championship.": Ibid.
248. "kind of a paycheck player.": Interview with Jeff Pearlman, May 20, 2015.
248. "just didn't care.": Interview with Gary Cohen, December 21, 2015.
248. only what's on the scoreboard.": Interview with Steve Jacobson, January 22, 2015.
248. "There's nothing wrong with that.": Interview with Marty Noble, February 25, 2015.
249. My addiction is life.": Interview with Kevin Mitchell, March 27, 2015.
250. No. Impossible.": Pearlman interview.
250. we're not even having this discussion.": Pearlman interview.

251. protect guys against themselves.": Interview with Bob Ojeda, March 8, 2011.
252. But it should not have been a one-time thing.": Ibid.

Chapter 16: Tilting at Windmills

253. would rank higher than those Mets," he said.: Interview with Rob Neyer, March 28, 2015.
253. only one-time champion in the top 10: Rob Neyer and Eddie Epstein, *Baseball Dynasties: The Greatest Teams of All Time*. (New York: W. W. Norton, 2000), 364–67.
254. an extraordinary balance of pitching and hitting.: Bill James, *The Bill James 1987 Baseball Abstract* (New York: Ballantine, 1987), 80.
254. 1986 World Series as number two.: David Schoenfield, "Remember the '80s: The Iconic Moments," ESPN.com, July 7, 2009, http://sports.espn.go.com/espn/page2/story?page=remember80s/partone/090706.
254. intend to be back here next year.": Dave Anderson, "Cub Fan Praises a Few Mets," Sports of the Times, *New York Times*, November 13, 1986, www.nytimes.com/1986/11/13/sports/sports-of-the-times-cub-fan-praises-a-few-mets.html.
255. That's what it felt like.": Interview with Heather Quinlan, July 8, 2014.
256. "You've got about one second to live, buddy!": "*Blue Velvet* (1986) Quotes," IMDB.com, www.imdb.com/title/tt0090756/quotes.
256. 20 years away from Derek Jeter's rookie year.": Interview with Len Berman, March 30, 2015.
256. to gravitate toward the Yankees.": Interview with Adam Rubin, March 12, 2015.
257. but it should be sustainable because of the starting pitching.": Interview with Adam Rubin, November 18, 2015.
258. another good reason to hate New York.": John Shanahan, "Pirates-Mets Rivalry Has Mayors Crossing Swords," Associated Press, July 9, 1988, www.apnewsarchive.com/1988/Pirates-Mets-Rivalry-Has-Mayors-Crossing-Swords/id-e28ad6469aaed13673e3c6cd99218fbd.
258. They still have fans that don't want to give up on them.": Interview with Steve Jacobson, January 22, 2015.
258. "Keith, it's a pleasure to pay the money.": Joseph Durso, "Hernandez Signs 5-Year Pact," *New York Times*, February 11, 1984, www.nytimes.com/1984/02/11/sports/hernandez-signs-5-year-pact.html.
259. in a market where we're able to afford it.": Jason Diamos, "The Mets Agree to Make Piazza Baseball's Richest Player; Leiter Says He Is Close to a $32 Million Deal," *New York Times*, October 25, 1998, www.nytimes.com/1998/10/25/sports/baseball-mets-agree-make-piazza-baseball-s-richest-player-leiter-says-he-close.html.
259. "I was going back to my old job.": J. Frank Cashen, *Winning in Both Leagues: Reflections from Baseball's Front Office* (Lincoln: University of Nebraska Press, 2014), 90.

260 to purchase the team if it was ever sold.": Ibid., 179.
260. when debt was canceled out: Richard Sandomir, "Owners of Mets Make a Deal," *New York Times*, August 14, 2002, www.nytimes.com/2002/08/14/sports/baseball-owners-of-mets-make-a-deal.html.
260. had $550 million tied up in almost 500 accounts.: Serge F. Kovaleski and David Waldstein, "Madoff Had Wide Role in Mets' Finances," *New York Times*, February 1, 2011, www.nytimes.com/2011/02/02/sports/baseball/02mets.html?_r=0.
261. Mets lost a reported $70 million in 2011: Steve Kettmann, *Baseball Maverick: How Sandy Alderson Revolutionized Baseball and Revived the Mets* (New York: Atlantic Monthly Press, 2015), 154.
261fn. interest in 2000.: Cork Gaines, "The Crazy Contract the Mets Gave Bobby Bonilla Was Actually Incredibly Smart," *Business Insider*, July 2, 2013, www.businessinsider.com/chart-contract-new-york-mets-bobby-bonilla-2013-7.
261. or don't have at this point.": Interview with Marty Noble, February 25, 2015.
262. never been around anything like that.": Interview with David Lennon, March 12, 2015.
262. will happen when the team wins.": Interview with Ed Coleman, May 13, 2015.
263. hear the owner say, "We're snakebitten, baby.": Jeffrey Toobin, "Madoff's Curveball," *The New Yorker*, May 30, 2011, www.newyorker.com/magazine/2011/05/30/madoffs-curveball.
263. instead of 65 percent of $1 billion.": Interview with Howard Megdal, June 2, 2015.
263. the mess he created in Los Angeles Craig Calcaterra,: "Frank McCourt Turned a $1.278 Billion Profit on the Sale of the Dodgers," Hardball Talk, NBCSports.com, April 23, 2013, http://hardballtalk.nbcsports.com/2013/04/23/frank-mccourt-turned-a-1-278-billion-profit-on-the-sale-of-the-dodgers.
263. survive a cash crunch in late 2010.: Richard Sandomir, "The Dodgers, the Mets and the Commissioner," *New York Times*, April 30, 2011, www.nytimes.com/2011/05/01/sports/baseball/01dodgers.html?_r=0.
264. debt balloon payments. Against Citi Field.": Megdal interview.
264. far outstrips the money coming into, for instance, the Rockies, Twins, and Brewers.": Howard Megdal, "Mets Have Obligations to Live Up to Promises Made to Fans. *USA Today Sports Weekly*, November 18/-24, 2015.
264. not the way a big-market team behaves.": Lennon interview.
265. I was sure that was going to be us.": Interview with Greg Prince, December 31, 2014.
266. "That's a long time.": Interview with Rich Gedman, August 12, 2014.

Chapter 17: Kid's Curtain Call

267. end up in the Hall of Fame.": Blue Jays/Mets exhibition game from Montreal, CSN via MLB-TV, March 28, 2015.
268. He would have liked half and half.": Interview with Sandy Carter, October 21, 2014.
269. thought the pastor was talking about.": Bill Staples and Rich Herschlag, *Before the Glory: 20 Baseball Heroes Talk About Growing Up and Turning Hard Times into Home Runs* (Deerfield Beach, FL: Health Communications, 2007), 151.
269. "protect my amateur status.": Ibid., 152–53.
270. going to see my mom and dad in heaven.": Sandy Carter interview.
270. and football at UCLA in 1972.: Staples and Herschlag, *Before the Glory*, 159.
270. plus an extra $7,500 when he reached the majors.: Gary Carter with Phil Pepe, *Still a Kid at Heart: My Life in Baseball and Beyond* (Chicago: Triumph Books, 2008), 14.
270. chose Carter as the best pick for '72.: Christina Kahrl, "Fifty Best MLB Draft Picks from Past 50 Years," ESPN.com, June 8, 2015, http://espn.go.com/mlb/story/_/id/13023443/mlb-draft-50-best-picks-50-years.
270. You're going to be an All-Star catcher for 10 years.": Blue Jays/Mets exhibition game from Montreal, CSN via MLB-TV, March 28, 2015.
270. watched the veterans play cards.: Carter with Pepe, *Still a Kid*, 19–21.
271. "no one ever said *the*.": Interview with Marty Noble, February 25, 2015.
271. they lost 107 games.": Dick Williams and Bill Plaschke, *No More Mr. Nice Guy: A Life of Hardball* (San Diego: Harcourt Brace, 1990), 207.
272. between 1977 and 1984.: Jonah Kerri, *Up, Up, & Away: The Kid, The Hawk, Rock, Vladi, Pedro, Le Grand Orange, Youppi!, The Crazy Business of Baseball & the Ill-Fated but Unforgettable Montreal Expos* (Toronto: Random House Canada, 2014), 202–207.
272. Carter the first big domino to fall.": Kerri, *Up, Up, & Away*, 208–209.
272. John McHale settled the deal.: J. Frank Cashen, *Winning in Both Leagues: Reflections from Baseball's Front Office* (Lincoln: University of Nebraska Press, 2014), 126.
272. They were great.": Sandy Carter interview.

272fn. than Gary Carter upon signing his 1982 deal.: Murray Chass, "Carter's New Pact: 7 Years, $14 Million," *New York Times*, February 16, 1982, www.nytimes.com/1982/02/16/sports/carter-s-new-pact-7-years-14-million.html.

273. They did a lot of damage.": Interview with Christy Kearce, October 21, 2015.
274. 'Show me this, tell me that.'": Sandy Carter interview.
275. how special those times were for me.": Interview with Kimmy Bloemers, June 7, 2015.
275. had his number retired as well.: Steve Dorsey, "Palm Beach Atlantic Posthumously Honors Gary Carter," *Palm Beach Post*, April 25, 2015.

275. It's not like there's so many retired.": Sandy Carter interview.
275. Kearce added, finishing the thought. :Kearce interview.
276. done everything but retire his number.": Interview with D. J. Carter, March 5, 2015.
276. Sounds good enough to me.": Bloemers interview.
277. We were the same age.": Interview with Keith Hernandez, December 22, 2014.
277. He's sorely missed.": Interview with Tim Teufel, March 12, 2015.
277. bond over something you did. Together.": Interview with Jeff Pearlman, May 20, 2015.
277. It doesn't mean anything.": Interview with Len Berman, March 30, 2015.
277. That's what I'll always remember about him.": Interview with Randy Niemann, May 29, 2014.
278. good character, even godliness.": Interview with Ed Hearn, March 27, 2015.
278. Try not to ask too much out of them.' He was the best.": Interview with Davey Johnson, March 31, 2015.
279. fit in with the cool kids in the smoking section.": Pearlman interview.

Sources

More important than anything was the ability to have every game and detail from the 1986 season and other years, plus searchable data, available at my fingertips—more than I ever imagined possible as managing editor in an age when seven-pound behemoth baseball encyclopedias ruled the earth. All stats, standings, and other baseball-related numbers for this book come via Baseball-Reference.com. Ah, what future colleagues John Thorn and Pete Palmer unleashed in the 1980s.

Numbers are great, but it was crucial to hear from people with memories or impressions on the subject matter. Not everyone I talked to was included in the book due to space. Likewise, not everyone contacted was willing to talk, but that makes me all the more indebted to those who agreed to share their experiences and expertise. Thank you all. Many interviews were done over the phone, others took place in person, a handful were lengthy e-mail exchanges, and a couple were very brief, but I appreciate everyone who took time to discuss a team still worth talking about.

Interviews

Wally Backman, Len Berman, Charlie Bevis, Kimmy Bloemers, D. J. Carter, Sandy Carter, Gary Cohen, Ed Coleman, Mark Feinsand, Pete Flynn, Rich Gedman, Peter Golenbock, Ed Hearn, Keith Hernandez, Whitey Herzog, Bob Heussler, Kevin Horrigan, Ricky Horton, Steve Jacobson, Davey Johnson, Christy Kearce, Jerry Koosman, David Lennon, Josh Lewin, Howard Megdal, Kevin Mitchell, Michael Mitchell, Roger Mooney, Rob Neyer, Randy Niemann, Marty Noble, Bill Nowlin, Bob Ojeda, Jesse Orosco, Jeff Pearlman, Richard Puerzer, Greg Prince,

Heather Quinlan, Ed Randall, Ed Romero, Howie Rose, Adam Rubin, Shannon Shark, Ed Sherman, Mark Simon, Art Spander, Rusty Staub, John Stearns, Tim Teufel, John Thorn, Gary Thorne, and Mookie Wilson.

Books and Articles

1986 Remember When . . . A Nostalgic Look Back in Time. Birmingham, AL: Seek Publishing.

Angell, Roger. *Season Ticket: A Baseball Companion*. New York: Random House, 1989.

Appel, Marty. *Pinstripe Empire: The New York Yankees from before the Babe to after the Boss*. New York: Bloomsbury, 2012.

Bevis, Charlie. *Doubleheaders: A Major League History*. Jefferson, NC: McFarland & Co., 2011.

Bock, Duncan, and John Jordan. *The Complete Year-by-Year N.Y. Mets Fan's Almanac*. New York: Crown Publishing, 1992.

Brand, Dana. *Mets Fan*. Jefferson, NC: McFarland & Co., 2007.

Burman, Howard. *Season of Ghosts: The '86 Mets and the Red Sox*. Jeffersonville, NC: McFarland & Co., 2013.

Carter, Gary, with Phil Pepe. *Still a Kid at Heart: My Life in Baseball and Beyond*. Chicago: Triumph Books, 2008.

Caruso, Gary. *The Braves Encyclopedia*. Philadelphia: Temple University Press, 1995.

Cashen, J. Frank. *Winning in Both Leagues: Reflections from Baseball's Front Office*. Lincoln: University of Nebraska Press, 2014.

Chuck, Bill, and Jim Kaplan. *Walkoffs, Last Licks, and Final Outs: Baseball's Grand (and not-so-grand) Finales*. Chicago: ACTA Sports, 2008.

Cosell, Howard, with Peter Bonventre. *I Never Played the Game*. New York: William Morrow and Co., 1985.

Darling, Ron, with Daniel Paisner. *The Complete Game: Reflections on Baseball, Pitching, and Life on the Mound.* New York: Alfred A. Knopf, 2009.

Devine, Bing. *The Memoirs of Bing Devine: Stealing Lou Brock and Other Winning Moves by a Master GM*. New York: Skyhorse, 2011.

Edelman, Rob. "M. Donald Grant." In *The Miracle Has Landed: The Amazin' Story of How the 1969 Mets Shocked the World*, edited by Matthew Silverman and Ken Samuelson. Hanover, MA: Maple Street Press, 2009.

Gooden, Dwight, and Ellis Henican. *Doc: A Memoir*. Boston: Houghton Mifflin Harcourt, 2013.

Gorman, Lou. *High and Inside: My Life in the Front Offices of Baseball*. Jefferson, NC: McFarland & Co., 2008.

Harvey, Doug, and Peter Golenbock. *They Called Me God: The Best Umpire Who Ever Lived*. New York: Gallery Books, 2014.

Hearn, Ed, with Gene Frenette. *Conquering Life's Curves: Battles, Baseball & Beyond*. Dallas: Masters Press, 1997.

Helyar, John. *Lords of the Realm: The Real History of Baseball*. New York: Villard Books, 1994.

Hernandez, Keith, and Mike Bryan. *If at First: A Season with the Mets*. New York: McGraw-Hill, 1986.

Herzog, Whitey, and Kevin Horrigan. *White Rat: A Life in Baseball*. New York: Harper & Row, 1987.

Izenberg, Jerry. *The Greatest Game Ever Played*. New York: Henry Holt, 1987.

James, Bill. *The Bill James 1987 Baseball Abstract*. New York: Ballantine Books, 1987.

Johnson, Davey, and Peter Golenbock. *Bats*. New York: G. P. Putnam's Sons, 1986.

Kanarek, Jacob. *From First to Worst: The New York Mets, 1973–1977*. Jefferson, NC: McFarland & Co., 2008.

Kerri, Jonah. *Up, Up, & Away: The Kid, The Hawk, Rock, Vladi, Pedro, Le Grand Orange, Youppi!, The Crazy Business of Baseball & the Ill-Fated but Unforgettable Montreal Expos*. Toronto: Random House Canada, 2014.

Kettmann, Steve. *Baseball Maverick: How Sandy Alderson Revolutionized Baseball and Revived the Mets*. New York: Atlantic Monthly Press, 2015.

Kiner, Ralph, with Danny Peary. *Baseball Forever*. Chicago: Triumph Books, 2004.

Kiner, Ralph, with Joe Gergen. *Kiner's Korner*. New York: Arbor House, 1987.

Koppett, Leonard. *The New York Mets*. Rev. ed. New York: Collier Books, 1974.

Kuhn, Bowie. *Hardball: The Education of a Baseball Commissioner*. New York: McGraw-Hill Book Company, 1988.

Lang, Jack, and Peter Simon. *The New York Mets: Twenty-Five Years of Baseball Magic*. New York: Henry Holt and Co., 1986.

Leach, Terry, with Tom Clark. *Things Happen for a Reason: The True Story of an Itinerant Life in Baseball*. Berkeley: Frog Books, 2000.

MacCambridge, Michael. *America's Game: The Epic Story of How Pro Football Captured the Nation*. New York: Anchor Books, 2005.

Madden, Bill (Commentary). *Daily News Scrapbook History of the N.Y. Mets 1986 Season*. New York: Collectors Marketing Corp., 1987.

Madden, Bill. *Steinbrenner: The Last Lion of Baseball*. New York: Harper, 2010.

Mass, A. J. *Yes, It's Hot in Here: Adventures in the Weird, Wooly World of Sports Mascots*. New York: Rodale, 2014.

McCollister, John. *The Good, the Bad, and the Ugly: Heart-Pounding, Jaw-Dropping, and Gut-Wrenching Moments from Pittsburgh Pirates History*. Chicago: Triumph Books, 2008.

Mitchell, Michael. "'Recorded Games of Frustration': Win Expectancy and the Boston Red Sox." In *SABR Baseball Research Journal* 42, no. 1 (Spring 2013).

Neyer, Rob, and Eddie Epstein. *Baseball Dynasties: The Greatest Teams of All Time*. W. W. Norton, 2000.

Nolan, Martin F. "From Frazee to Fisk: Park Is Unique, So Is Its History." In *The Red Sox Reader*, rev. ed., edited by Dan Riley. Boston: Houghton Mifflin, 1991. Originally published in the *Boston Globe*, October 6, 1986.

Pearlman, Jeff. *The Bad Guys Won*. New York: HarperCollins, 2004.

Prato, Greg. *Just Out of Reach: The 1980s New York Yankees*. CreateSpace, 2014.

Prince, Greg. *Faith and Fear in Flushing: An Intense Personal History of the New York Mets*. New York: Skyhorse, 2009.

Rose, Howie, with Phil Pepe. *Put It in the Book! A Half-Century of Mets Mania*. Chicago: Triumph Books, 2013.

Shaughnessy, Dan. *At Fenway: Dispatches from Red Sox Nation*. New York: Three Rivers Press, 1996.

Shaughnessy, Dan. *One Strike Away: The Story of the 1986 Red Sox*. New York: Beaufort Books, 1987.

Skirboll, Aaron. *The Pittsburgh Cocaine Seven: How a Ragtag Group of Fans Took the Fall for Major League Baseball*. Chicago: Chicago Review Press, 2010.

Sowell, Mike. *One Pitch Away: The Players' Stories of the 1986 League Championships and World Series*. New York: Macmillan, 1995.

Spander, Art. "The Same Old Story." In *The Art Spander Collection*. Dallas: Taylor Publishing, 1989.

Staples, Bill, and Rich Herschlag. *Before the Glory: 20 Baseball Heroes Talk About Growing Up and Turning Hard Times into Home Runs*. Deerfield Beach, FL: Health Communications, 2007.

Strawberry, Darryl, with John Strausbaugh. *Straw: Finding My Way*. New York: Ecco, 2009.

Tango, Tom, Michael Lichtman, and Andrew Dolphin. *The Book: Playing the Percentages in Baseball*. TMA Press, 2006.

Thorn, John, and Pete Palmer. *The Hidden Game of Baseball*. Rev. ed. New York: Doubleday, 1985.

Thorn, John, Pete Palmer, and Michael Gershman. *Total Baseball*. 7th ed. Kingston, NY: Total Sports, 2001.

Weinreb, Michael. *Bigger Than the Game: Bo, Boz, the Punky QB, and How the '80s Created the Modern Athlete*. New York: Gotham Books, 2010.

Williams, Dick, and Bill Plaschke. *No More Mr. Nice Guy: A Life of Hardball*. San Diego: Harcourt Brace Jovanovich, 1990.

Wilson, Mookie, with Erik Sherman. *Mookie: Life, Baseball, and the '86 Mets*. New York: Berkley, 2014.

Periodicals

1986 National League Championship Series Mets Scorebook

1986 Official 25th Anniversary Mets Scorebook

1987 Mets Information Guide

2015 Mets Media Guide
Airways News
Billboard
Boston Globe
Capital New York
Chicago Tribune
Fort Lauderdale Sun-Sentinel
Gainesville Sun
Harvard Crimson
Liberty Champion
Los Angeles Times
New York
New York Daily News
New York Post
New York Times
New Yorker
Newsday
Orlando Sentinel
Philadelphia Inquirer
San Francisco Examiner
Seattle Times
The Sporting News 1986 Baseball Yearbook
Sports Illustrated
Time
USA Today Sports Weekly
Wall Street Journal
Washington Post

Websites

all-that-is-interesting.com
apnewsarchive.com
baseball-almanac.com
baseballanalysts.com
baseball-reference.com
boxofficemojo.com
businessinsider.com
cbssports.com
census.gov
cgi.superstation.com
classictvhits.com
dailymotion.com
dailyscript.com
designobserver.com

espn.go.com
faithandfearinflushing.com
fangraphs.com
grucci.com
hardballtalk.nbcsports.com
imdb.com
law2.umkc.edu
mentalfloss.com
miscbaseball.wordpress.com
nationalpastime.com
nbcsports.com
neverforget69.com
ocf.berkeley.edu
papergreat.com
retrosimba.com
sabr.org/bioproject
sbnation.com/longform
setlist.fm
space.com
sportslistoftheday.com
statemaster.com
studiousmetsimus.blogspot.com
ssa.gov
thedailybeast.com
ultimatemets.com
vimeo.com
youtube.com

Video

DVD

The New York Mets 1986 World Series Collector's Edition. (Games 1 through 7, plus Game 6 of the '86 NLCS and a bonus DVD of interviews.) Official MLB DVDs, A&E Home Video, 2006.

Online

"10-27-1986 Letterman: Rich Hall, Michael Sergio." YouTube video posted by "zschim," August 22, 2015. https://www.youtube.com/watch?v=4jiw4rzszy4.

"1986-07-22 Mets at Reds." WLWT-TV. YouTube video posted by "ClassicMLB11," January 17, 2014. https://www.youtube.com/watch?v=dljM3PyIiXI.

"1986 All Star Game @ Houston." YouTube video posted by John Quinn, January 21, 2015. https://www.youtube.com/watch?v=TrC1BrP8Y64.
"*1986 Mets: A Year to Remember*." SportsChannel/Rainbow Home Video posted by "congerz83," July 25, 2013. www.dailymotion.com/video/x129dhn_1986 mets-a-year-to-remember_sport.
"1986 NLCS 1 . . . Dwight Gooden." YouTube video posted by "ace kuroda," July 30, 2013. https://www.youtube.com/watch?v=LncDacAu9bA.
"1986 NLCS 1 . . . Mike Scott." YouTube video posted by "ace kuroda," July 30, 2013. https://www.youtube.com/watch?v=LGfkVlDzuJg.
"1986 NLCS, Game 3: Astros @ Mets." YouTube video posted by MLBClassics, October 1, 2010. https://www.youtube.com/watch?v=OnWikVkgSJM.
"Al Capone's Vault." YouTube video posted by "davidgideon," April 30, 2006. https://www.youtube.com/watch?v=P84OKTUx6LY.
"Battle Lines - 1986 World Series - Red Sox/Mets." YouTube video posted by "atomjackfuser," October 7, 2013. Originally aired on ESPN Classic, October 29, 2003. https://www.youtube.com/watch?v=8fEPmxQgZnw.
"Bob Costas on 1986 World Series." Archive of American Television. YouTube video posted by John Strubel, June 19, 2013. https://www.youtube.com/watch?v=BxHL-mIW8vY.
"E:60 Bill Buckner Behind the Bag." Originally aired October 25, 2011. http://espn.go.com/video/clip?id=7152345.
"E:60 Oil Can Boyd." ESPN video posted June 12, 2012. http://espn.go.com/video/clip?id=7882764.
"Seinfeld - Pilot." *The Seinfeld Chronicles* pilot episode. Vimeo video posted by "Marie." https://vimeo.com/82691805.

Index

Italicized page numbers indicate photographs.

About the Author

Matthew Silverman is the author of *Swinging '73: Baseball's Wildest Season*, *New York Mets: The Complete Illustrated History*, *Mets Essential*, *100 Things Mets Fans Should Know and Do Before They Die*, and *Best Mets: Fifty Years of Highs and Lows from New York's Most Agonizingly Amazin' Team*. He also cowrote the Mets, Cubs, and Red Sox books in the *By the Numbers* series. He served as associate publisher for Total Sports Publishing, working with Major League Baseball, the National Football League, and *Sports Illustrated*. A longtime member of the Society of Baseball Research, he was lead writer, editor, and spokesman for *Baseball: The Biographical Encyclopedia*. Profiled in the *New York Times* and elsewhere, Silverman has been interviewed on ESPN radio, NPR, SportsNet New York, WFAN, and for numerous other programs and publications. He blogs regularly at Metsilverman.com and lives with his family in High Falls, New York.